TO DR. Richard Meyers,

" With Best Wishes "

12 Sep 2005

Dr. Susilo Bambang Yudhoyono
PRESIDENT OF THE REPUBLIC OF INDONESIA

Transforming Indonesia

Selected International Speeches

WITH ESSAYS
BY INTERNATIONAL
OBSERVERS

Transforming Indonesia
Selected International Speeches

ISBN 979-99864-0-0

Author   : Dr. Susilo Bambang Yudhoyono
Editor   : Dino Patti Djalal
Publisher   : Office of Special Staff of the President for International Affairs
Cover Design : Yusuf
Layout   : Joni Hadi, Ivan Novianto, Purwandari Dyah Hapsari
First Edition : 2005

Printed by PT Gramedia Jakarta
The content of the book is not guaranteed by the printing company

"Our greatest challenge is to transform –
not just change– Indonesia"

President Susilo Bambang Yudhoyono

THE PRESIDENT
OF THE REPUBLIC OF INDONESIA

Foreword
by
President Susilo Bambang Yudhoyono

On October 20, 2004, I was sworn in as Indonesia's sixth President—
and the first to be directly elected by the voters. Thus began a new
historical chapter for Indonesia. As I raised my hand to say my oath,
I remember thinking that every person who assumes the Presidency
is an infant. I was in awe of the enormity of the challenges that lay
ahead, but I was also fully conscious of the potentials of a directly
elected President to deliver change and transform the nation that
has become the world's third largest democracy. And I knew that
along the way difficult decisions would have to be made. What
President Soekarno said —that being President is the loneliest job—
is entirely true.

This past year has been a rough roller coaster ride for Indonesia. I
would even say that it is one of our Republic's hardest years since
independence. We had to endure the loss of some 200,000 of our
brothers and sisters who lost their lives in a matter of minutes
due to the tsunami of December 26, 2004. We suffered from a

series of earthquakes. Yet, through all the trials and tribulations, we remained focused on the agenda for change, accelerated the wheels of the economy, intensified political reforms, aggressively fought corruption, kept our nation's spirits high, and above all, we managed to stay on course. We also raised Indonesia's international profile and strengthened our diplomatic activism. All in all, we emerged from the crisis a more resilient nation, and I believe we laid a good foundation to make Indonesia--as I promised during the elections--safer, more prosperous, more just, more democratic.

This book contains a collection of my speeches delivered for international audience. They cover wide-ranging topics, from terrorism to poverty, tsunami to corruption, democracy to education, globalization to infrastructure, security to investment. These speeches were delivered in many places : Jakarta, Bali, Medan, Canberra, Santiago, Washington DC, Tokyo, Singapore, among others.

What I hope to achieve through these speeches is to define Indonesia's new thinking and project the new spirit that emerged after the 2004 elections. A key challenge for my Government in our first year has been to translate the tremendous expectations, energy and optimism into real policy measures that will promote growth and stability. In the process of doing this, the inter-connection between our national objectives and international activities becomes stronger. I am a firm believer that to attain our domestic priorities, we need greater—not lesser—engagement with the outside world.

From reading the materials in this book, I hope readers will get the sense that Indonesia remains steadfast in our commitment to an independent and active foreign policy. I also hope readers will appreciate that Indonesia is very much an outward-looking country eager to make a difference as we promote peace and cooperation in the international arena

Every generation needs to find its voice. My only hope is that the ideas and messages expressed in these speeches and statements will add to the voice of the present generation. Here is where I remind my fellow countrymen that one way to measure our nation's vitality is by determining to what extent we have become part of the global marketplace of ideas.

In this book, I am honored that a number of distinguished international experts have graciously contributed their thoughts on Indonesia's recent development. In the following pages, you will see insightful commentaries from Kishore Mahbubani, Prof. Don Emmerson, Timothy Ong, Ed Masters, Prof. Takashi Shiraishi, Adam Schwarz, Greg Sheridan, Dr. Michael Williams, and Karim Raslan. Indonesia is fortunate to have them as friends, and I hope to read more of their work on Indonesia.

This book is dedicated to the good people of Indonesia, because it is from their courage and strength that I find my inspiration and draw my energy to serve this vast country of great promise.

Enjoy the book !

Dr. Susilo Bambang Yudhoyono

Editor's Note

The work for this book began in February 2005 when President Susilo Bambang Yudhoyono commissioned his staff to produce a collection of his major international speeches. The book would be published in August 2005 to coincide with our Independence Day celebration. The publication would also mark President Yudhoyono's first year in office.

We could not have met such a tight schedule if President Yudhoyono had not constantly encouraged us and checked on our progress. I speak for the rest of the team in expressing our admiration to President Yudhoyono for inspiring us with his words and his deeds. He makes us believe that we are working for a cause far larger than ourselves.

We are also grateful for the support of Cabinet Secretary Pak Sudi Silalahi. And thanks, Pak T.B. Silalahi, for your valuable advice —you are an angel. The same goes for my colleague, Pak Kurdi Mustofa, who makes good things happen, and Pak Andi A. Mallarangeng who always lend us his helping hand.

To the team who completed this project, I am particularly thankful. Thank you, Ivan Novianto, for faithfully managing our mountain of files and for working so hard with Purwandari Dyah Hapsari to ensure a successful result. My able staff Denny Abdi, Tri Sukma Djandam and Landry Haryo Subianto, assisted by Anita Wardhana, did excellent research to obtain reports and analyses on Indonesia, many of which are quoted in this book. I appreciate our meticulous proof-reader, Prof. Hasjim Djalal, for spotting the typos, spelling, and grammatical errors. I also wish to thank our photo editor, Deniek Sukarya, for his superb editing job. Dudi Anung Anindito, Abror Rizki, Armaya Thohir, and Deniek Sukarya deserve special praise for their wonderful photographs, which capture the essence of President SBY's dynamic personality. Garibaldi Sudjatmiko, Iwan Djalal and Eko Rachmadi get the credit for preparing the DVD attached at the back of this book—on time, and Yusuf did wonderful job for designing the cover. We also thank the Indonesian embassies abroad that sent some of the news clippings used in this book. And thank you, Pak Sudjadnan Parnohadiningrat (Secretary-General of the Foreign Ministry), for helping the embassies meet our deadline.

There are those who might say that this book suffers from an overdose of optimism. To this, we plead guilty. An unavoidable consequence of working with SBY is not only getting infected with his seemingly boundless energy, but also with his belief that a positive outlook is always better than negativism or cynicism. If anything, we hope that the optimism and the "can do" spirit reflected in the speeches and commentaries in this book will prove contagious for readers as well.

Dr. Dino Patti Djalal

Table of Contents

SELECTED INTERNATIONAL SPEECHES BY PRESIDENT SUSILO BAMBANG YUDHOYONO

MEMORABLE SPEECHES BY SUSILO BAMBANG YUDHOYONO
BEFORE HIS PRESIDENCY

Essays by International Observers on Recent Developments in Indonesia

Kishore Mahbubani
Prof. Donald K. Emmerson
Timothy Ong
Edward Masters
Prof. Takashi Shiraishi
Adam Schwarz
Greg Sheridan
Dr Michael Williams
Karim Raslan

By Kishore Mahbubani *

Indonesia:
Seizing a new window of opportunity

recently met an Indian diplomat who accompanied an Indian Minister when he called on a senior Clinton Administration official just as Indonesia's financial crisis was unfolding in 1998. The first question this senior American official posed to the Indian Minister was: "By the way, how significant is this country called Indonesia? I have spent my whole day working on it."

This lack of awareness of Indonesia's strengths and significance is not confined to Washington D.C. but it is still shocking. As the world's fourth most populous state, the most populous nation of Muslims with a secular constitution and now the second largest democracy outside the West, Indonesia should naturally loom large in the global imagination. This book of essays by President Susilo Bambang Yudhoyono, the first directly elected President of Indonesia, is therefore timely and should be widely read.

---

* Kishore Mahbubani is the Dean of the Lee Kuan Yew School of Public Policy in Singapore. He is the author of "Beyond the Age of Innocence: Rebuilding Trust between America and the World" and "Can Asians Think?" (which now has a Bahasa edition). These are his personal views.

The recent story of Indonesia is remarkable. Clearly, Indonesia went through seven lean years between 1997 and 2004. The prospects looked so grim that many respected academic analysts predicted gloom and doom. Two Australian scholars, Paul Dibb and Peter Prince, warned in 2001 that "The regional base for ethnic and economic jealousies in Indonesia lends substance to fears of a national breakdown along the lines of Yugoslavia or the former Soviet Union."[1] An American-based scholar, Rajan Menon, issued a similar warning: "Indonesia is staggering like a heavyweight boxer who has absorbed too many blows in too many places. A faltering economy, a fractious and feeble central government, communal war and secessionism could culminate in the state's collapse and the country's fragmentation."[2]

But Indonesia did not collapse. Instead, it showed remarkable resilience and strength by bouncing back to hold remarkably peaceful elections in 2004, defying all predictions. This success was obvious. Less noted was the resolve of the Indonesian people in the seven lean years. Traditionally, economic collapse is followed by social unrest and mass migration overseas. And Indonesia did experience a serious economic downturn. As the World Bank noted: "No country in recent history, let alone one the size of Indonesia, has ever suffered such a dramatic reversal of fortune."[3] Yet, Indonesians did not leave their country, not even the ethnic minorities. This is remarkable. Philippines' per capita income

[1] Paul Dibb and Peter Prince, "Indonesia's Grim Outlook," Orbis, Vol. 45, No. 4 (Fall 2001), p. 625.
[2] Raja Menon, "Another Year of Living Dangerously," The National Interest, No. 65 (Fall 2001), p. 101.
[3] Dibb and Prince, p. 629.

is higher than Indonesia's but in per capita terms, its emigration is far higher. All this demonstrate that the Indonesians' sense of nationhood is strong.

The strong mandate that President Susilo received from all corners of a geographically, ethnically and culturally diverse nation also sent a signal of a community wanting to come together to demonstrate national resolve. They decided to place their trust and confidence in President Susilo. So far, despite the inevitable problems of governing a large developing country, the new President has not let the Indonesian people down. Instead, he has begun tackling some critical challenges head on. He is making the battle against corruption the centerpiece of his reform agenda, bravely taking unprecedented steps such as prosecuting senior government officials. He also displayed political courage in pushing through unpopular, but timely and necessary, policies such as the reduction of fuel subsidies in his first few months in office. On the economic front, President Susilo has embarked on a three-prong economic strategy of "pro-growth" (revitalising the business and investment climate), "pro-jobs" (creating jobs for the people), and "pro-poor" (reducing poverty). Despite significant external challenges (such as high world oil prices), his efforts have improved international confidence and helped Indonesia re-emerge on the radar screens of international investors. On the political front, President Susilo, who is Indonesia's first democratically elected President, has recently overseen the first ever direct local elections. President Ronald Reagan once quoted a famous saying by Lao Tze: "Manage a state as you cook a delicate fish: Do not overdo it." So far, President Susilo seems to be heeding this advice, showing respect and understanding of Indonesia's remarkable diversity.

Indonesia's progress was suddenly set back by the devastating earthquake and tsunami that struck Aceh province on 26 Dec 2004. Here, President Susilo demonstrated his leadership and statesmanship in rallying his fellow Indonesians and the international community to respond to the crisis. President Susilo skilfully chaired the Special ASEAN Leaders' Summit on Earthquake and Tsunami in January 2005 and managed to secure substantial pledges of assistance from the international community. His crisis management skills came through clearly in his efforts to marshal the Indonesian military. police, and other relevant agencies to work hand-in-hand with the international community to rebuild the lives of the affected communities in Aceh.

Still, many major challenges remain to be addressed. Despite the improving economy, FDI flows have not returned to pre-1997 levels. Indonesia is lagging behind China and India. Terrorism remains a challenge (although, as the 7/7 bombings showed in London, no country is immune). The legal system needs strengthening. This list should not be surprising. The larger the country, the longer the list of challenges. In today's small globalized world, some of the challenges of leadership come from overseas. Often the West can set domestic agendas, as it once did for Indonesia and East Timor. Hence, it is vital for Indonesia to continue retaining the trust and confidence of the international community, both on the governmental and non-governmental fronts. Life is never a smooth road. Indonesia will hit some bumps inevitably. This is why international confidence is a key factor.

The good news for Indonesia is that the international climate for promoting development has never been more propitious. Globally, there is a consensus developing around the key principles of good governance: political stability, free market policies, rule of law, transparency and accountability in the public administration. Indonesia does not need to reinvent the wheel. The Lee Kuan Yew School of Public Policy, of which I am privileged to be Dean, will be happy to share its experience, if called on to do so. On the geopolitical front, there is also a strong international consensus that the world has a vital stake in Indonesia's peace and prosperity. The warm reception that President Susilo received during his visits to the United States and Japan as well as to regional countries showed both the confidence in President Susilo's leadership as well as the new global commitment to Indonesia's success.

There is therefore a reasonable possibility that the past seven lean years will be followed by seven fat years. Strong leadership is always key. President Susilo is clearly winning greater confidence. Business Week, in its 11 July 2005 edition, named President Susilo as one of the "stars of Asia" agenda setters, and confidently pronounced that Indonesia, for the first time since the overthrow of Soeharto, has a leader "who might just pull it off." Both the world and the region are rooting for Indonesia's success. This book of essays can both inspire and motivate the people of Indonesia to seize the new window of opportunity that has opened for them.

****

Prof. Donald K. Emmerson *

Rebalancing Indonesia?

L eaving aside the qualifications that a fuller account would require, Indonesia's three decades under President Suharto could be summarized as an experiment in development without democracy. Although the experiment failed, in the end, for many reasons, one could argue that Suharto's system fell into a chasm of its own making: the widening gap between the economy as it raced ahead and the polity as it was held back.

Beginning in 1998, this sequence was reversed. Democracy outran development. Nationwide, Indonesians voted in democratic elections four times—once in 1999 and thrice in 2004. An executive-heavy constitution once deemed sacrosanct was amended four times—in effect, revamped. Notwithstanding some limits and setbacks, political freedoms flourished, the army's political role shrank from dominance to relevance, and a radical effort to decentralize authority spread political competition throughout the archipelago.

---

* Prof. Donald K. Emmerson is a senior fellow at Stanford University where he also heads the Asia Pacific Research Center's Southeast Asia Forum.

By 2004 one could speculate that post-Indonesia was veering toward a yawning gap that had reversed Suharto's dilemma, as the reforming polity pulled the country forward while a laggard and corrupted economy kept it back.

Nine months into an administration scheduled to last five years is too soon to conclude that Indonesia's sixth president, Susilo Bambang Yudhoyono, or SBY, will become known for having closed the second gap without reopening the first one—by achieving and sustaining development with democracy.

Recent signs of an improving economy are encouraging. Growth accelerated sharply to a 6.4 percent year-on-year pace in the first quarter of 2005, the best such rate since Suharto's fall. Forecasts for all of 2005 soon surged. Morgan Stanley Economics (MSE), for example, enlarged by one-fifth its prediction for current-year economic growth, from 4.5 to 5.4 percent.

In 1998 Indonesian GDP fell 13 percent. From that severe contraction the economy moved through a low-growth phase driven less by investment than consumption. Now, finally, capital inflows are burgeoning. Foreign direct investment (FDI) approvals are plans not transfers. But their year-on-year near-doubling to US$ 4.9 billion in the first third of 2005 certainly is good news.

SBY became president in October. These are the first economic data to arrive for periods on his watch. "While we believe it is premature to proclaim the arrival of a structural investment boom,"

MSE concluded, "the proactive efforts of the new government to improve the investment climate have vastly improved growth and confidence."[1]   Not all would agree with the adverb "vastly." But MSE's assessment itself signals the positive difference for potential investors that SBY appears to have made.

Economic growth and socioeconomic development are not synonymous. The former merely makes the latter possible. SBY's quantitative target is 6.6 percent average annual economic growth. But he wants, as he puts it, "quality growth"—the kind that will enable Indonesians to halve rates of poverty and unemployment by 2009. Improving the business climate, he has said, is a means to that higher and longer-term end.[2]

Of all the obstacles to achieving development with democracy in Indonesia, the most formidable are corruption and insecurity. On these fronts also, SBY has been vocal. Rather than treating such ills as abstract priorities, he has taken specific measures, focused on particular targets, and sought to rally public opinion. "In many provinces," he noted recently, "we have put corrupt local bureaucrats, political leaders and parliamentarians, majors, and even a governor in jail for their wrongdoings. Many government officials now have to think twice."[3]

---

[1] Daniel Lian (MSE), "Indonesia: A Well-Deserved Forecast Upgrade," 29 June 2005.
[2] "Yudhoyono's 'Triple-track' Strategy," Asian Business/Online Extra, 4 July 2005.
[3] Ibid.
[4] Muninggar Sri Saraswati, "Susilo Texts Millions in Antidrug Campaign," The Jakarta Post, 29 June 2005.

At the inauguration of his new national police chief in July, while calling for action against illegal logging, street crime, and transnational terrorism, SBY urged the new head of the force to battle corruption in its own ranks as well. (The previous chief of police had failed to meet a 100-day deadline laid down by SBY for the arrest of two alleged Malaysian terrorists who remain at large.) Meanwhile the Corruption Eradication Commission has proven itself willing to take on high-profile cases.

Perhaps the weakest link in the apparatus of reform in Indonesia are the country's courts. Judges can still be bought. Verdicts can be erratic. Violators of human rights have gone unpunished, or underpunished. A judiciary that is neither clean nor independent cannot implement the rule of law. Thoroughgoing legal reform may be the president's next major challenge.

Whatever the outcome of SBY's campaigns on behalf of a growing economy with less poverty, cleaner government, and a more secure society, one thing is clear: Susilo Bambang Yudhoyono, the first directly elected head of government in his country's history, has mobilized the presidency to communicate with the Indonesian people.

This new presidential style was illustrated on 28 June during a ceremony at the state palace to commemorate an International Day Against Drug Abuse and Illicit Trafficking. SBY used the occasion to send a text message to millions of users of all the major mobile-phone service providers in Indonesia. "Stop drug abuse and drug-related crimes right now," the message ran. "Let us preserve and build a healthy, smart and progressive nation."

Different observers will interpret this anecdote differently: cynically, admiringly, or with an intermediate mix of skepticism and appreciation. In the eyes of busy Indonesians already wearied by spam in cyberspace, SBY's exhortation may have been just one more intrusion. Others, however, may have read the message as evidence that their president cared enough to call.

The answers to many key questions will influence the course of SBY's presidency in months to come. Two such questions come quickly to mind:

First, looking back on the earthquake and tsunami that devastated so much and so many in northwestern Sumatra at the end of 2004, will Indonesians be proud of their government's response? Will the massive aid funneled into the country have been used to good effect? Will the disaster have in some sense swept the deck to enable, finally, a stable accommodation between Aceh's rebels and Jakarta's politicians? Or will efforts toward relief and conciliation fall victim to indifference, malfeasance, and intransigence—undermining SBY's cell-phone subtext that the country's leaders really care?

Second, will decentralization, including "blossoming" (pemekaran)— the sometimes volatile process of carving new jurisdictions out of old ones—animate the base of society in ways that dovetail with, or diverge from SBY's priorities and policies? Will the direct election of governors, mayors, and district heads weaken or strengthen his hand, and how? If and as "blossoming" reduces the average ethnoreligious diversity of Indonesia's provinces, districts, and cities, will conflicts and insecurity thrive or abate?

Today Susilo Bambang Yudhoyono is being challenged not only to rebalance Indonesia by reviving its underperforming economy and thus helping legitimate its newly democratic polity. He and his government are also under pressure to improve public and personal security and, no less important, to establish, embody, and protect the moral integrity of public persons and institutions. To call this multi-tasking Herculean is to belabor the obvious.

Judgments of SBY will continue to differ. So will expectations. That is as it should be in a democracy. What cannot be doubted meanwhile is that Susilo Bambang Yudhoyono is helping, with energy and innovation, to make the future history of Indonesia.

****

Timothy Ong *

President Yudhoyono:
A pivotal leader for a pivotal state

n 1999, at the height of the Asian financial crisis, a group of
American scholars surveyed the developing world to identify key
countries they considered to be 'pivotal states'. They defined a
pivotal state as a key country whose future affects the future of its
region and the world.[1]

Of the nine countries these scholars identified as pivotal states,
one was from Southeast Asia. This was a remarkable country of
extraordinary contrasts comprising 17,000 islands stretching 3,200
miles from east to west. A nation of 224 million people, it is the
world's fourth most populous nation and third largest democracy.
It is also the world's largest Muslim majority nation with three-
quarters as many Muslims as all the Arab countries combined. The
pivotal state from Southeast Asia they identified is the Republic of
Indonesia.

---

* Chairman of Asia Inc Forum and Deputy Chairman, Brunei Economic Development
  Board.
[1] The Pivotal States: A New Framework for U.S. Policy in the Developing World
  edited by Robert Chase, Emily Hill and Paul M. Kennedy

Few nations have had a past more turbulent than Indonesia's. Forty years ago, Indonesia was one of the poorest countries in the world with the lowest income per head in Asia – one third of China and India. Twelve years ago, after three decades of rapid growth, the World Bank considered Indonesia to be one of eight most successful economies in Asia together with Japan, South Korea, Taiwan, Hong Kong, Singapore, Malaysia and Thailand. Eight years ago, Indonesia experienced a complete reversal of fortune when its economy collapsed and millions of Indonesians plunged into poverty. At the end of 1998, Indonesia stood at the brink of political and economic collapse but it was not to be.

Eight years from the Asian financial crisis and despite the recent Tsunami disaster that killed 128,000 and left half a million homeless, Southeast Asia's pivotal state is demonstrating an unexpected resilience.

Despite gloomy prognostications, its fledgling democracy is alive and well. Indonesia's first ever direct presidential elections concluded in September 2004 was largely peaceful and honest. The contest was between politicians and parties of secular outlook; the Islamists were mostly shunned by the electorate.

Indonesia's economy is stable and growing. The economy is growing at its fastest pace since 1996, up 6.4% year-on-year in the first quarter. Growth is projected at 5.5% in 2005. The debt to GDP ratio has been significantly reduced from 99% in 2000 to 53% in 2004. Foreign direct investment commitments in the first four months of this year have nearly doubled to $5.5 billion compared to the same period in 2004. Income per head today is higher than it was before the financial crisis.

Will Indonesia whose recent history is filled with tragic disappointments fulfill its promise as a pivotal state? At this time much depends on the man whom Indonesians voted overwhelmingly and directly to become the sixth President of Indonesia. Dr Susilo Bambang Yudhoyono took office in October 2004 with a reputation for intellectual brilliance, integrity and a cautious approach to decision making.

Dubbed the 'thinking general', Dr Yudhoyono had graduated from the Indonesian Military Academy in 1973 at the top of his class, studied extensively in the United States and obtained a PhD in agricultural economics by dissertation two days before his presidential victory was announced. His reputation for integrity was underlined by key choices he made in the course of his political career before becoming President. He served as Minister for Security and Political Affairs under both President Abdurrahman Wahid and President Megawati Sukarnoputri and left both administrations over issues of principle. As for his cautious approach to decision making which his critics have characterized as indecisiveness and made much of, this reflects an abiding preoccupation with adhering to the rules and being above board on all things.

Dr Yudhoyono's performance in the near term will be largely measured in terms of his success in meeting three pressing challenges. Firstly, his resolve in waging war against corruption. If he sustains the present momentum that has so far seen two former ministers detained for questioning and a former provincial governor jailed, he will add immeasurably to his political capital and stamp his authority as the leader Indonesia needs.

Secondly, Dr Yudhoyono will need all his considerable political skills to manage the expectations of a nation hungry for change and desperate for economic relief. Nowhere are these political skills more badly needed than in the area of economic reform where there are unavoidable tradeoffs between popular support and much needed unpopular decisions. How the present challenge of fuel subsidies that (at current oil prices) are threatening to blow out the state budget will have a significant bearing on Dr Yudhoyono's standing as an economic reformer and manager.

Thirdly, Dr Yudhoyono will need to build quickly the institutional capacity required to translate his vision and his will into concrete results. Combating corruption will require effective law enforcement and a legal system that works. Economic reform will require the technocratic expertise to ensure proper sequencing of policy changes and careful distribution of the costs as well as a civil service capable of implementing change honestly and efficiently. Having vision and will is necessary but insufficient. Sustainable change requires that vision and will are accompanied by the capacity to execute.

Just over a 100 days into his presidency, Dr Yudhoyono spoke in Singapore of the different ways a country's greatness can be measured. He expressed at the time his conviction that the true measure of a country's greatness lies in its ability to adapt to changing times and new challenges.

Can Dr Yudhoyono lead the changes Indonesia needs if it is to fulfill its promise as a great pivotal state? It is obviously too early to come to a decisive conclusion. But present indications are promising and growing numbers of people in Indonesia and beyond are cheering him on. One thing is abundantly clear: the region and the world have a strong vested interest in his success and the success of the pivotal state he leads. President Yudhoyono of Indonesia deserves all the support we can give him.

****

Edward Masters *

A Different Indonesia

Addressing a group of business leaders at the U.S. Chamber of Commerce in Washington on May 26, President Susilo Bambang Yudhoyono started by saying he wished he did not have to stand at the rostrum and make a speech because he had been told that "a President looks wiser when he is sitting down with his mouth shut." Fortunately he did not follow this advice but went on to deliver a speech on Indonesia's new policies which by the end had the audience standing and applauding,

This was only one success of SBY's busy visit to Washington on May 24-27, 2005. The President, Ibu Ani and their party arrived in Washington on the late evening of May 24 on a Garuda flight under conditions which might have been considered auspicious in Indonesia but not in the United States. The American pawang was apparently not as powerful as those in Indonesia, and the party arrived after the long trip from Jakarta in a fierce rainstorm. The

* Co-Chairman of USINDO Board of Trustee. Former President of the U.S.-Indonesia Society, U.S. Ambassador to Indonesia, President of the National Policy Association, and Senior Vice President for International Affairs of the Natomas Company. Former Adjunct Professor at the School of Advanced International Studies (Johns Hopkins University) and the Fletcher School of Law and Diplomacy (Tufts University)

welcoming party waiting at the airport was thoroughly drenched, but they rallied and put the best face on welcoming the first directly elected president of Indonesia on his first presidential visit to the U.S. capital.

During the next two days President Yudhoyono met with President Bush, had lunch with Vice President Cheney, talked with a number of key cabinet members and leaders of the Congress, met with additional businessmen and the Indonesian community, and together with President Bush met in the White House with members of the Asian Pacific Heritage organization representing Americans of Asian descent.

President Yudhoyono's major public appearance was at a gala dinner hosted by The United States-Indonesia Society (USINDO) and attended by 500 guests representing government and private sector opinion leaders. The President used the occasion not only to stress the importance of the U.S.-Indonesia bilateral relationship but also to emphasize that "the 2004 elections changed Indonesia for good" and that the nation is now returning to an internationalist role after several years of preoccupation with domestic issues. "We are trying," he said "to do the right things."

Speaking as a friend, President SBY also had some words of advice for the United States. "The present and future world order will be determined by how America uses her enormous power and, more importantly, how she shares and allocates her resources to promote peace and prosperity." He suggested that the United States project its "soft power" of culture, education, business, etc., rather than "hard power" that may provoke "resistance and sometimes resentment." The speech was interrupted many times by applause, and one guest with a background in journalism said she had heard many presidential speeches and this was the best ever.

The two presidents, who had previously met at the APEC meeting in Chile, hit it off well. American and Indonesian observers who participated in the meeting were uniform in agreeing that the atmosphere was warm, friendly and constructive. The Joint Statement issued at the end of the meeting sets the stage for strengthened co-operation on a broad range of issues. President Bush and other American leaders expressed their deep sympathy for the tragic earthquake and tsunami which caused such widespread death and hardship for the Indonesian people only two months after SBY assumed the presidency. Bush pledged $400 million for relief and reconstruction, and much more than that has been raised by private organizations, business firms and individuals.

While not new, it is noteworthy that Bush in the Joint Statement reiterated U.S. support for Indonesia's territorial integrity and U.S. opposition to "secessionist movements in any part of Indonesia." He noted that "a strong, united, democratic, and prosperous Indonesia will serve as a force for stability and progress in Asia and beyond." Speaking to the press after their meeting Bush said," Indonesia will play a large role...in helping us understand that great religions should co-exist in a peaceful way."

In the Joint Statement, the two presidents "underscored their strong commitment to fight terrorism" but also "endorsed cultural and educational exchange visits and interfaith dialogue as a way to promote...mutual understanding." Specifically, they pledged to "expand opportunities and improve the quality of higher education for Indonesian students, including by increasing the number... studying in the United States." This is particularly gratifying to USINDO, the Indonesian Embassy, and officials in Jakarta who have been working for several years to expand opportunities for Indonesian students at U.S. universities.

Overall there is no question that this highly successful visit reaffirmed that Indonesia is the cornerstone of U.S. relations in Southeast Asia. It strengthened the partnership between the world's second and third largest democracies and also the personal ties between the two presidents, who are scheduled to meet again later this year at APEC or the UN General Assembly. As shown by SBY's frank comments in Washington, there are still significant differences between Washington and Jakarta reflecting their differing perspectives on world affairs. But it seems clear that the two sides have found a broad area of common ground on which to work together. It may not be going too far to suggest that SBY is one of the Muslim leaders with whom George W. Bush is most comfortable and with whom he has close rapport.

The December 26, 2004 earthquake/tsunami provided a tremendous distraction from domestic programs during much of SBY's first year in office, but nonetheless I believe important progress has been made in at least four key domestic areas. First, the SBY government has strengthened democracy to the point where any turning back to old ways of governing now seems unlikely. The Yudhoyono administration is open and accessible, although the well-intentioned release by the President of his cell phone number to the public led so many Indonesians to exercise their domestic rights that the system has had to be institutionalized. The presidential staff has been strengthened and lines of responsibility and communication clarified in a way not seen in Jakarta for some years.

The administration also seems to be working better with the Dewan Perwakilan Rakyat than has been the case for some time. In short, Indonesia has become a prime example of how democracy can be brought peacefully to an important Muslim-majority nation.

Secondly, and of special importance domestically and internationally, SBY has followed through on his campaign pledge to attack Indonesia's endemic corruption. Action has been taken against a number of senior government officials and managers of state enterprises but also against lower level bureaucrats, tax evaders and illegal loggers, among others. Much remains to be done, but the view is gaining ground that Indonesia has changed and that the rampant corruption of the past will no longer be tolerated. This will support another of SBY's goals, the creation of jobs and the accompanying need for increased foreign investment.

In the third place, a good start has been made in introducing structural reforms that will bring government closer to the people, provide better coordination in policy formation, and reduce "unofficial channels" which have complicated orderly administration at times in the past. Particularly noteworthy, and important for further strengthening U.S.-Indonesian military ties, are continued military reforms by the SBY government to bring the TNI and its private businesses more directly under civilian control. Finally, building on progress made by the previous administration, the SBY team has continued to strengthen economic growth, which by early 2005 was running at six percent. The rupiah, while reacting occasionally to domestic or external developments, remained relatively stable, interest rates were manageable, and inflation was at the single digit level. SBY was also starting to win back foreign investors who were previously deterred by political uncertainty, corruption, and bureaucratic impediments. Revival after a lapse of eight years of the U.S.-Indonesia energy dialogue, a result of SBY's Washington visit, should open the way for renewed investment in this vital sector which will reduce Indonesia's growing oil import bill.

Personally President Yudhoyono is emerging as a firm administrator, a man who can be tough when needed (as for example in holding the line on cutting the fuel subsidy against popular opposition), and a man of personal compassion. This compassion was shown when one of his first acts after arriving in Washington was meeting with Mrs. Patsy Spier, the widow of one of the teachers killed in an ambush of their vehicle in Papua in 2002.

Major problems remain, but the SBY administration has made a good start toward a more active and constructive role for Indonesia internationally and increased stability, openness, and orderly reform domestically. Indonesia today is different than it was before SBY. And the change has been much for the better.

****

Prof. Takashi Shiraishi *

Reinventing Indonesia

A year has passed since Susilo Bambang Yudhoyono assumed the presidency of the Republic of Indonesia.

Installed in October last year, Yudhoyono is the first president to be elected directly by the Indonesian people. By all accounts a good listener, he is very patient, cautious, and hands-on as far as management is concerned.

But he is also, in many ways, the first post-Suharto president. Since Suharto stepped down in 1998, the three other presidents—B.J. Habibie, Abdurrahman Wahid, and Megawati Sukarnoputri—had largely defined themselves and their administrative agenda in relation—and often opposition—to Suharto.

Yudhoyono represents a new type of Indonesian political leader. He is one of the first politicians to understand the importance of the

* Vice President and Professor, National Graduate Institute for Policy Studies (GRIPS), Japan

democratic process, to which the public and public opinion matter. He is, in other words, the first president to listen to the people.

He is also a reformer. One of the top military leaders in the final years of the New Order, he, together with General Wiranto, led the Indonesian military during the period of transition from Suharto's dictatorship to the current democratic regime. He was instrumental in calling for reforms aimed at dismantling the military's socio-political function, which had long been used to justify the military's central role in supporting the authoritarian government.

The Indonesian people were disillusioned with Megawati's failure to live up to her promise of reform, and clamored for change. It is true that Megawati's government succeeded in stabilizing the economy. But it failed to achieve economic growth that was high enough to create jobs for the nearly 2.5 million people entering the labor market every year. Her administration was marked by widespread corruption. Military reform stalled. The conflict in Aceh worsened when Megawati imposed martial law and adopted a military approach to Aceh.

In his presidential campaign, Yudhoyono called for change, and projected himself as a man of will and leadership. He rightly identified the economic question as the fundamental issue that Indonesia now faces. His winning the election shows how much Indonesians actually hope for a better future.

There is no question that democracy is alive and well in Indonesia. Parliamentary elections held in April as well as the two rounds of presidential elections in July and September were held peacefully, fairly, and freely.

But democratization has changed Indonesian politics in a fundamental way. Along with the presidency and the military, the parliament and political parties have now emerged as competing power centers. Yudhoyono has had to negotiate with these power centers to advance his policy agenda, which include, first of all, maintaining Indonesia's territorial integrity and adopting a political solution in Aceh, and second, formulating economic policies aimed at improving the investment climate and overcoming the economic crisis, and finally, instituting judicial reform, fighting corruption, and addressing problems of law and order.

Despite these challenges, Yudhoyono's track record during his first year has been impressive.

When Yudhoyono came to power, the parliament was evenly divided. But with the election of Vice President Jusuf Kalla as chairman of Golkar in December last year, the great majority of parliamentary members now support the government and the opposition is in disarray. The military leadership has also changed with Yudhoyono allies, including the current army chief of staff, now filling strategic positions.

Some pressing issues remain, however.

The newly formed cabinet is clearly a product of delicate political negotiations and compromises typical of democratic systems of government. More important is the question of the division of labor between the president and his vice-president. A product of economic development under Suharto, Jusuf Kalla has built his empire as a leading pribumi (native non-Chinese) businessman and Golkar politician. The archetypal businessman-politician whose business is business, Jusuf Kalla has a strong voice in the current government. Other interests, represented particularly by Islamic and Islamist parties, can not be ignored, either.

Yudhoyono made it clear in his inaugural address that Indonesians should not expect any easy and rapid solution to the country's pressing problems.

He has signified his willingness to work toward a political approach to resolve the conflict in Aceh. The earthquake and tsunamis that hit Aceh provided an opportunity for Yudhoyono to push for his initiatives. Overriding opposition from his own administration as well as from sections of the parliament and military, he approved the introduction of foreign NGOs and troops for emergency relief efforts, and opened informal negotiations with the separatist Gerakan Aceh Merdeka (now ongoing in Helsinki) to address one by one the contentious issues involved. His ability to bring about a political solution to the problem Aceh will be the biggest test of his leadership.

The government is now working to improve the investment climate for medium and long-term economic growth. This strategy is preferable to the alternative of creating jobs through government-funded public works, an alternative unsustainable in the long run. There is domestic resistance to foreign firms doing business in Indonesia, as seen in the parliament's opposition to the ExxonMobil deal in Cepu and Cemex's attempt to acquire a stake in Semen Gresik. But Yudhoyono has shown his commitment to improving investment climates by personally meeting with business leaders. Approvals for foreign investment reached almost US$5 billion in the first four months of this year, up 50 percent on the same period last year.

The president and his attorney general have also demonstrated their will to tackle big corruption cases and bring the guilty parties to justice through investigations of a provincial governor, an election commissioner and the head of a partially state-owned bank, among others.

The government is on the right track. The more this government shows that it is in charge, the more public trust it will generate. Indonesia is a project, begun in the 1920s by Sukarno's generation and inherited by Suharto's generation. Yudhoyono needs to reinvent this project not only to maintain the integrity of Indonesia and bring prosperity to the Indonesian people, but also and most importantly to regain the people's faith in the republic.

****

Adam Schwarz *

Charting a New Course for Indonesia

I ndonesian politics in 2005 has again proved the old adage that a year is a long time in politics. As President Susilo Bambang Yudhoyono moves towards the end of his remarkably successful first year in office, it's hard to believe that just 18 months ago he wasn't even a candidate in the presidential election planned for September 2004.

It remains early days for the Yudhoyono administration, and the obstacles to returning the country to sustainably high rates of economic growth are many and complex. Yet there is no denying that President SBY has brought a welcome sense of energy, optimism and professionalism to Indonesian politics. For the first time in many years, Indonesians sense a steady hand on the till of government.

The emergence of SBY as a presidential candidate in 2004 and his eventual victory represented a turning point for Indonesian

* Adam Schwarz is a management consultant based in Singapore. He is the author of the seminal work on contemporary Indonesia, A Nation in Waiting: Indonesia's Search for Stability.

democracy and suggest a maturation of Indonesian politics more generally. SBY's vision of a "New Indonesia" is an appealing one to both Indonesians and Indonesia-watchers worldwide. Before returning to a discussion of that vision, it's worthwhile to review briefly SBY's sudden and recent emergence into the political realm, for it says a great deal about Indonesians' yearning for different and better leadership.

As 2004 opened, there was a remarkable lack of excitement in the air regarding the upcoming presidential campaign. In many respects, the Indonesian elections were shaping up as a carbon copy of the 1999 elections: same parties, same candidates, same expected result. In some countries, such predictability would be seen as a good thing. But not Indonesia. The seven years of democratic governance since the fall of ex-President Suharto were not without their successes, especially in consolidating democratic and civil freedoms. But the three presidential administrations which came between those of Presidents Suharto and Yudhoyono were generally seen as deeply flawed. None were able to generate the economic growth rates and job creation that Indonesians were demanding. None had made much progress on building the strong institutions that market economies need to succeed. None had come close to developing momentum behind a credible anti-corruption program. The prospect of another five years of similar economic management was sending investors fleeing for the exits.

But in March 2004, Indonesian politics broke from its trajectory and headed off in another direction. In that month, Coordinating Minister for Security Affairs Yudhoyono resigned from the cabinet of then President Megawati Sukarnoputri and declared his candidacy for president. In the beginning, few gave SBY much hope of winning. After all, he had never before run for public office. He was loosely associated with the newly formed Democrat Party, but that party lacked the infrastructure and name recognition of Indonesia's bigger, more established parties. The big political parties were thought to have a lock on the parliamentary electoral process, and thus on the selection of the nation's president. As a result, the incumbent President Megawati, who headed the biggest of the political parties, the Indonesian Democratic Party of Struggle, was widely believed to be headed for a near-certain re-election.

But those observers who joined the Megawati bandwagon had missed two crucial changes in Indonesian politics: one legal and one cultural. The legal development was the relatively unheralded constitutional reform from a few years earlier that created two separate elections for the parliament and the president. The reform gave Indonesians the opportunity to choose a president directly and greatly weakened – to a degree not fully appreciated even today – the hold of Indonesia's political parties over the political process. This crucial legal change returned the locus of political power to the Indonesian voter. By opening the opportunity for new blood to enter the political arena without requiring the consent of Jakarta-based political party leaders, this legal reform broke the back of the elite-centered political system created and nurtured by former President Suharto for three-and-a-half decades.

The shift in Indonesia's political culture was even harder to discern. Indonesian voters used to be routinely described as politically apathetic and inordinately faithful to their political parties. These descriptions were not without solid historical evidence. Voters had an extremely limited role to play in the highly regulated politics under President Suharto, and so apathy toward the formal political process was hardly surprising. Indonesians also used to be described as subject to 'primordial' politics, in which families, villages and communities stayed loyal to a political party regardless of its policies or, for that matter, its political fortunes. This so-called political reality naturally reduced the incentive for political party officials to understand and address the concerns of ordinary voters.

But both of the descriptions turned out to be less true than once believed. Following Indonesia's return to democratic politics in 1998, Indonesians' political apathy disappeared in a hurry. Voter interest and turn-out rose dramatically. Acutely aware of what they had been deprived of for so long, Indonesians were decidedly interested in using their electoral rights once they had been granted those rights again. Similarly, the notion of Indonesian voters as unmoveably loyal to a particular political party regardless of its track record also turned out to be an exaggeration, if not a fundamental misconception. Indonesians, it became obvious in 2004, did indeed care about the performance of their political leaders and, moreover, they didn't think that highly of the performance of the incumbent leaders. While familiar patterns emerged in the parliamentary elections earlier in 2004, the presidential elections later in the year revealed a far more fluid set of voters. President SBY's astonishing victory in the presidential elections of September 2004, with more than 60% of the vote, demonstrated an intense desire by Indonesians for a different sort of leadership and perhaps even a different sort of Indonesia.

What accounted for SBY's extraordinary appeal to the Indonesian voter in the 2004 elections and the continuing support he has enjoyed into his first year in office? In what ways is he a fundamentally different politician than the three post-Suharto presidents who preceded him? One obvious difference is SBY's long-term view of where he wants Indonesia to go and become, his managerial talent for leading large organizations, and his disciplined personal workstyle. Secondly, the widely traveled SBY is at home in the world; he has a keen understanding of both geopolitical dynamics and the economic implications of globalization. Thirdly, he gives both rhetorical and practical support to the critical role that the private-sector business community must play in Indonesia's economic recovery. Fourthly, he acknowledges and understands the critical importance of reforming and building the country's political and economic institutions. Fifthly, he is a pragmatist at heart, with a non-ideological, results-driven political orientation. And finally, he is a modern politician in his understanding of the need for continuous and effective communications with important stakeholders and constituencies.

These attributes reveal themselves in numerous ways. SBY's regular interactions with foreign leaders are well-planned and focused on outcomes. His appointment of several business leaders to his cabinet has greatly improved the richness of the dialogue between the Government and business community, and reduced the sense that the two were working against each other. Although much more needs to be done, SBY has given an important and real push to the goals of judicial reform and tackling the scourge of corruption. His pragmatism was on full display after the tragic tsunami which struck the coast of Aceh and North Sumatra at the very end of

2004, leaving over 130,000 dead and more than 30,000 missing. Despite contrary advice from some nationalists, Islamic groups and military officers, SBY did not hesitate in welcoming assistance from foreign militaries, governments and non-governmental organizations. By keeping his focus on the needs of the victims in the tsunami-affected areas, SBY won a great deal of admiration both from the Acehnese as well as the international community. By mid-2005, Jakarta's adept handling of post-tsunami relief and reconstruction helped paved the way to a long-awaited peace deal with Acehnese separatists, and promised an end to almost thirty years of conflict.

To be sure, much more needs to be done before Indonesia can reclaim either the economic growth rates or regional stature and leadership it enjoyed prior to the financial crisis of the late 1990s. For all its recent steps forward, Indonesia's democracy remains a work in progress. As with all transitions from authoritarian rule, Indonesia's democracy will need time before the risk of recidivism disappears. The government bureaucracy is bloated, inefficient and in parts outright disfunctional; transforming the bureaucracy into a modern civil service perhaps ranks as SBY's most difficult yet most critical task. Only with a much more efficient public sector can SBY hope to fulfill his ambitious reform agenda. Corruption of course remains an entrenched problem, and a major disincentive to new investment. The decentralization program which devolves political and economic power to Indonesia's provinces and districts is correct conceptually but poses an enormous capacity challenge for regional administrations. The risk of a rising wealth gap across regions cannot be discounted. In addition, a number of risk factors facing Indonesia are external to the country and beyond the control of the SBY administration: the price of oil, the continuing openness of global and regional trade patterns, the health of the global economy, political rivalries within Asia, to name just a few.

But against these risks are numerous opportunities for Indonesia to progress in political, economic and diplomatic terms. Most of these opportunities are well-known: among others, geographic and demographic size which give Indonesia geopolitical clout and an attractive market for investors; rich endowments of agricultural and mineral resources; and a set of political traditions which have enabled this multi-ethnic, multi-linguistic, multi-religious archipelago to hold together and grow as a nation. To this mix comes the undoubted leadership skills of President Yudhoyono. The positive change in how the average Indonesian views the future since the election of President SBY demonstrates once again the essential truth that there is no substitute for top-quality leadership in the business of nation-building.

****

Greg Sheridan *

A New Indonesian Renaissance ?

T he first time I interviewed Susilo Bambang Yudhoyono as president of Indonesia our meeting was delayed for a short while. SBY had just been comforting the grieving relatives of Australian servicemen and women who had lost their lives in a helicopter crash on the Indonesian island of Nias. The Australians had been there to help with tsunami relief and reconstruction work. The president was affected by the emotion of meeting the relatives and wanted some time to himself, to reflect and to recover from the task of offering solace to people sick with grief.

When we did meet, later that night, he was his usual infinitely courteous self. A general who is courteous to everyone he meets is worthy of comment in any context, but one who, after everything he has been through, can be moved by the grief of others, even beyond that of his own countryman, is a large hearted leader.

SBY is a fascinating mixture of all the different influences a modern Indonesian president could be subject to. He is that rarest

---

* Greg Sheridan is the foreign editor of The Australian and author of Cities of the Hot Zone, a Southeast Asian Adventure.

of creatures, an intellectual with a popular touch and a good administrative record. When he was Coordinating Minister for Politics and Security he was the go-to minister in the Indonesian Government. He was the minister who could get things done - more than that he had a certain gravity and credibility in the way he explained policy on a day to day basis. People understood what he was talking about and had faith that he was telling them the truth.

Naturally everyone who follows Indonesian politics had been aware of SBY for years but it was at this time that he established himself with a wider international as well as Indonesian audience. The presidencies of Abdurrahman Wahid and Megawati Sukarnoputri were turbulent times and SBY was like the stable rock around which the eddies and currents of political reform and the clash of ideas swirled.

Like many others, I will never forget the speech he delivered at the first anniversary of the Bali bombing, an outrage which killed 202 people on Indonesia's beautiful tourist island. SBY had written the speech himself and it was eloquent and personal and powerful. Everyone who heard it that day was moved. He said in part, of all the people of all the different nationalities who died in the Bali bombing: ``They were our sons, our daughters, our fathers and mothers, brothers and sisters, our cousins, our best friends, our soul mates. And they were all innocents.''

But he didn't neglect the hard political truths of terrorism and he spoke that day truth to power, when he said of the terrorists who had carried out the bombing: ``These diabolical men and their brand of evil simply have no place in our society. They belong in our darkest dungeons, locked away beneath our children's playgrounds. History will condemn them forever."

We were all looking for leadership that day, and we all found it in SBY.

But Indonesia's sixth president is much more than someone who can speak the truth. He is really a bundle of paradoxes. He has a PhD in agricultural economics and a personal library of several thousand books. This is exceptionally rare in a successful political leader. An intellectual who is also a capable administrator is almost a specimen to be preserved in a museum for its rarity value.

Similarly he is a soldier who served in East Timor and had many and tough commands. He was also a military reformer in the thick of Indonesia's always complex military politics. Yet he is also a poet of considerable technical accomplishment and deep feeling. Not only is he a poet but he enjoys warbling a tune or three in front of a karaoke machine.

He is an ardent nationalist, deeply proud of Indonesia and its historic struggle for independence and national unity, just as proud as any soldier and president should be. Yet he also did several post-graduate degrees in the United States and is effortlessly comfortable in any cross cultural transaction with the West.

No single one of these things is especially remarkable by itself, but put all together they are a remarkable combination.

Certainly it is easy to make the case that SBY is the best prepared for the job of all the individuals to have become president of Indonesia. He had long cabinet experience before he got the top job, he had a long record in the military, he had the academic qualifications, he had founded a political party and he decisively won a two-stage democratic election for the presidency, the first such direct election in Indonesia's history.

Now his countrymen, and the world, hope for a lot from SBY. Indonesia's journey from the last days of Suharto to now has been a turbulent one, but several themes emerge. One is the growing sophistication of the political class and the political process, which has tried different electoral systems but now seems settled on a good one, and which has managed to make workable compromises throughout. Another is the enduring commitment to democracy in the new Indonesia. People want it and they are learning how to make it work. Yet another is the resilience and recuperative power of the economy.

As an Australian I understand that Indonesia is an immensely important nation. The wider world should understand this better too. There are more Muslims in Indonesia than in the entire Arabian Peninsula. Indonesia is now not only the world's most populous Muslim nation but its third largest democracy. Indonesia has so much of value to say to the world about development and democracy and the ability of a multi-ethnic nation to build a unified society.

Of course, the Indonesian genius extends far beyond this, through the literature and the arts to the irrepressible Indonesian sense of humour, which has often relieved difficult times.

Now there is a chance that Indonesia will re-emerge fully onto the main stage of global history, where it belongs. The truth is, the world needs the national Indonesian genius, the tendency to moderation, the inclusiveness.

For those of us who love Indonesia, who seem to have had infinite gifts of wisdom and friendship from so many of its people, we rejoice at the sight of this potential Indonesian renaissance. We're glad that its national leadership is in such capable hands, and that, through this volume, more people can begin to understand Indonesia and its leader a little better.

****

Dr Michael Williams *

Indonesia: The Road Ahead

Six weeks after President Susilo Bambang Yudhoyono's inauguration, I had the good fortune to come to Jakarta as Special Envoy from Prime Minister Tony Blair to meet the new President. I had met him before in Bosnia in the mid 90's when he was head of UN military observers and I was Director of Information for the UN, but this was the first time we had met since he had become President. It was a very positive meeting. President Yudhoyono described some of his plans for Indonesia. He talked, among other things, about his commitment to fighting corruption, to renewing infrastructure, to seeking a "new deal" for Aceh, his interest in the Middle East Peace Process, and the important role that Indonesia could play internationally as a newly modern democratic state with the world's largest Moslem population. The breadth of the

---

* Dr Michael Williams did his Ph.D thesis on Indonesian politics at the School of Oriental and African Studies, London University. He has been Senior Commentator/ Editor on East Asia for the BBC World Service, Director of Human Rights UN Mission to Cambodia, Director for the Office of Children and Armed Conflict at the UN and Special Adviser to the British Secretary of State for Foreign Affairs.

conversation showed how much he wanted to achieve for Indonesia during his Presidency. In turn, I assured him of Britain's strong commitment to Indonesia and what he was seeking to achieve.

Afterwards I was struck by having come to Jakarta on UN Human Rights Day (10 December). Despite the shortcomings in many areas, the country had been transformed since I knew it in the 1980s. There was a functioning National Human Rights Commission, freedom of the press, and an obvious popular enthusiasm for the agenda of "demokrasi" and "reformasi".

The successful peaceful holding of first legislative elections and then - for the first time ever - direct Presidential elections showed that Indonesia had arrived at a turning point. Democracy had come of age in the world's largest Muslim country. In his inaugural speech on 21 October, President Yudhoyono had emphasised that Indonesia had passed one of the most important tests of its history. The elections had been "the most ambitious, the most difficult and the most complicated electoral marathon in the world". The nation had successfully conducted them in a "democratic, fair, orderly and peaceful" manner. It had also accomplished the transfer of Presidential power constitutionally and democratically. The EU and the Carter Centre were among the first to congratulate Indonesia. The President's challenge is to consolidate democracy and to accomplish the agenda of reform. He listed the many difficult challenges, political, social and economic that his government needed to overcome and set out the immediate first steps needed to do so. His aim was for Indonesia to continue to grow as a "democratic, open, modern, pluralistic and tolerant nation".

This collected book of his speeches, sets out President Yudhoyono's vision for Indonesia and what he is aiming to accomplish. The challenges facing him have been made even greater by the terrible tragedy of the tsunami that struck Aceh and North Sumatra on 26 December last year. Fortunately, this tragedy has served to increase international sympathy and solidarity with Indonesia. In my own country, Britain, ordinary members of the population reacted with unprecedented concern and generosity by contributing more than $500 million for relief and reconstruction. President Yudhoyono's personal leadership of the response to the emergency paved the way for the international community. I came back to Jakarta in early January with our Foreign Minister, Jack Straw, to attend the special regional leaders' meeting that President Yudhoyono had called.

Despite that tragedy the President has sought at the same time to address both the domestic and foreign policy agendas for Indonesia. As a result I believe respect for Indonesia internationally is higher than at any time for decades. The President's speeches represent a wide-ranging effort to articulate a comprehensive vision for the future of Indonesia both at home and abroad. As the leader of the world's third largest democracy, he has recognised that for any democratic leader to succeed in today's open societies, he must explain his policies to the people and win their support. The days when Indonesian leaders could simply tell people what to do and arbitrarily enforce this are happily over. Given the size and complexity of this giant archipelagic nation, he is rightly seeking the consensus needed to unite people and motivate them.

At home the President has set out his determination to address the problem of poverty in a country where over half the people still live on less than $2 a day. The doctorate that he gained while he was fighting the Presidential elections, is appropriately on the subject of help to the rural poor. His ambitious programme of economic reform and development addresses the fundamental need to raise the national growth rate so that poverty can be made history in Indonesia. His commitment to combating corruption and promoting human rights provides an essential and encouraging under-pinning to this economic policy.

Fifty years ago Indonesia was the focal point for the first Afro-Asia meeting in Bandung. In his opening address to the Asian African Summit on 22 April this year, President Yudhoyono emphasised to the assembled Asian and African leaders his belief that national success depended on "good governance". He urged that the two continents of Asia and Africa should aim to promote just, democratic, accountable and harmonious societies that protected human rights and basic freedoms. This was a courageous and important statement and greatly deserved the applause that it received.

In the same address, President Yudhoyono also noted that, in contrast to 1955, Asia and Africa now saw the world as "much more sympathetic to their problems". They should aim to "connect with" not "confront" others. In his 19 May speech to the Indonesian Council on World Affairs, he further described Indonesia as having a "brand of nationalism that is open, confident, moderate, tolerant and outward-looking". This modern, internationalist approach is one which we in Britain greatly welcome and to which we would wish to respond positively. It is an approach that I believe can help lead Indonesia back to the important place in international affairs that its size and geographical position have long merited. As a long time friend and student of Indonesia and its people, I am delighted to have been given this opportunity to contribute one of the introductory articles to this book. I hope that it will provide readers outside of Indonesia with a greater understanding of where this important country and its new President hope to go. I would like to wish both President Yudhoyono and Indonesia the very best in their endeavours.

****

Karim Raslan *

Susilo Bambang Yudhoyono : A Malaysian Perspective

There is strange sense of déjà vu for Malaysians observers of Susilo Bambang Yudhoyono's Presidency. President Susilo's gracious and understated manner may seem old-fashioned and out-of-date to visitors from Europe and America constantly bombarded by George W. Bush's homilies and Tony Blair's international barn-storming.

However from the vantage of Kuala Lumpur where Prime Minister Abdullah Badawi now holds sway, President Susilo's low-key charms are reassuringly familiar. Both are god-fearing, decent family men who have slowly but steadily risen to prominence almost despite the corruption and venality of their respective political elites.

Indeed the two men seem to wield power in a similar, very Asian way. Whilst both leaders won tremendous electoral victories in

---

* Karim Raslan is a Cambridge University educated. A lawyer, columnist and author.

2004, neither believes in using the popular mandate immediately. Rashness is an anathema to both. Instead they have sought to consolidate their support and move slowly – pushing their key objectives, most notably their strong anti-corruption programs whilst ensuring that these policies don't get bogged down by bureaucratic resistance and or inertia.

The reform of institutions such as police, the judiciary and the military are critical for both men not to mention the professionalisation and rationalization of lumbering state owned enterprises. However, Susilo in particular has been very patient in addressing these challenges – waiting for the right time and the right candidate for the job.

Both men recognise the enormous burden of trust placed upon them. Certainly, President Susilo is well aware that his countrymen have endured six years of relative turmoil and that his election was to a large extent a vote for stability and gradual change. In this respect he knows that he must act in a measured and principled fashion, selecting policies and making appointments that are evolutionary in nature rather than revolutionary, nurturing the republic's democracy and good governance over time.

Leading by example Abdullah Badawi and Susilo have used the popular perception of their honesty and integrity as a beacon for others to follow. At the same time they also tapped into traditional cultural and pre-Islamic values. Susilo has projected Javanese virtues of self-effacement and the respect of elders whereas for Badawi, Malay gentlemanliness and dignity have been uppermost. Moreover both are conciliatory figures who are more than willing to reach out to their predecessors and even their enemies if need be in interests of the nation as a whole.

Interestingly, the combination of a commitment to good governance and the perception of integrity as well as a projection of deeply-rooted cultural values has made both men attractive figures with Islamic constituencies that are far more conservative and traditional than they themselves are. This support has given them an important advantage in an era of increasing religiosity as both men have endeavoured to promote moderate and progressive Islamic values. Ironically, the same factors have also been contributed to the popularity and trust they enjoy amongst non-Muslim minorities who see the two leaders as bulwark against extremism.

However, their measured and consensual approach to solving political and economic problems has drawn criticism. The reluctance to push through half-baked policies and the insistence on listening to differing opinions has exasperated many who have become used to decades of decisive if authoritarian leadership. Still, an all-too keen awareness of popular sentiment (certainly in the case of oil subsidies) has at times stymied some reforms.

Nonetheless, political foes are unwise to underestimate either man. The quiet and unassuming approach that they have adopted has in fact led to a gradual accumulation power and authority, augmenting their electoral mandates whilst also ensuring a society-wide, buy-in of their most cherished policy initiatives.

Both men are unflinching in their opposition to corruption and whilst Indonesia's challenges are admittedly more serious, newspapers in two countries are crammed with news reports of legal proceedings initiated against administrators, politicians, bankers and corporate figures.

Given the similarities in the way they manage power and their continuing popular appeal, its perhaps unsurprising that a warm and mutually reciprocal friendship has developed between the two men. An element of personal chemistry has brought them together but their commitment to shared ideals has served to cement that friendship, leading in turn to a period of unusual closeness between Jakarta and Kuala Lumpur.

In the past there has been a degree of creative tension and at times even military clashes between the two majority Muslim nations. Sadly our shared cultural and religious heritage has often been a barrier to mutual understanding. At the same time the very different leadership styles and political cultures in Kuala Lumpur and Jakarta have made cooperation difficult.

However, a resurgent Indonesia under Susilo's leadership has been warmly received in Kuala Lumpur. Having looked on at the events of 1998 and the fall of Suharto with barely concealed anxiety, Malaysians are relieved to stand alongside an Indonesia that is increasingly strong, stable, prosperous and democratic. Unlike others, Malaysians see no value in arbitraging or leveraging off a weakened Indonesia. The Mahathir era maxim of 'prosper thy neighbour' remains a key aspect of Malaysian foreign policy.

Moreover Malaysia also acknowledges that a revitalized Indonesia will, in turn seek out a more prominent place on the global stage. A less confident man than Premier Abdullah might feel slighted by the altered situation but his diffident manner and pragmatism has meant quite the opposite. The recent Asia-Africa Summit is a clear indication of the republic's growing confidence and strategic importance. As the world's fourth most populous nation, the largest majority Muslim state and a regional titan, Indonesia's international profile must inevitably be on the rise.

Moreover the President's fluency in English, his principled manner as well as his willingness to lead have meant that he will is steadily becoming the de facto 'leader' of ASEAN, speaking for the regional grouping whilst also articulating an Indonesian position on global affairs. Certainly, in geopolitical terms a resurgent Indonesia adds greater heft and credibility to ASEAN, positioning the association as vital balancing force in an Asia dominated by emerging giants to the north and west, namely China and India.

Bilateral disagreements are to be expected between two close neighbours, but recent history indicates that they now stand a far greater chance of a peaceful resolution. During the Ambalat dispute earlier this year, for example, the more nationalistic elements in Indonesia, were poised for aggression. Despite internal pressure, Susilo was able to work with Malaysian premier Abdullah Ahmad Badawi to reach a diplomatic solution. The two countries saw the same spirit of co-operation at work when Malaysia tried to address the long-standing problem of illegal foreign workers. Both issues involved high stakes in domestic politics, but Susilo proved adept at negotiating the local scene while keeping foreign relations intact.

The strength of the ties between Susilo and Abdullah Badawi has been an enormous boon for many Malaysian companies who are beginning to realize the limited prospects of their local market. Substantial Malaysian investments in Indonesia will only serve to augment these bonds as more and more Malaysians discover the archipelagic nation. At the same time investment from Malaysia presents Indonesia with a welcome opportunity to diversify its sources of foreign direct investment.

However, the two countries cannot depend on the rapport between the two men forever. Inevitably both sides will have to start developing deeper ties, building friendships and business partnerships across the Straits of Malacca, tapping into the shared cultural and religious roots with greater sincerity and focus.

Finally, Malaysia and Indonesia – two majority Muslim and plural nations can demonstrate to the world that Islamic polities can be successful, prosperous and stable. In an era much troubled by civilizational discord and conflict, two understated, mild-mannered gentlemen, President Susilo and Premier Abdullah perhaps hold the key to good governance, religious harmony and democracy in the Muslim world.

****

"We held the free and fair elections in our terms, in our own way, with our own resources. No one can dispute that, the Indonesian people have full ownership of our democracy."

President Susilo Bambang Yudhoyono
Washington DC, USA , May 25, 2005

Selected International Speeches

By
President Susilo Bambang Yudhoyono

1

"The Challenge of Security for The World Economy"

Speech delivered at the APEC CEO Summit

Santiago, Chile
November 20, 2004

♦ ♦ ♦ ♦ ♦

Assalamualaikum Warahmatullahi Wabarakatuh,
Excellencies,
Ladies and gentlemen,

Let me begin by expressing how grateful I am to be here today to share my thoughts in a distinguished forum attended by world leaders in government and business.

I have been asked to speak in this session about "the challenge of security for the world economy".

It goes without saying that security and prosperity are two sides of the same coin. But since 9/11, the dynamics between them are changing. The demands for greater security are affecting economic activities and business costs like never before. The world economy, particularly APEC economies, must now strive to find the right balance between security concerns and open trade.

I think all of us here today concur on the basic objectives that we seek for the world economy. The bottom line is that we want a stable, safe environment conducive for the international economy.

- A conducive environment means the maintenance of security at all levels--national, regional and international.
- A conducive environment demands a healthy climate for investment and trade. We all want our productive forces to inter-connect, grow and expand, so that the incomes of our citizens can also grow.
- And a conducive environment requires a secure and efficient flow of goods, peoples and services within and across borders.

The problem is that, for now and the foreseeable future, our economies must function in an international system which is fraught with threats and turbulences.

- Terrorist groups continue to prey on our economies, seeking to strike a damaging blow to us with minimal resources.
- Non-traditional security threats are becoming prominent.
- Trans-national crimes are growing in all its aspects, from narcotics trafficking to money laundering, people smuggling to illegal logging.
- This is compounded by the increasing disparity between the haves and the have-nots, between developed and developing countries.
- And the spectre of conflicts, be they old and new conflicts, inter-state conflicts or intra-state conflicts, continue to cast a worrying shadow over us.

The sum of all this is an *unsettling sense of global insecurity*. Yes, some of us can talk proudly of successful elections, or of great military victories, or about phenomenal rises in GDP, or about export growth, or about expanding and integrating markets, or about outstanding human development index. Still, these things do not erase an uneasy feeling which many of us feel about the present and future state of international and national security.

We see this unsettling sense of global insecurity in many developing countries, which are falling farther behind the developed countries. We detect this jitteryness in many developed countries, which are becoming increasingly worried about public security and terrorist threats. We notice it in the restlessness felt throughout the Islamic world. We see it being reflected in the travel warnings to many nations across the globe. We see it in the rising flow of illegal migrants between borders. And we feel it in the phenomenal rise in the price of oil recently.

This situation presents great challenges for the world economy in a variety of ways. Allow me to highlight at least **6 security challenges for the world economy** which in my view require the attention of policy-makers and business leaders.

First, is the challenge of striking a satisfactory **balance between security concerns and open trade**. Our economic infrastructure needs to be guarded and well-protected against terrorist attacks but not at a cost or burden to business in such a way that trade flows will cease to exist. It is not an easy matter to balance the need for increased security and our goals to reduce transaction cost in the APEC region by 5% by the year 2006.

Second, is **the challenge of building a greater resilience.** The economies of the world must develop a capacity to withstand the devastating effect of terrorist attacks and rebound quickly.

In the last 3 years, we in Indonesia were hit by 3 major bomb attacks : the Bali bomb in 2002, the Jakarta Marriott bomb in 2003, and the Kuningan bomb this year. All of them were devastating- -the worst being the Bali bomb which killed over 200 people of various nationalities. But we recovered much better after each attack. And for each attack, it took less effort to rebound than the previous one. Look at our political stability, our stock market, our exchange rate, tourism industry, flow of travel, and the economy in general. All indices bounced back much more quickly following each terrorist strike.

Ultimately, resilience is the responsibility of each Government. But any country experiencing distress will still need a helping hand from its international friends. Gestures of support and solidarity can go a long way in strengthening resilience. Hard working Indonesians in the service industry have complained that the travel warnings on Indonesia badly hurt their livelihood, and many of them think they are being unfairly, though unintentionally, punished for what the terrorists are doing. But we were also touched by the simpathetic gesture of a number of foreign residents who decided to stay in my country no matter what. That display of solidarity is not only appreciated by Indonesians, it also sends a strong signal to terrorists that they will not scare us into changing our way of life.

The third challenge is **evolving the right kind of security cooperation.**

While terrorism has been around for a long time, fighting modern-day terrorists today is a new experience for all of us. To deal with it, we need to change the way we think about national and international security. During the Cold War, governments ensured their national security by *keeping* intelligence from each other. In the post-911, post-Bali, post-Riyadh, post-Madrid world, we can ensure our security only by sharing our intelligence with one another. To fight terrorists who ignore borders, Governments must evolve a different security culture. Our police, intelligence, immigration officials must be able to work together extensively. The community of nations must evolve a new global security culture where the norm is for all law enforcement agencies to cooperate with one another. This is what Indonesia and Australia did when we co-sponsored a number of regional conferences on people's smuggling, money laundering and counter-terrorism.

Fourth, **is the challenge of promoting security for all**.

Security can sometimes be a zero sum game, but it does not always have to be that way. Governments must take care to ensure that its quest for security does not lead to the insecurity of others. On the contrary, we must strive to achieve an international condition where the enhancement of one's security also leads to the security of others.

No one country can achieve security by locking itself and insulating others. Just like we cannot have a world where prosperity is segregated, nor can we have a community of nations where security is enjoyed only by some. The world economy must spread prosperity and security for all.

Promoting "security for all" has a deeper dimension: that is, security for individuals. Governments must ensure not just security of the state but also human security, that is, the safety of individuals within the state. It is not sufficient that the state is secure if some of its citizens insecure, unsafe, and unprotected.

Fifth, is the challenge of promoting greater inter-changes and openness. Of course, in this uncertain and dangerous world, there is a definite need to control access into one's borders. But if we seriously intend to unite the world in peace and progress, we will need more, not less, inter-changes across borders and oceans. We need to exchange our students, our teachers, our business actors, our artists, our religious figures, our politicians, our NGOs, our tourists, our citizens. We need to keep the gates closed for criminals and terrorists, but we need to keep it wide open for the creative and productive forces of society.

The world economy must therefore ensure, for its own good, that measures to promote greater security also produce greater inter-changes between the peoples of the world.

The **sixth challenge is promoting tolerance building.** In this restless world where the factors of ethnicity and religion are becoming more prominent, we have to redefine the concept of "security" and the concept of "development" so as to include tolerance building.

Yes, it is important to promote and defend freedom. But in my view it is even more important to promote tolerance, for without it freedom can become twisted and warped. Many problems of security can be traced to ignorance and a lack of tolerance. A more tolerant society is often more secure, and thereby more free and able to pursue their development goals. This is why Indonesia and Australia are jointly sponsoring an inter-faith dialogue next month in Yogyakarta, Indonesia to facilitate a constructive discourse between religious leaders from various countries.

I have explained what I think are the security challlenges for the world economy. Yet, at this CEO Summit, what I am really interested in is the question of what business leaders—that is, all of you—can do to promote a more peaceful world.

Here is how I believe the movers and shakers of the business world can do their part to help our mutual goal of strengthening security and prosperity.

First, you can help the world deal with globalization better. As the engine of this globalized world, the business community can help us better understand, accept and embrace globalization.

You can help us preventing globalization from becoming something that divides, marginalizes, and de-humanizes.

You can help see to it that globalization does not pit us into conflict, but instead can become a tool for empowerment: empowerment of the poor, empowerment of local communities, empowerment of minority groups.

You can help turn globalization into a positive force, one that can bring governments and businesses to join hands rather than to confront one another.

By doing this, you will help the world tackle the root causes of terrorism, which often take the forms of poverty, alienation, ignorance and injustice.

How do you do this? Well, you can start, as the saying goes, by "walking the talk". That means developing good corporate social responsibility. For trust to develop between businesses and local, if not global, communities, there must be a mutually reciprocal relationship. The community must feel that commercial entities give back as much as they take, and help them in their time of need. This can mean lending a hand to educational programs, or making sure that your enterprise does not endanger the environmental health of the community. Paying attention to your community's well-being can simply mean the difference between conflict and harmony.

Corporations can also be more generous in sharing their technology. Part of the discontent with globalization stems from a sense of inequity, exploitation, and a growing social gap. Almost half of the world's population lives on less than $ 2 a day. Amongst many of these communities, almost half of all their children are malnourished.

Let's reverse this deplorable statistic. Let's help the UN accomplish its mission of halving the numbers of people struggling on less than a dollar a day.

Companies can do their part by closing the gap, in concrete terms, sharing some of the knowledge that has led them to good fortune. Much of this technology—be it hardware or software—does eventually become common knowledge anyway, adopted by the mainstream. Bringing about this learning curve earlier to local communities can prompt a reserve of goodwill that is immeasurable in terms of numbers.

If you want your investment to serve you well, you must also invest in people. You must help communities boost their human resources, providing training programs, scholarships, and other educational opportunities. You must address the public's perception that globalization is turning societies into unskilled labor forces. You must convince them that a more educated and skilled workforce is as much your objective as it is theirs.

Corporations are regarded by most of the population as a wellspring of wealth. Hence it is your responsibility to transform this perceived "plenty" into "opportunity" for those around you. Corporations are in a strategic place to bridge this great divide between poverty and prosperity—make the most of that opportunity, and you may just see this prosperity become even greater.

So this is my message to all of you : let us join hands, let us partner with one another—governments hand in hand with the private sector—to promote security and prosperity.

Let us do our best to think of and realize solutions that will make our families safer, our economies prosper, and our countries secure.

Thank you, and God bless you.

Santiago, Chile, November 20, 2004

"Experts assess that over the course of the next decade and a half Indonesia may revert to high growth of 6 to 7 percent, which along with its expected increase in its relatively large population from 226 to around 250 million would make it one of the largest developing economies. Such high growth would presume an improved investment environment, including intellectual property rights protection and openness to foreign investment."

(Report of the National Intelligence Council's 2020 Project: Mapping the Global Future, December 2004.)

"Southeast Asian leaders once calibrated popularity based on economic growth and the number of rural clinics per capita. Not anymore. Popularity today is determined by how successfully a leader wages war on corruption...So leaders like Thaksin, Abdullah and Yudhoyono, if they fail to make measurable progress, face defeat at the next election. The good news is that none of these leaders have so far backed away from their pledge to wage war on corruption...Yudhoyono has perhaps taken the boldest strides... corruption won't be defeated by simply taking heads. Institutional reform is needed badly." —Michael Vatikiotis.

(International Herald Tribune, 13 July 2005)

"A constructive approach may mean many things. It also means putting to rest a siege mentality, wild conspiracy theories, excessive suspicion, an overly defensive attitude, or the fear that the world is out to get us."

President Susilo Bambang Yudhoyono
Jakarta, May 19, 2005

"We in Indonesia have embarked on a very ambitious decentralization program, because we know that our country cannot grow unless the provinces and the districts (kabupaten) also grow."

President Susilo Bambang Yudhoyono
Medan, March 10, 2005

PHOTO BY ANUNG

"I must admit that these expectations at the beginning were too high. After my first 100 days, I think the people are developing more realistic expectations."

President Susilo Bambang Yudhoyono
Sydney, Australia, April 5, 2005

2

"Promoting Tolerance, Harmony and Peace through Inter-faith Dialogue"

Keynote Address delivered at a Dialogue
on Inter-faith Cooperation

Yogyakarta
December 6, 2004

♦ ♦ ♦ ♦ ♦

Excellencies,
Distinguished Participants,
Ladies and Gentlemen,
It is an honor and privilege for me to address this unique and special forum.

It is a forum which serves as a communion of people of faith, who are engaged in an important process of dialogue and sharing to chart the way forward to community building and harmony.

Let me commend both the Government of Australia and the Muhammadiyah for working closely with the Government of Indonesia through our Department of Foreign Affairs in bringing to reality this dialogue.

I am particularly delighted that Australia and Indonesia are, once more, working intensively to promote the security and stability of our region.

The Muhammadiyah has for many years now served as a forceful voice of mainstream and moderate, intellectual Islam. As such, it is a very credible advocate of Islam as "Rahmatan al Alamin," or God's mercy upon a troubled world. The Muhammadiyah is certainly a natural partner to any endeavour at any dialogue between and among the religions of the world.

I am heartened to see so many faiths and religious traditions represented in this gathering. Though we hold various religious beliefs and live by different faith traditions, we are all united here by a common faith in the power of dialogue and cooperation in an atmosphere of mutual trust and acceptance.

Our coming together here is an affirmation of our common humanity. In a dialogue like this, there is no need for anyone to give up or defend his religious convictions. There is no need for anyone to surrender the uniqueness of his faith. Instead, this dialogue recognizes and affirms the wisdom of casting aside prejudices and enmities.

This inter-faith dialogue that you are embarking on is particularly significant against the backdrop of a volatile world that we live in. It is an unsettling world still punctured in some areas by ethnic and religious tensions, by communal violence, by prejudice, by misunderstanding and miscommunication.

And when ethnic and religious prejudice is compounded by economic and political rivalries as well as by mutual grievances deemed unforgivable, the resulting situation can be explosive.

The solution is not to deny that there are differences between people—nothing can be gained by such denial of reality. Pluralism is a fact of life not only between adherents of different religions, but often also between groups within the same religion.

Instead, the course that we should take is to affirm a deeper, greater and more important reality—and that is our common humanity. We are all children of the same providence on a journey to the same destiny.

Therefore, within the fold of humankind, there is a place for everyone. The things that make us different from one another can be regarded as assets that can be pooled in order to achieve a common purpose.

This idea of variety within a unity is especially meaningful to us Indonesians, who live by our national motto, "Bhinneka Tunggal Ika"-- we are many but we are one.

We are all here today because we believe in tolerance as an imperative to human and social development.

We all know that tolerance does not easily and naturally happen. It has to be deliberately cultivated and nurtured so that it becomes an important part of the framework of society.

Tolerance cannot grow on the soil of ignorance. That makes education equally an imperative. In Indonesia, therefore, students have to take courses in religion from primary to university level. They must have sufficient knowledge not only about their respective religions but also about other religions.

Moreover, our Constitution provides that it is the obligation of the state to promote the religious life of the people. Hence, Indonesia is not a secular state in the Western tradition. For us, a harmonious relationship among religions must be nurtured, as it is one of the most important building blocks in the process of our national development.

We must not look at development as a purely economic process. It has a very broad sociocultural and spiritual aspect. We must not be merely concerned with lifting people from their poverty. We must also redeem them from narrow-mindedness, from prejudice and intolerance, and from the poverty of their spirit and their ideas. Tolerance-building is very much part of development.

Apart from the issues of prejudice and intolerance, a number of other intractable problems also demand to be addressed by a dialogue like this. These include the tensions, conflicts and acts of violence that all together deprive humankind the peace and security that it longs for.

And there is one exceedingly heinous form of violence that we must grapple with, and that is the scourge of terrorism.

To my mind, terrorism today must be regarded as the enemy of all religions.

Terrorists are well organized, well funded and are highly skilled in sowing mayhem and fear through the slaughter of innocents. They never operate in a social vacuum; they establish safe havens and bases of operations among the people. There, they fan the flames of real or imagined grievances and pass themselves off as champions of the downtrodden.

On the other hand, people of faith like you are committed to bring enlightenment and the most positive human values like tolerance and compassion to wherever hatred and prejudice rear their ugly heads.

People of faith like you have the responsibility to bring your message of truth, unity and hope deep into the grassroots of society. And that message will resonate strongly among peace-loving people at all levels.

In the end, the forces of light, reason and hope must overpower the forces of darkness, despair and violence.

And, indeed, a commitment to and a preoccupation with community building can be one of the most effective antidotes to the culture of violence and destruction that terrorists promote and practice.

One of the great attractions of becoming a community is the feeling of security that it generates.

In a community, there are no masks: members communicate frankly and honestly with one another. More than just tolerating one another, they rejoice together and grieve together, according to their fortunes and misfortunes. Above all, they are responsible to and for one another. That is what makes the community so effective and progressive.

And the people most qualified to lead in the building of communities are the people of faith, such as yourselves, whose life's calling is to spread and foster enlightenment and humanitarian values.

You have a wide agenda in this dialogue, but it is my fervent hope that in the course of your discussions, the beginnings of some practical strategies for building true communities at the grassroots level will come to the surface.

It is also my hope that you will be able to move toward the establishment of a permanent forum for the exchange of ideas and insights to help us understand and effectively deal with the fundamental problems of the human condition in our time. At any rate, I trust that this dialogue will be the beginning of a truly meaningful engagement that will include many more nations, apart from the 14 already represented here.

May your discussions be fruitful. I now declare this dialogue open.

Yogyakarta, December 6, 2004

> *"Now that Indonesia has a president who looks like a hands-on leader rather than a symbolic figurehead, it's time for the country to revive its role in regional and world affairs. This is important, because without Indonesia's presence and responsible leadership, Southeast Asia's chemistry is thrown out of balance and it becomes a region diminished in the eyes of the world. More broadly, without Indonesia, the non-Muslim world finds it hard to imagine Muslim society as tolerant and secular. Just look what happened when Indonesia was out of the picture. While Indonesia was preoccupied with economic crisis and a messy transition to democracy these past six years, ASEAN lost the economic weight it once had."* —Michael Vatikiotis.
>
> (The Jakarta Post, 2 November 2004)

"I call on GAM at all levels, where ever they are, to terminate this conflict, to come to permanent peace with dignity, and to work together to rebuild Aceh under the framework special autonomy."

President Susilo Bambang Yudhoyono
Singapore, February 16, 2005

"We have to redefine the concept of 'security' and the concept of 'development' so as to include tolerance building."

President Susilo Bambang Yudhoyono
Santiago, Chile, November 20, 2004

"I know economic plans generally have pros and cons. For my part, I would like to think that my economic vision based on the Triple Track Strategy has 3 pro's : pro-growth, pro-employment, pro-poor."

President Susilo Bambang Yudhoyono
Jakarta, January 19, 2005

3

"...remember what Spiderman said..."

Remarks at The Opening Ceremony of
The 1st International Junior Science
Olympiad (IJSO)

Istana Negara, Jakarta
December 6, 2004

♦ ♦ ♦ ♦ ♦

Good afternoon everybody,

My name is Susilo Bambang Yudhoyono.

I am so happy to welcome all of you to Istana Negara, or "State Palace", which is a very historic building and a very special place for the Indonesian people.

So much of the history of Indonesia, so many important things has happened in this building. This is where I swear-in my Cabinet Ministers, where I receive foreign ambassadors, and have meetings with world leaders.

And because all of you are so special, so very talented, we decided to have the opening ceremony of the First International Junior Science Olympiad here in this palace. You can tell your parents that you are sitting in a room where Presidents and Kings and Prime Ministers usually sit. That is how special you are.

This is the First International Junior Science Olympiad, an international science competition for junior high students. I cannot begin to express how much my heart is filled with pride and joy to find myself here today with the best and the brightest students from all over the world.

As President, my job is simply to open this ceremony, but the real star of this event is you.

I know many of you have traveled far from your home country to compete at this Science Olympiad. Your parents must be so proud of you. Your teachers must be so proud of you. Your country must be so proud of you.

You know, even though I am older than you, I am also a student. A few months ago, after several years of hard studying, I was fortunate enough to finally complete my Doctorate degree at the Bogor Institute for Agriculture. So you see, I too have a great love for science. And perhaps because of this, my Education Minister has asked me to give you a few words of advise, from one scientist to another scientist. So here it is.

I think the most important thing I want to tell you is to be thankful for the special gift of learning that God has given you.

As a life-long student, I have learned a powerful lesson : no matter who you are, no matter where you come from, no matter how rich or poor, city-boy or village-girl, no matter your skin color or family background, each and everyone of us has the same capacity for learning. We all have the same brain cells. It is up to each and every one of us how we use this gift from God. You can choose to use your mind to become a smarter person, or you can simply waste it by closing your mind. It is all up to you. But I know from experience that those who succeed in life, those who are able to reach their dreams, and those who change the world, are always the ones who can take advantage of this gift of learning.

The other important thing I would tell you is to never, ever stop dreaming. Never stop imagining. Never stop thinking. Never stop wondering. Never stop being curious. Never stop asking questions. Never stop trying to search for answers.

This is the only way by which you will know more, and understand better, not just about science, but about life in general, and also about your own self. No wonder that the most important inventions of the world, the ones who change the fate of mankind, always come from curious minds who never stop asking "why" and "how". We must always remember what Albert Einstein once said: "imagination is more important than knowledge". So keep your mind wide open, because you have no idea how creative you can be once you pump the power of knowledge into your brain cells. The fact that you are here, competing in a prestigious international junior science olympiad, means that you have used the power of your mind more effectively than the average students to master science.

Finally, while it is obvious that all of you are talented in the field of science, it is even more important for you to know how to apply your knowledge so that you can use that knowledge to make life better, to help others, for the good of society. Remember what

Spiderman said in that movie : "With great power, comes great responsibility." Well, whether you are a Spiderman, or President, or science student, that is very true : "with great power, with great knowledge, comes great responsibility".

You are all here because you are so talented, so gifted, so smart. I am amazed to think of what you will know in the next 5 years, or the next 10 or 20 years. Do not get tired of gaining more knowledge, and always use your knowledge wisely. I want to share with you a saying that I think you will find useful in the years ahead. The saying goes : "20 years from now, it will not matter how your hair looked, how well you danced and what brand of jeans you wear. What will matter is the knowledge you gained and how you apply it in your life." As you move on in life, I hope you will remember this.

In the next few days, all of you will be part of something very special. Your knowledge and skills in science will be tested. You will be competing with the best and the brightest in the field of science. And by competing with the best, you will only get better. I know that all of you will come out from this Olympiad a better scientist.

This junior science olympiad will end on December 14, but I hope that the friendships that you will make during this exciting international event will last a life time, and will change your life. And that is another thing that I have learned in my life : knowledge will bring you far, but friendships, even farther. If you come away from this conference with better knowledge and better friends, you will go far in life.

I trust that all local Olympiad Committee members are working very hard to make your stay in Indonesia as enjoyable as possible. I must tell you, Indonesia is a wonderful country : we are a people who love life, who love peace, who love progress, and who love science. We are now in the middle of the rain season, but that will not stop you from seeing and feeling warm hearts everywhere you go.

I am therefore pleased to declare the International Junior Science Olympiad open. My very best wishes to all of you, and please also convey my respect to your parents and your teachers, along with our thanks for sending you to this important Olympiad. Tell them something they already know : that we are all so very proud of you.

Good luck, everyone !

Thank you.

Jakarta, December 6, 2004

"*The new government's ability to deal with the tsunami's devastation is an important test of its effectiveness.*"—Morton Abramowitz and Stephen Bosworth.

(The Jakarta Post, 20 April 2005)

"*In his repeated announcements of an anti-corruption campaign that he will lead, SBY is symbolizing something important. If his gestures are supported by real action from the Anti-Corruption Court, progress is possible. But SBY cannot simply order a ban on corruption and then watch it take effect across his vast nation.*" —Merle Ricklefs.

(Australian Financial Review, 20 May 2005)

"Good governance is what will fulfill the promise of freedom that our fathers struggled for. And good governance is what will truly "liberate" Asia and Africa, and unleash our true potentials."

President Susilo Bambang Yudhoyono
Jakarta, April 22, 2005

"I can also tell you that even though Indonesia is undergoing a tremendous change after the introduction of regional autonomy, the oil and gas industry is and will still be at the hand of central government."

President Susilo Bambang Yudhoyono
Jakarta, January 18, 2005

"I truly believe that the best way for a country to grow is to produce a system whereby its citizens can have equal access to justice. By doing this, we are not only promoting equality, we are also advancing equal opportunity."

President Susilo Bambang Yudhoyono
Bali, May 4, 2005

4

"Creative Partnership in Energy and Mining : Confronting Opportunities and Global Challenge"

Keynote Speech at the Gala Dinner of
The Bimasena : The Mines and Energy Society
Conference 2004

Jakarta Convention Center, Jakarta
December 12, 2004

♦ ♦ ♦ ♦ ♦

Bismillahirrahmanirrahim
Assalamualaikum Warahmatullahi Wabarakatuh.

Excellencies,
Distinguished Participants,
Ladies and Gentlemen,

I am honored to be here to address an important conference attended by the leaders of energy community. Let me begin by bidding all of you, especially friends of Indonesia who have come from overseas, a warm welcome to Indonesia.

I am especially delighted to see so many prominent dignitaries in our midst tonight.

I recognize and honor Dr. Mahathir Muhammad, the great nation-builder, and a visionary leader who helped transform Malaysia's Petronas into the world-class oil company that it is today.

And I recognize and honor Professor Subroto, the doyen of the Indonesian energy community. We are honored to have you with us tonight.

I must admit that I have come here tonight in a rather somber mood. This afternoon, I returned from Alor, East Nusa Tenggara, an island which was hard hit by a major earthquake last month. It was heartbreaking for me to witness the physical destruction and devastation caused by the earthquake.

But I was also inspired by the strength of character of the good people of Alor, who turned up by the thousands to welcome us. They remain in high spirits, and, with government support, they are working hard to rebuild their homes, infrastructure and community.

As we gather here tonight in good comfort, I would humbly urge you to also think of our unfortunate brothers and sisters in Alor and also in Nabire, Papua, who are suffering and trying hard to return to a normal life. I hope you can find a way to help them in any way you can.

Having said that, I wish to commend Bimasena Mines and Energy Society and Indonesian Institute for Energy Economics for organizing this important international conference on energy and minerals, and thank you also for inviting me to say a few words tonight.

To me, this evening feels very much like a homecoming. As you know, when I left military service, my very first civilian job was to serve as Minister of Mines and Energy under President

Abdurrachman Wahid. Back then, it felt like I was transported to a new universe, from managing soldiers and tanks to managing hydrocarbons and coal and oil rigs. But I truly loved that job. I made many friends, many of whom are here tonight, and I learned a lot about the dynamic, restless and innovative world of energy industry. I can say to you that energy issues remain close to my heart to this day.

But beyond sentimental reasons, I cannot stress enough the importance of energy issues for the livelihood of our nation. Almost everything we do in our national development is dependent on it.

This year, we in Indonesia definitely feel the burden of a difficult situation for the international oil market, in a year marked by erratic volatility and high prices. This fluctuating trend has been driven by a combination of factors on both the demand and supply sides, whose effects have been compounded by strong speculative activities in futures market.

Governments around the world have been troubled by the dramatic rise in the price of crude oil, which recently broke the US$ 50 mark, and just a few days ago was at US$ 33,78. For us in Indonesia, this presents a major problem, because our national budget is based on the assumption that the price of oil would be at USD$ 24 per barrel—a big gap from what it is today. You also know that besides being an oil and gas exporter, Indonesia, for the domestic consumption purpose, does import crude oil and gasoline. You can just imagine the tremendous pressure inflicted on our development budget by this fluctuating oil price.

That is why our good friend Minister Purnomo, who returned yesterday from an OPEC meeting in Cairo, is losing a lot of sleep and a lot of hair these days in his intense efforts, as President of OPEC, to seek prices that are sustainable for long-periods, prices that can withstand heavy pressure from the market, especially excessive speculative activity.

But whatever happens, and whatever changes that will be made to the oil subsidies, one thing is for sure : my Government is committed to ensure affordable energy for the poor in Indonesia. This means that Government subsidies for solar and kerosene, which are widely used by the poor, will be maintained.

That is the commitment I have made to my people, and that is the commitment that I will keep.

The international energy situation serves as a reminder to us of the need to ensure energy security for Indonesia, for the short-term, medium-term and long-term. Our national development depends on our ability to achieve this.

Achieving long-term energy security is no easy task : it is estimated that without new reserves being found, Indonesia's oil reserves will last for merely another 11 years.

The good news of course is that, as we all know too well, that there are many hydrocarbons deposits out there just waiting to be found. Exxonmobil's major oil find in Cepu is exciting news to all of us. And between January and September this year, we have had several oil finds, both onshore and offshore, such as in

Papua, South Sumatra, and East Kalimantan. We look forward to hearing many more good news from the field.

And that is why we want to work with you, members of the energy community, to explore and exploit the tremendous hydrocarbons and coal potentials in Indonesia.

We know full well, of course, that it takes two to tango. While you go out to take the risk in explorations, the Government can offer you a more open, relaxed and attractive policies that is much friendlier to investors.

I am pleased to inform you that Indonesia's oil and gas sector is now in the process of being reformed and restructured, with the aim of modernizing the industry and placing it on a more competitive footing.

In the upstream side of oil and gas sector, an implementing body, BP Migas, now has the authority for supervision and controls the upstream oil and gas industry. This implementing body, which works closely with the Department of Energy and Mineral Resources, will streamline the way in which the upstream oil and gas sector is managed by the Government and will closely monitor investment levels to ensure that terms and conditions are internationally competitive.

With regards to the downstream oil and gas sector, we have a new oil and gas law that seeks to establish non-regulated, open and competitive downstream oil and gas market, whilst maintaining continual supply and affordability of petroleum fuel prices.

We hope that the new oil and gas law, Law no. 22 / 2001, will create very substantial investment opportunities in the downstream oil and gas sector, including refinery, storage, distribution, and trading. We are certainly eager to attract more investments from foreign and domestic energy companies as a way to introduce much-needed competitiveness that may drive down costs. Such investments are also needed to fund the improvement and expansion of infrastructure.

As part of oil and gas restructuring program, the Government has changed Pertamina from the state enterprise to the limited liability company. This reflects our strong commitment to create efficient and transparent oil and gas sector by ensuring that all players, including Pertamina, can compete on the basis of level playing field.

We are also undertaking restructuring program in the electricity sector. The new electricity law (Law Number 20 Year 2002) has been implemented to promote greater efficiency through the introduction of competition and to create conducive investment climate in electricity sector.

The Government will also strengthen regulations and improve legal certainty to create a more conducive business climate for the private sector. And as part of efforts to improve transparency and efficiency of the power sector, the Government will separate social mission from commercial mission. Social mission will be the responsibility of the Government.

The new electricity law also provides a level playing field for all players, various investment schemes through the introduction of competitive electricity market, distribution of risk among the players, greater role for regional Government, and protection of public and consumers interests.

Meanwhile, Indonesian coal policies are set to increase coal production to meet ever increasing domestic coal demand on a sustainable basis, and to enhance coal competitiveness in the international market. We also seek to ensure that the growth of the coal industry is consistent with the concept of sustainable development and environmental protection.

For us, coal is strategic commodity that has a crucial role to meet the need of domestic energy demand as well as export revenue.

In saying all this, I must tell you that I am aware of your issues, your stories, your occasional difficulties. I have listened to many inputs, comments and suggestions as to how we can best reform our energy and mining sectors. And I will be very keen to learn of fresh ideas emanating from your discussions tomorrow.

For my part, I wish to reassure you that I will do my best to remove major barriers in this important sector. I know a lot of you have tax issues on your mind. Well, on this issue, I have asked to review and study of the existing tax and customs policy to find a more sound and proper policy which I hope will boost more investments in the years to come.

On the issue of legal certainty, I have also met with the Indonesian governors, and I have urged them to develop a more sound, coherent and better-coordinated policies, not only within their own province, but also among provinces, and with the national policy.

I also understand that we need to harmonize many regulations and policies issued by various ministries in order to avoid policy contradictions or overlaps. We will work hard to ensure that policies and development strategies in this sector be more effective and well-targeted, and more investor friendly.

In the following days, I trust that you will have a very productive discussions involving the best minds in the energy and mines community on the various issues, challenges and strategies related with the country's energy sector development. I have several messages for you to consider in your deliberations.

First, do invest in Indonesia for the long-term. Notwithstanding what happens to the international oil market, I hope you will stick with us through the highs and the lows. I promise you that if you stay with us for the long-term, in time you will harvest the rewards accordingly.

Secondly, do invest in our people. Our people is our best asset. They are intelligent, diligent, adaptable, hard-working, and warm, and if you give them a chance, they will not let you down. So invest in our good people and I promise you, your investment will pay off.

Thirdly, do not be shy to share your know-how and new and advanced technology with your local partners. We are all aware of the power of technology as a tool of progress and empowerment for individuals and societies. A few months ago, I had a tele-conference with some young Indonesians who operated one of the most technologically advanced offshore oil rigs in Natuna. They proudly told me that there are so many young dedicated and bright Indonesians working in the energy field. And these young men and women are able to serve as spearheads in such a sophisticated and competitive industry. We need to see more of these empowerment stories.

Fourth, invest in the good earth. I have always believed that if we seriously put our mind to it, we can avoid conflict between industry and ecology. Rapid technology innovations are allowing industries to progress without harming the environment. All of us should do everything we can to promote both the industry while protecting the environment within the context of sustainable development.

The bottom line is that we, the Government, want you, the energy community, to succeed. Your success means more jobs, more energy supply, more infra-structure, more prosperity, and more revenues for the Government.

Which is why I warmly welcome the signing of 46 investment oil and gas contracts that we have just witnessed tonight. It is a good step in the right direction, and I wish all the best to the participating companies in their endeavors.

So let us continue to build on this cooperation.
We want you to be here with us for the long-term.
We want you to help us ensure energy security for short, medium and long-terms.
We want you to be our partners in development.
And we want you to have profitable business in Indonesia.

Thank you for your attention, and I wish you all a very good deliberations.

And by praising Allah Almighty, Bismillahirrahmanirrahim, I am pleased to declare this conference open.

Assalamualaikum Warahmatullahi Wabarakatuh.

Jakarta, December 12, 2004

"Running Indonesia—a fractious nation of 240 million people from more than 350 ethnic groups spread over some 17,500 islands—is a tough job at the best of times. But the country's new President, Susilo Bambang Yudhoyono, is taking over at a particularly difficult juncture."—Simon Elegant and Jason Tedjasukmana.

(TIME Asia Magazine, 8 November 2004)

"For the first time in our history we have finally gotten democracy locked-in. Our elections last year in 2004 was the second free and fair elections since 1999. We have achieved a point of no return in our democratic development."

President Susilo Bambang Yudhoyono
Tokyo, Japan, June 2, 2005

"And despite the uphill battles that await us, I have a very strong feeling that the Indonesian nation will continue to beat the odds and grow from strength to strength. And why not, they have had lots of practice."

President Susilo Bambang Yudhoyono
Jakarta, January 24, 2005

5

"Building Indonesia's Infrastructure : Opportunity, Partnership, Progress"

Keynote Address delivered at
the Indonesia Infrastructure Summit 2005

Shangrila Hotel, Jakarta
January 17, 2005

♦ ♦ ♦ ♦ ♦

Excellencies,
Ladies and gentlemen,
Dear friends,

Let me begin by welcoming all of you to this important conference on infra-structure. Especially to our international friends, I bid all of you a warm welcome to Indonesia. I hope you already feel at home here in my country, because after today we want you to make Indonesia your home, the home of your next investment. I am sorry : I could not resist making that sales pitch, but I promise you will hear more of it later.

I wish we could meet today under happier circumstances. We gather here today in the midst of the most trying moment in the history of Indonesia : we are all still living the nightmare of the aftermath of the horrific earthquake and tsunami of last December 26th.

We have all seen the tragic scenes of grief and sorrow from our television. In fact, the worst day of my Presidency was when I saw with my own eyes the senseless death of my people and terrible devastation in Lhoksemauwe, Banda Aceh, and Meulaboh.

What I hope you will see and remember out of this horrible nightmare is the triumph of the human spirit. We hear countless heroic stories of soldiers who died while trying to save lives; we hear of a pregnant woman who survived at sea for days while keeping her unborn baby alive; we hear of rescue workers who braved the tsunami waves to save others; we hear of the courage of survivors who are determined to get on with life despite losing everything.

And to this day, the whole of Indonesia is united in tears and deeds : Indonesians of all age, from all walks of life and from all parts of the country are trying to do whatever they could to show solidarity with their brothers and sisters in Aceh and North Sumatra. Clearly, the tsunami disaster has brought out the best in our national character : unity, compassion, solidarity, selflessness, sacrifice.

I want all of you to know that as you engage with my country, this is a spirit and quality of resilience that you will see in the great people of Indonesia.

Through each of you, our friends from all over the world, I also want to thank you and your respective Government and people and organizations for the tremendous international support, simpathy and solidarity shown for the Indonesian people in these trying times.

I easily admit that the tsunami disaster in Aceh and North Sumatra has consumed my Government attention and it is a matter of certainty that the task of rebuilding the devastated communities will continue to be our national priority.

But the other point is equally important : what happened in Aceh and North Sumatra does not in any way detract or distract my Government from achieving the things that we intended to do when we came into office : that is, to change Indonesia for the better. To make Indonesia more democratic, more prosperous, more just, more peaceful. In fact, the tsunami has only added greater urgency for us in achieving these national objectives.

Ladies and gentlemen,
You have all come here to discuss infrastructure development in Indonesia.

I stand here before you today to speak about 3 (three) themes that will be central to your deliberations : opportunity, partnership, progress. I think these 3 themes sum up the essence of what we are trying to do and what can be achieved by all of us, if we put our heads and resources together. And yes, this is where I begin my sales pitch to you.

First, opportunity.

When I was sworn-in as President in October last year, we set forth several economic targets to be achieved at the end of my Government's term.

We aim to decrease unemployment rate from 9.5 % in 2003 to 5,1 % in 2009.

We aim to reduce poverty rate from 16.6% in 2004 to 8.2% in 2009.

And we aim to accelerate economic growth from 4.5% in 2003 to 7.2% in 2009 so that in the next five years, the economic growth will achieve the average of 6.6 % per year;

Big ambitions ? Yes. Is it easy ? No. Are they achieveable ? Certainly !

But as we took stock of our situation, our resources and our shortcomings, one glaring problem emerged : infrastructure, or more precisely, the lack of it thereof.

Blame it on the financial crises, blame it on other things, but the hard fact is that in the past few years, we hardly saw new roads, new toll roads, new ports, new telephone lines, new power plants. And according to conventional wisdom, poor infrastructure has been a key barrier to investment.

I do not tell you these things to paint a glass half empty. On the contrary, I tell you these things because I see a glass half full. Like all of you, I am an optimist who try to see an answer in every problem, unlike the pessimist who see problem in every answer. And one of the answers to our economic future is clear enough : get more investments in infrastructure.

Because of the financial limitations of the Government, and because the Government's role will mainly be as regulator and facilitator, our efforts to mobilize new investments in infrastructure is increasingly relying on the participation of the private sector, both domestic and international.

Here is where you come in. And here is why we are inviting all of you to this Infrastructure Summit conference in Jakarta. We invite you to be our partners. We invite you to take advantage of the huge opportunity to invest in our economy. We invite you to prosper together with us.

Beneath all the numbers and figures I mentioned earlier, lie your opportunity : opportunity to invest, opportunity to grow with us, opportunity to profit.

And If you wish to remember any phrase of my speech tonight, I hope it will be this : "a new partnership". I do not speak of "partnership" as a fancy slogan or as a buzzword. I speak of "new partnership" as a concept that underscores my personal commitment and my Government's determination to promote a strong environment for business and enterpreneurship in Indonesia. We offer you this new partnership in a variety of ways.

To promote this "new partnership", my Government is improving our tax policy and administration, including the improvement of the Draft Law on Taxation to reflect fair, efficient and clear principles.

We are pursuing trade and industry policies that aim to increase competitiveness, decrease costs, and removing those distortions that have obstructed investment and economic activities as a whole.

To improve and increase the supply of infrastructure, we are developing a stable and clear policy framework where the private sector can engage in effective partnership with the government, secure in the knowledge that the charges and tolls that generate income will be free of arbitrary political interference.

And as we proceed to implement a number of infrastructure programs, my Government is committed to provide the private sector with a healthy environment and firm project-by-project support as per tendered contracts, to implement supporting investments. Indeed, the most recent deregulations serve as clear examples of our determination to attract, enable and safeguard private sector investment. The international and domestic private sectors are now encouraged to invest on almost equal terms in new companies and projects in all of the industry.

My Government is also improving the workforce market, to make it more flexible so as to provide more employment openings.

For the medium-term, my Government is enacting programs to support greater private sector involvement through public-private partnership in infrastructure services and by removing all bureaucratic bottlenecks which currently inhibit private sector involvement.

My Government will also focus our own resources increasingly on sectors which are not commercially viable - such as rural roads and specific investments that help the poor and remote communities. My Government will see to it that the poverty alleviation program will be based on the improvement of access and quality of education, health and basic infrastructure such as water, road and irrigation. After all, we in Indonesia value infrastructure in terms of its contribution for promoting equity, justice and the general prosperity of society.

Furthermore, we continue to improve the legal climate for private sector investment, enshrined under the Capital Investment Law.

I happily note that the international component of investment is rising in response to a well established environment of sound fiscal and monetary management, freedom to enjoy the returns on investments, and a continual rationalizing of investment policies and procedures.

And since I know a lot of you have a great interest in macro-economic stability, I can tell you that to maintain and sustain the macroeconomic stability, my Government is developing a fiscal policy to encourage economic growth prudentially; diminishing the risk of burden and public debt fluctuation; and improving expenditure cost of the government to favor poverty alleviation (pro-poor fiscal policy).

Ladies and gentlemen,

If we capitalize on the opportunity and harness our partnership, I am utterly convinced that we can make great progress together.

We know from experience that infrastructure is a key driver for our prosperity. I recall that between 1975 and 2002, Indonesia was able to achieve more than 30 years of robust growth precisely because of the high spending on infrastructure, and this also had the effect of decreasing poverty, from 64 to 18 percent.

We know that today the private sector can play an increasingly important role in offering investment, expertise, and improving competition.

So you will understand why I attach such great importance to infrastructure in my long-term development strategy, and why this topic of infrastructure never tires me. And given the disparity in the levels of development between the provinces, my Government is committed to pursue a policy of "infrastructure for all", that is, to allocate investments in infrastructure in the more developed regions as well as to the less developed areas.

So there you have it : opportunity, partnership, progress.

In the next 2 days, you will be able to flesh out the details of the various opportunities that await you, how to develop partnerships, and how we can progress together.

You will have various briefing sessions, Q and A sessions and break-out groups where my Ministers will be totally at your disposal. And please, you don't have to be gentle with them. Feel free to rough them up. And I hope by so doing, you will know from our response that we mean business.

I began this speech with a sad note on the tsunami. I wish to end it with an upbeat word on the power of collaboration, which is the reason why we are engaged here today. Throughout my whole life, as a student, as a soldier, as a Government official, as a politician, and now as President, I have learnt much about the value of collaboration as a way to unlock the secret of success.

The power of collaboration is the power to create, the power to build, the power to change. I can only hope that through this infrastructure summit, each and everyone of you will find your own ways to many more collaborations that will allow us all to achieve great things to come.

With Indonesia's tremendous resources; with my Government's strong support; with your capital, technology and expertise; with the talents of Indonesian people; with the huge market potential out there, and with our long term partnerships, I believe that we can do very well to harness our respective productive potentials.

I now come to the most pleasant part of my speech, and that is to let you get on with your work. In the name of Allah SWT, Bismilahirrahmanirrahim, I declare the "Indonesia Infrastructure Summit 2005" open.

I wish you all success in your deliberations.

Thank you.

Jakarta, January 17, 2005

"The landslide election in October last year of Susilo Bambang Yudhoyono may have marked a turning point in Indonesia's economic fortunes"—Greg Waldron.

(Singapore Business Review, May, 2005)

"Equity investors expect that Susilo Bambang Yudhoyono (SBY) will induce a "feel-good" factor among businessmen and investors, revive the investment cycle, lower the unemployment rate, and improve purchasing power"

(JPMorgan Indonesia Equity Research Report, 21 October 2004)

"As well as graft and terrorism, Gen Yudhoyono faces a long-running rebellion in the Sumatran province of Aceh, a lesser insurrection in Irian Jaya and the need to bring the military more fully under civilian control. Such an agenda is a mighty challenge to the authority of this personable but largely unproven ex-soldier. He has a democratic mandate in Indonesia's history. We wish him success."

(The Daily Telegraph, 21 October 2004)

"It is your responsibility to transform this perceived 'plenty' into 'opportunity' for those around you. Corporations are in a strategic place to bridge this great divide between poverty and prosperity."

President Susilo Bambang Yudhoyono
Santiago, Chile, November 20, 2004

"Our international identity must be rooted in a strong sense of who we are. We cannot be all things to all people. We must know who we are and what we believe in, and project them in our foreign policy."

President Susilo Bambang Yudhoyono
Jakarta, May 19, 2005

6

"A Strong Gas Industry for Indonesia"

Speech at Indogas 2005 :
The 2nd International Conference and Exhibition

Jakarta Convention Center, Jakarta
January 18, 2005

◆ ◆ ◆ ◆ ◆

Bismillahirrahmanirrahim
Assalamualaikum Warahmatullahi Wabarakatuh

Excellencies
Distinguished Participants
Ladies and Gentlemen,

I am pleased to be here today to welcome and meet old and new friends from the energy community from Indonesia and from all over the world.

You all know that I consider myself one of you: the rewarding experience and valuable contacts which I made during my stint as Minister for Mines and Energy a few years ago remain with me to this day. That is why, as a life-long member of the energy community, it was a very easy decision for me to agree to address this forum, because, frankly, I see it as a personal home-coming.

You will notice that my welcome this morning is very much tinged with enormous grief and sadness resulting from the disastrous earth quake and tsunami in Aceh and North Sumatra. I know you all share our grief and sorrow. I speak for the Indonesian people in expressing our heartfelt gratitude for the tremendous outpouring of sympathy, support and solidarity from all our international friends. It is in moments like this that I am reminded of Gandhi's creed that we may belong to different nationalities but our truest "nationalism is humanity".

You will be interested to know that life in Aceh is improving, gradually but surely. Lots remain to be done, but people in Banda Aceh are now starting to go to Friday prayers again at Baiturrahman mosque, children are starting to attend emergency classes, the homeless in emergency camps are being looked after, the sick are being tended to, and most of the dead have been buried. In February, Insya Allah, I plan to inaugurate the construction of thousands of low-cost housing in Meulaboh.

You may ask what do the Acehnese need now. Well, I can tell you for sure that what they need most now is the promise of a future and an opportunity to reclaim their livelihood. We need to let the Acehnese know that they are not alone. And I have no doubt that the private sector, particularly our friends in the gas industry here tonight, can have its own constructive role in helping and rebuilding the stricken communities in Aceh and North Sumatra. Ladies and Gentlemen,

I note that you have chosen the theme "The New Era of Indonesia's Gas : A Business Perspective" for this conference.

It is an aptly chosen topic.

The development of the gas industry in Indonesia is a priority for my Government's energy policy.

Oil and gas have been the largest source of energy for domestic use. Oil and gas are also critical source of foreign exchange, of government income as well as a crucial energy source for industries.

But as oil reserves become scarce, gas is certain to become more prominent relative to oil in our energy use. Of course, the fact that reserves life for gas field is longer than oil field gives gas an added edge over oil. And as our population grows, and our economy expands, the demand for gas will only rise. A strong gas industry therefore is vital to the growth of the Indonesian economy.

Our gas development policy is driven by a vision to create an efficient, dynamic, transparent, environmentally friendly, competitive and world-class Indonesian gas industry which can support Indonesia's sustainable economy and promote greater prosperity for our people.

Our gas industry is promising, but we have a lot of work to do to speed up its development. And here, a number of challenges confront us.

To begin with, we have a situation where the location of gas reserves are sparsely scattered throughout the Indonesian archipelago, creating cost and logistical constraints on the development of the industry.

We are experiencing a marketing constraint because the large gas reserves are geographically remote from the major domestic markets centered on the island of Java. Compounding this is the fact that we still face a lack of infrastructure, and this can pose significant problems since the supply of gas is dependent on the factor of infrastructure.

We are faced with the fact that the ability of domestic consumers to purchase natural gas at an unsubsidized market price is still very limited.

And we also see that exploration expenditures are generally down. For various reasons, the gas discoveries for the past few years have not been developed to help meeting the energy needs for domestic as well as exports.

These challenges are of course not insurmountable. We have the resources and will and expertise to overcome them. I am sure this is a point that will become even more obvious in your discussions at this Forum.

While the future prospects for gas are good, I do understand that your investment decisions are driven by a number of considerations.

Believe me : every business people who come to see me give me an earful of what they think should be done by the Government.

So I do hear you.

And my Government is responding with clear policy measures.

In order to create a more conducive investment climate, my government is synchronizing policies and regulations in order to avoid policy-overlap.

We are now considering some significant changes to the Tax Law and the Investment Law that would speed up the process of investment approvals.
Because legal certainty is vital to your business, my Government will do all we can to ensure legal certainty for your investments in Indonesia.

We will also honour contract sanctity for gas contracts to strengthen a predictable and secure environment for your investment in Indonesia. This applies also to the existing LNG contracts, where Pertamina was appointed as the seller. However, with regard to new contracts, we open the possibility of the role of sellers other than Pertamina. Such a policy reflects government's responsiveness to the emerging buyers market, where there is a shift from monopolistic to a more competitive market.

My Government is also working very hard to ensure that stability and security is well-maintained across the country. We know that security and stability are prominent considerations in your investment decisions. We intend to strengthen security through close co-operation among all stakeholders : the government, the people, and you in the business community.

I can also tell you that even though Indonesia is undergoing a tremendous change after the introduction of regional autonomy, the oil and gas industry is and will still be at the hand of central government. This is aimed at ensuring certainty and bureaucratic efficiency in your dealings with the Government on oil and gas issues, which are very strategic and vital to our economic growth and development.

In parallel with this, we will also ensure that your investments in oil and gas will not be burdened by additional and unnecessary levies. And therefore investors can develop their business plan and cost estimates with much greater certainty.

Regarding your concerns over the law and fiscal regulations in the gas industry, my Government is now in the process of reviewing all existing fiscal regulations including deferring value-added tax during the exploration stage; whereas refunds for value-added tax and exemptions for import duty in the upstream gas industry will be implemented.

I have also asked Minister for Energy and Mineral Resources to amend the domestic market obligation for gas, which was recently rejected by the Constitutional Court. In this process, we will need the inputs from the stakeholders and we will also value learning your views on this particular issue during this conference.

You can also make good use of the enactment of Government Regulation No. 35 Year 2004 and Government Regulation No. 36 Year 2004 to provide more security to oil and gas investments, in particular on awarding extensions of work contracts well before the end of the contract period.

All in all, I believe your investment will also benefit from the increasing signs of improvement in the Indonesian economy. The growth rate this year is estimated to reach 5.5 percent with an inflation rate of 5-7 percent, slightly lower than last year's inflation rate. The Rupiah exchange rate to the US dollar is now much less volatile and the shares index has passed the 1,000 level. Our foreign exchange reserves are also increasing. With such positive macro-economic indicators, combined with the steadily improving political and security climate, I am confident that Indonesia will regain its position as a favored destination for investment.

The international scene also promises good prospects for gas. For the foreseeable future, we can bet that the world is still very much dependent on oil and gas energy sources. The economies of East Asia and in the Asia Pacific region will grow, though at different pace, but nonetheless they will demand greater supply of oil and gas. And concerns of the impact of fuel emissions on the global environment will bode well for the future for gas as a clean source of fuel.

With all this, we can therefore expect to see a lot of actions in the gas industry.

And the proof is in the pudding, so to speak. In the last decade, gas producing countries including Indonesia are exporting more and more liquefied natural gas (LNG) to both the traditional markets of Japan, South Korea and Chinese Taipei and to newer markets i.e. People's Republic of China and the United States of America. Many LNG markets now no longer wish to be dependent on long-term contracts, and spot markets have begun to emerge in a number of countries that have gas storage capabilities. I am pleased that Indonesia will have a new LNG Train located in East Indonesia that will be used primarily for export purposes to increase foreign exchange. In the future, it will also be used for domestic gas needs.

In the next few days, we hope to hear lots of fresh ideas from you on how to best develop our gas industry for the future.

And while you deliberate on the future prospects of gas, I hope you will consider my message tonight, from one member of the energy community to another.

Join us in developing our domestic gas industry.

Join us to search for and develop new reserves in areas not previously exploited, such as in Eastern Indonesia.

Join our efforts to ensure and guarantee the sustainability of our gas supply and to develop its infrastructure.

Join us in our efforts to expand the current gas pipeline transmission and distribution networks.

Join us in exploiting existing gas reserves in the most efficient and the most environmentally-friendly energy ways as possible.

Join us in a productive partnership that is for the long term and mutually beneficial.

I now come to the pleasant of letting you get on with your work. In the name of Allah SWT, Bismillahirrahmanirrahim, I declare the INDOGAS 2005, The 2nd International Conference and Exhibition open.

I wish you all success in your deliberations and thank you.

Assalamualaikum Warahmatullahi Wabarakatuh.

Jakarta, January 18, 2005

"What happens to Indonesia will affect not only the rest of Southeast Asia, but also the rest of the wider Asia-Pacific region...Indonesia is first among equals of the ten states of Southeast Asia and a significant actor in the wider region of East Asia and the Pacific... Indonesia's diplomatic history further increases its significance to Southeast Asia"—John Bresnan.

(Robert Chase, Emily Hill, Paul Kennedy, The Pivotal States: A New Framework for U.S. Policy in the Developing World (New York: W.W. Norton & Co, 1999).

PHOTO BY ANUNG

"If you want your investment to serve you well, you must also invest in people."

President Susilo Bambang Yudhoyono
Santiago, Chile, November 20, 2004

"There is a very simple reason why I am pro-business. Pro-business means pro-job, it means pro-growth, and by extension it means pro-poor because of the jobs created by business."

President Susilo Bambang Yudhoyono
Tokyo, Japan, June 2, 2005

7

"Accelerating The Wheels of The Indonesian Economy"

Opening Remarks at The Opening of
The 14th Meeting of The Consultative
Group on Indonesia

Istana Negara, Jakarta
January 19, 2005

◆ ◆ ◆ ◆ ◆

Excellencies,

Dear friends of Indonesia,

I am pleased to welcome all of you to Jakarta to attend the 14th meeting of the Consultative Group on Indonesia (CGI).

You might have noticed that the weather this time of year is gloomy and the public mood after the tsunami is rather somber. But let me assure you that the spirit of our nation is high, our commitment to democracy is strong, our will to reform is unwavering, and our determination to progress is steadfast.

I stand here before you as Indonesia's first-directly elected President, presiding over a country which had just accomplished the world's most complex and most ambitious free multi-party elections, with over 100 million voters participating. That fact alone speaks volumes about how far Indonesia's political landscape has changed, and how much our democratic transition has progressed.

We take pride in our democratic development, but this is no time for complacency. The challenges facing my Government and the entire people in Indonesia remain enormous. At the same time, we are also compelled to manage great expectations from our people. You know, our media is intensely focusing on the first 100 days of my Government. Well, I wish I could say to them : "It's not the first 100 days that are difficult. It is the whole 5 years".

You will notice immediately that this year's CGI is different from previous ones. For one, the President of Indonesia this year is different, and on that note, let me state for the record how much I appreciate all the good work of President Megawati Soekarnoputri and her Cabinet. I intend to build on my predecessor's accomplishment to bring greater prosperity for Indonesia.

But what makes this year's CGI particularly significant is that it is being held in the wake of the unspeakable loss of life and destruction from the earthquake and tsunami of December 26th 2004. We are meeting in the midst of the most difficult period in our nation's history.

The devastation in Aceh and North Sumatra is literally beyond our imagination. I still remember traveling by helicopter from Banda Aceh to Meulaboh, a distance of some 240 km, and seeing how the tsunami literally flattened everything to the ground. And it was obvious even from the air that before December 26th, the long coastlines in Western Aceh were once populated by a long stretch of vibrant communities.

As of now, we know that there are over 100,000 dead and 40,000 missing. There are about 500,000 homeless people in the emergency camps, and thousands of tsunami orphans. Perhaps we will never know the exact scale of the human casualties.

The most urgent task now is that of providing emergency relief, and then to proceed with the phase of rehabilitation and reconstruction which will take between 3 to 5 years. We will need to give the stricken communities in Aceh and North Sumatra their livelihood back, but beyond that they also need to achieve emotional healing to recover from the collective grief.

In this forum, you will have the chance to get detailed assessments from my Ministers regarding the extent of the damage, and the preliminary plans for rehabilitation and reconstruction. We look forward to hearing your inputs and cooperation in our efforts to rebuild Aceh and North Sumatra after the tsunami.

I should remind you that at the Special ASEAN Leaders Meeting on the Aftermath of the Earthquake and Tsunami, held in Jakarta a few weeks ago on January 6, Governments and international organizations expressed their commitment to global solidarity to help the victims of the tsunami, to support national programs for rehabilitation and reconstruction and to prevent future disasters by establishing a regional early warning system in the Indian Ocean. They also made commitment to pledge funds for the programs agreed at the Tsunami Summit in Jakarta. I hope that the CGI will take this into consideration.

But Aceh and North Sumatra will only be part of your discussions. At your meeting this year, you will have a full agenda of issues critical to Indonesia's well-being.

The theme of this CGI meeting is "Accelerating growth toward just and equitable society". This theme of course fits in perfectly with my Government's vision as we proceed with our economic development.

My Government is a firm believer in the notion that "growth" and "equity" must go together. And my Government is equally determined to see to it that "prosperity" and "poverty" should not be allowed to go hand-in-hand.

I particularly welcome the fact that this is the first Indonesia-led CGI meeting. The Indonesian Government has set the agenda of this year's meeting and has formulated its own borrowing strategy. With this background, we expect that as partners we will work together to ensure that our decisions on the loan programs and projects match the economic and social needs of Indonesia.

My Government was elected into office with a strong mandate for change. I campaigned on the platform for a more democratic, peaceful, prosperous and just Indonesia. Of course, there is nothing exclusive about such a platform, as this is what all of us in this room want to see for Indonesia.

Since assuming office, I have started the wheels of government to achieve that vision. And we have been fortunate to be able to build on sound basics.

Despite various obstacles to economic performance, and the threat to global conditions posed by high oil prices, the economy performed better than what was expected in 2004.

The inflation was low, interest rate fell, the stock prices surged to the highest level in the history, and economic growth in 2004 reached close to 5%, the highest since the crisis in 1998.

To further promote prosperity in Indonesia, my Government is implementing what I would call the Triple Track Strategy.
- The first track is to achieve sustainable higher economic growth through a combination of strong exports and increased investments, both domestic and foreign.
- The second track is to stimulate the performance of the real sectors to create employment.
- And the third track is to promote the development of the rural economy and agriculture to alleviate poverty.

I know economic plans generally have pros and cons. For my part, I would like to think that my economic vision based on the Triple Track Strategy has 3 pro's : pro-growth, pro-employment, pro-poor.

The good news is that investment and export growth have started to pick up. However, the macroeconomic stability has not yet been translated into tangible job creation. We still see many shortcomings in the real sector. The economic recovery has not been accompanied by a sufficient increase in job opportunities. This is a key challenge for the next five years, namely how to accelerate sustainable economic growth by consolidating micro-reform while maintaining macro-economic stabilization.

I hope that CGI discussions this year will yield constructive measures that would help my Government in achieving this triple track strategy.

If we remain on track with the Triple Track Strategy, we will be able to meet the economic targets set by my Government immediately upon assuming office.

In the next five years, we aim to decrease open unemployment rate from 9.5 % in 2003 to 5,1 %.

We aim to reduce poverty incidence from 16.6 % in 2004 to 8.2 % in 2009.

And we aim to accelerate economic growth from 5.5 % in 2005 to 7.6 % in 2009 so that in the next five years, the economic growth will achieve an average of 6.6 % per year;

These targets can only be achieved if we maintain low inflation, fiscal sustainability and stick to the economic reform strategy. Economic growth can only be accelerated if we increase productivity in every sector of the economy. And such an increase in productivity will only take place if macro-economic reforms are continued and synchronised with various refoms at the micro level. You can be assured that my Government is actively pursuing various reforms to improve investment climate, to ensure flexibility of the labour market and to combat corruption in order to reduce high cost economy.

The Indonesian government is committed to continue the legal reform process, for example by issuing a decree on combating corruption, establishing the Oversight Body on the Attorney General's Office (Komite Pengawas Kejaksaan), and fighting against smuggling. All these efforts are aimed at ensuring the security and certainty of investments in Indonesia.

The Government has also taken bold steps to improve infrastructure, by establishing a public-private participation forum, which opens up infrastructure for private participation. In this regard, I am pleased to inform you that in the past 2 days the Government held a successful Indonesia Infrastructure Summit here in Jakarta attended by about 700 businessmen from 22 countries.

In all this, the role of foreign financing will be valuable. We will cover some of the financing needs from new investments, domestic and foreign. There is also room for loans, but they must be effectively allocated to serve our socio-economic priorities. And presently, our priorities are concentrated on sectors which promise high productivity and high returns, such as exports and infrastructure. We need to ensure that resources are not wasted on unproductive sectors. I ask the CGI to consider this in your discussions on bridging the financing gap.

In the next few days, you will have rich discussions on issues affecting Indonesia's future: the general macro-economic situation, governance, decentralization, poverty, security, health and education, aid effectiveness, forestry and environment, justice, legal reform and anti-corruption agenda, investment climate and financial sector reform, as well as reconstruction needs for Aceh. It is an extensive and exhaustive list. I have instructed all of my Ministers concerned to take an active role in the discussions, and

I hope you will make use of this opportunity to provide them with constructive policy ideas and suggestions. After all, for us, this is the real value of the CGI, as a forum between the Indonesian Government and the stake-holders where we can exchange views, review developments, and do a temperature check on policy direction and the outcome of our development strategy.

Since it began its work, the CGI has played an important role in our national development, and I am confident that you will remain our close and reliable partners in the future. My Government, and the governments before me, recognize and value our mutual co-operation and partnership over these past years.

Finally, I am convinced that, despite the tsunami crises, Indonesia has gained a momentum to once again become an economic success story. Indonesia can achieve this if we all work together with the right spirit of cooperation based on mutual respect and equitable partnership.

I wish you all the best in your deliberations, and I expect to hear a successful report on your work today and tomorrow.

Thank you.

Jakarta, January 19, 2005

"The business mood is better than it has been in Indonesia at any time since the financial crisis in 1998"—Joe Bartlett, President, AMCHAM Indonesia.

(AMCHAM Indonesia Press Release, 25 February 2005)

"My Government is committed to ensure affordable energy for the poor in Indonesia. This means that Government subsidies for solar and kerosene, which are widely used by the poor, will be maintained.

That is the commitment I have made to my people, and that is the commitment that I will keep."

President Susilo Bambang Yudhoyono
Jakarta, December 12, 2004

"Indonesia now has a unique opportunity. For the first time in possibly more than a decade, we have the opportunity to take ownership and responsibility to lock in economic and structural reforms that will lift Indonesia's growth rate, create jobs and reduce poverty."

President Susilo Bambang Yudhoyono
Jakarta, January 24, 2005

8

"Towards Democratic Stability and Democratic Prosperity for Indonesia"

Speech at CNBC Strategic Forum

Dharmawangsa Hotel, Jakarta
January 24, 2005

♦ ♦ ♦ ♦ ♦

Excellencies,
Distinguished guests,

Assalamualaikum Warahmatullahi Wabarakatuh,

Good morning to all of you.

I am glad to see so many of you here today, and I wish to thank CNBC Strategic Forum for organizing our gathering today.

This is the fourth time in a week that I am addressing an audience of corporate leaders. I trust that you will take it as a clear sign of how much I am counting on the private sector to be the engine of our economic progress.

I must say, however, that my most poignant moment of the week was last Friday, when I joined thousands of Acehnese for Idul Adha prayers at Baiturrachman grand mosque in Banda Aceh.

The Baiturrachman I prayed at last Friday was very different from the dysfunctional Baiturrachman I visited 2 days after the tsunami, a time of chaotic desperation where dead bodies piled its courtyard. Today, Baiturrachman provides a powerful spiritual sanctuary for Acehnese who want to find emotional healing from their agonizing collective grief.

At the present moment, we are still in the emergency relief phase. By the end of March, we hope to complete the key objectives of the emergency relief phase, which means, finding and burying the dead, relocating the emergency camps, sheltering all the homeless, preventing the spread of diseases, clearing-up the rubbles, connecting the roads, re-functioning the local government, rebuilding the vital infrastructure.

By March 26, we will evaluate the progress made as we proceed to the next phase, which is the long term rehabilitation and reconstruction of Aceh, at which point we will make operational adjustments accordingly based on our needs and capability.

We are deeply thankful to all the soldiers, the police, the volunteers who have worked tirelessly and selflessly. They have done a tremendous job in the relief efforts.

I also want to thank the international community for the outpouring of sympathy, support and solidarity shown to Indonesia during this agonizing time.

Re-building Aceh will be among my Government's top priorities for the foreseeable future. And as we rebuild Aceh, I also wish to assure you that we are equally determined to press on with our national objectives.

And this is what I wish to speak to you about today : the story of a changing Indonesia and why you should be a part of it.

When I campaigned for the Presidency, I made a simple promise to the Indonesian voters : to make Indonesia more democratic, more peaceful, more prosperous and more just.

A simple concept, but a great challenge. A great challenge because it is not just a matter of making incremental progress, it is about transforming a country.

After 3 months in office, I remain as optimistic today about Indonesia`s prospects as I was before entering Government.

I know you need more than to just rely on my enthusiasm, so let me offer several reasons why you should also be optimistic about Indonesia`s prospects.
The FIRST reason is that Indonesia has continued to beat the odds as we took on great historical challenges.

We overcame excruciating financial, economic and social crises. We overcame a constitutional crisis, and went through several peaceful Presidential change-overs. We proceeded with the most far-reaching decentralizations by any standard. We consolidated our democratic transitions to the point of no-return. We restored freedom for the press, and scrapped all repressive political laws. We successfully conducted the most complex and most ambitious free multi- party elections anywhere in the world. We fought back strongly against cruel acts of terrorism. We are recovering from the most devastating natural disaster in living memory.

And above all, we managed to hold the country together.

All this is a tribute to the strength, resilience and adaptability of the Indonesian people.

I do not think there are too many countries out there that have gone through so much trials and tribulations, and have bounced back even stronger each time.

And despite the uphill battles that await us, I have a very strong feeling that the Indonesian nation will continue to beat the odds and grow from strength to strength. And why not, they have had lots of practice.

The SECOND reason to be optimistic is the factor of political stability and greater security.

Politically, the historic direct Presidential elections gave my Government a strong mandate, obtained directly from the electorate, to govern for the next 5 years until 2009. By implication, this means that there is no longer ambivalence in the relationship between the executive and the legislature. I am pleased that my Government has established stable, dynamic and constructive relations with the Parliament. I have very good working relations with Parliament speaker Agung Laksono, and I intend to maintain that for the rest of my term. And Vice-President Jusuf Kalla`s success to become chairman of Golkar, the largest party in Parliament, will significantly add more stability to my Government`s relations with the Parliament so that the nation can prosper and grow.

Of course, I fully agree that the Parliament has to stay critical to the Government, but ultimately we are all responsible for maintaining a healthy, stable political climate.

On the security front, we are moving resolutely to end separatist conflicts through peaceful means. In Aceh, after extending the civil emergency status in Aceh for 6 months, I offered dialogue with the Acehnese, and stressed the need to effectively implement special autonomy. After the tsunami, I immediately ordered the military to be on the defensive mode, challenged GAM to permanently terminate the conflict, and promised amnesty to GAM members who would be willing to lay down their weapons.

We are also pursuing the implementation of special autonomy in Papua. In fact, on the day of the tsunami, I happened to be in Papua, where I unveiled the Presidential Decree on the establishment of the much-awaited Council of the People of Papua (MRP), which will promote the cause of women, local customs and religion in that province.

Today, the security situation in both Aceh and Papua, and also in the troubled areas of Poso, Maluku and North Maluku are now stable and are improving day by day.

Meanwhile, we are actively continuing our fight against terrorists. We have captured more terrorists, including the bombers of

Kuningan. And while we continue to hunt known terrorists such as Dr. Azahari and Noordin Muhamad Top, we are also intensifying coordination between our intelligence, police, immigration and customs in our efforts to capture terrorists.

And, *alhamdulillah,* our Idul Fitri, Christmas, New Year and Idul Adha celebrations went by in generally calm and peaceful way.

A THIRD reason for optimism is that my Government is moving ahead with focus, direction and will.

I think you would agree with me that Indonesia now has a unique opportunity. For the first time in possibly more than a decade, we have the opportunity to take ownership and responsibility to lock in economic and structural reforms that will lift Indonesia's growth rate, create jobs and reduce poverty.

My Government's development strategy is based on what I call the Triple Track.

The first track is to achieve sustainable higher economic growth through a combination of strong exports and increased investments, both domestic and foreign.

The second track is to stimulate the performance of the real sectors to create more employment.

And the third track is to promote the development of the rural economy and agriculture to alleviate poverty.

The Triple Track Strategy is essentially pro-growth, pro-jobs, pro-poor.

With this Triple Track Strategy, we intend to reach our economic targets at the end of our term. By 2009, we aim to reduce the unemployment rate from 9.5 percent to 5.1 percent, and we seek to cut the poverty rate in half to 8.1 percent.

We also seek to increase growth in the average of 6,6 % per annum for the next 5 years. But we want to do more than to just pump-up numbers. We intend to create quality growth that creates good jobs for around two million new job seekers each year, let alone the millions of workers crowded into the more insecure informal sector.

We will promote growth by maintaining macro-economic stability through stable prices, fiscal sustainability and financial sector reforms.

We are also committed to fiscal policy consistency. We are targeting around 1 percent deficit for 2005 but a more gradual reduction in the deficit thereafter. We plan to balance the books in 2008. This strategy is consistent with reducing government debt ratio as well. This more gradual approach will provide us with a little extra room to make good on our promises of additional resources for our social sector programs and infrastructure development.

We are also committed to financial sector reforms. The government will continue to implement prudential reforms in the banking and financial sector. We will review and remove obstacles to growth of the non-bank financial institutions, and we will put in place systems to minimize the vulnerability of another systemic crisis.

My FOURTH reason to be optimistic about Indonesia is more specific to your needs, and that is : an improved business climate.

I know that you want to put your money where it can breed profitably, and so do we. We are aware of your business needs and considerations, and we are trying our best to address them. In the short term, we want to make it easier for you to invest and we also want to change perceptions about doing business in Indonesia.

Our strategy is to seriously tackle the business regulatory environment, streamline investment procedures and to reform institutions related to investment so they become facilitators and promoters of investment, not regulators.

We have begun already implementing changes in my 100 day program.

Let me highlight some examples.

We are modernizing our labor regulations. Of course, workers need social protection, but the direction in the last two years has been excessive by all standards. It is beginning to hurt employment and risks causing social exclusion of those who do not have access to these good jobs. We certainly need to balance the needs of formal workers for protection with the need to create good jobs.

We are also pursuing tax reforms, including reducing tax distortions, improving tax administration and procedures, and reform of tax disputes mechanisms.

We will also improve our customs and trade policies with promises to remove customs inefficiencies, eradication of corrupt practices and to harmonize import tariff rates.

We are pressing on with legal reforms and anti-corruption drive. You can see from media reports the proliferation in the number of investigations and prosecutions of civil servants and politicians on corruption charges in recent weeks.

We are also rigorously promoting infrastructure development. Last week, we had a successful Infrastructure Summit and it was well received by both foreign and domestic investors. One of our key objectives here is to improve the efficiency of existing infrastructure and utilities, increase investments and open up sectors to greater private sector participation. These areas include energy industry, telecommunication, clean water, rehabilitating rail transportation, increasing national road networks across the country and investment in rural roads.

And with regard to regional autonomy, we will focus on improving local government regulations and taxes so that they do not burden investors and citizens. We will focus on clarifying roles between the centre and regions in the areas of budgetary expenditures, management of infrastructure assets, economic and social policy implementation and ensuring free internal trade between regions.

With all these reasons, I hope you can see why I am optimistic about Indonesia`s prospects. It is hardly an exhaustive list of reasons, and each one of you can add your own reason to the list.

The key challenge in all this is to effectively connect and combine democracy with governance.

I have long realized that democracy does not come automatically in the same package with governance.

Democracy does not necessarily deliver us peace, prosperity, security, equity, national unity.

Democracy can only deliver these precious things to our lives if it is equipped by governance—good governance.

If there is disconnect between democracy and governance, you will have a dysfunctional democracy. The world is full of examples of democracies becoming unstable, democracies in decay, democracies in regression, democracies ruined by conflict and poverty. We do not intend to go that route.

I believe that if we establish a healthy connection between democracy and governance, two things will happen.

First, democracy will go hand-in-hand with stability, hence producing what I would call `democratic stability`.

And secondly, democracy will be blessed with prosperity, which means more growth, more employment, more equity and better standard of living overall. Hence, what I would call `democratic prosperity.

In these two instances, democracy will live up to its promise : the promise to deliver a better life, better freedom to all citizens.

I hereby invite you all to our house of democratic stability, and to be a part of our democratic prosperity.

By saying *Bismillahirrrahmanirrahim*, I now take great pleasure to declare the CNBC Strategic Forum : "The New Indonesia 2005 - Policy and Action" open.

Thank you.

Jakarta, January 24, 2005

"Susilo Bambang Yudhoyono is a different kind of Indonesian leader"—Patrick Walters, National Security Editor.

(The Australian, 5 April 2005)

"Susilo Bambang Yudhoyono, also known by his initials SBY, won over voters in Indonesia's first democratic elections with his image as a man of integrity, a strong communicator and firm leader in times of crisis."--Rachel Harvey.

(BBC News World Edition, 20 October 2004)

PHOTO BY ABROR

"The time for peace —real peace, permanent peace— is now. Those who continue to espouse conflict represent not the interest of Acehnese but only themselves."

President Susilo Bambang Yudhoyono
Singapore, February 16, 2005

"I think it is important for the US to project and emphasize more of its soft power".

President Susilo Bambang Yudhoyono
Washington DC, USA , May 25, 2005

9

"Indonesia : The Challenge of Change"

The President's Lecture Series organized by ISEAS

Singapore
February 16, 2005

♦　♦　♦　♦　♦

My good friend Prime Minister Lee Hsien Loong,
Excellencies,
Ladies and gentlemen,
Dear friends,

Thank you, Senior Minister Goh Chok Tong, for your kind words and for graciously agreeing to chair our session today. We remember you as an able statesman and a good friend of Indonesia, who did exemplary work carrying the baton from Singapore's remarkable leader, Lee Kwan Yew.

I wish to begin by thanking ISEAS for inviting me to give the President's lecture here today. Since elected President, I have given several keynote speeches at different forums, but this is the first time since I received my Doctorate degree that anyone has asked me to give a "lecture". As flattering as this is, I do not feel that I am in a position to lecture to an audience made-up of

Singapore's best brains. In fact, Singapore, being the world's most successful city-state, has a lot to tell the world about the lessons of governance.

I stand here today to speak about "the challenge of change for Indonesia".

All of you in Singapore know the meaning of "change" very well. I know of no other country in the world which has changed as rapidly and as frequently as Singapore. In the last few decades, you have transformed this island into a modern city-state, a world-class trading, manufacturing, financial center, thus making Singapore relevant -- relevant to the region, relevant to the world economy.

There are many ways to measure "greatness" in a nation, but history tells us that the measure of a country's greatness lies in its ability to adapt—adapt to changing times, adapt to new challenges, adapt to emerging trends, adapt to new terrains.

The examples are all around us.
- China is the important player that she is today because in the 1970's she changed course, adopted Four Modernizations, opened up to the outside world, and embraced market principles.
- Vietnam too realized after winning the Vietnam War that her future relevance would depend NOT on her superb military experience, but on her becoming economically competitive and on integrating herself with the region.
- The US is today the world's only superpower and the world's largest economy because over the last 2 centuries

she has demonstrated an uncanny ability to reinvent herself over and over again.

- And Chile, which I visited a few months ago while attending the APEC Summit, has rapidly transformed herself in the last decade or so to become one of the most successful recent examples of democratic governance.

Different countries adapt differently, but adapt they must.

Those who fail to adapt will be swept aside by history.

Just look at strong-state Yugoslavia, which is shattered to pieces because her superstructure was no longer capable to contain and pacify the disintegrating forces within her borders.

Change therefore is the essence of adaptability, the hallmark of progress, and for some, the necessary measure of survival.

For us in Indonesia too, we cannot escape the necessity to adapt, to change. And this is something that goes a long way back.
Our founding fathers learned the concepts of nation-state and nationalism, learned about constitutional Government and rule of law, learned about representative democracy, adopted the terminology "Indonesia", and mixed them all up to create the sovereign Republic of Indonesia.

In the 1960's, a new generation of Indonesians discovered a new term—"pembangunan", or development—and set in motion a long-term economic progress which in the next 3 decades would give Indonesia one of the highest growth in the region.

And at the end of the 20th century, another generation of Indonesians began yet another strategic adaptation, by launching "reformasi" which effectively set the country on the path of democratic transition.

My mission as the sixth President of Indonesia is to advance as far as possible Indonesia's democracy and reformasi. During the Presidential elections last year, a great number of Indonesian voters chanted "change", and in so doing the voters were expressing their desire to see greater clarity over the direction of the nation. What I promised the Indonesian voters were quite simple : to do my best to make Indonesia more democratic, more peaceful, more just, more prosperous. And I intend to keep that promise.

Indonesia is a country that can change in so many different ways. Which is why we have to avoid change for the sake of change. Upon assuming office, my immediate priority was to make sure that "change" be given direction, that change have a target and a plan, and that change have relevance to the lives of the people. For the first time, we have an elected Government that is mandated directly by the Indonesian voters, and for the first time since 1997, there is a Government that has the luxury to plan and execute for the full 5 years.

There are several challenges of change that I would like to highlight today. As I go through this list, I think you will find that some of them might be of some relevance to Singapore as well.

The first challenge is ensuring that Indonesia's present macro-economic stability leads to real improvement of the living standards of average Indonesians. This is easier said than done. The previous Government was able to deliver macro-economic stability, but for some reasons it did not translate into a feel-good factor and more employment.

To achieve this, my Government is adopting what I call the "Triple track strategy" :

- first, to promote growth through exports and investment;
- secondly, to promote employment by stimulating the real sector;
- and thirdly, to reduce poverty by promoting agriculture and rural development.

The triple track strategy is in essence pro-growth, pro-jobs, pro-poor.

Over the next 5 years, my Government is aiming an average annual growth of 6,6 %, but, more importantly, we want that growth to help reduce poverty from 16,6 % to 8,2 %, and we want that growth to half unemployment from 9,5 % to 5,1 % by 2009. We want growth to be coupled with equity, and we want to ensure that prosperity eradicates poverty.

The second challenge of change goes beyond numbers and statistics. There are some things that cannot be measured by numbers and statistics. Employment may rise, inflation may go down, and the GDP may go up, but none of these things mean much if the nation as a whole becomes insecure, if conflicts persist, if it loses its fiber, if it loses its sense of identity. That is why the real challenge of change is not just ensuring the growth of the economy, but also the growth of the nation. Not just economic growth, but national growth. My aim as President is to see to it that the Indonesian nation grows to be prosperous, but also resilient, competitive, peaceful and confident about itself and about its future.

All of you in Singapore know what I am talking about. In the 1960's, people who lived in this island had a hard time figuring out its identity. You experimented with different political arrangements before deciding to form your own independent sovereign Republic of Singapore. And from then on Singapore transformed itself into a coherent, vibrant nation. With decades of stability, effective leadership and nation-building, your economy grew, but your sense of national pride also grew.

Finally, the challenge of change is to bring out the best in Indonesia. What are the best things about Indonesia ? Our independence, our diversity, our tolerance, our simplicity, our openness, our love of family and community, our passion for unity and harmony, our rich spirituality, our neighborliness. These are the values that make us distinctly Indonesian. My grandparents and parents lived by them, and so should my generation and my children's generation. The more we change, the more we need to embody the essence of being Indonesian.

I have described to you some of the challenges of change that we face. After over 3 months in office, I remain as optimistic as ever about Indonesia's future. There has been intense focus in Indonesia on the performance of my Government in the first 100 days. I have listened to these criticisms as we plan our next moves. But we are only at the beginning of a long journey. We are running a marathon of 5 years, not a sprint for 100 days.

I have no doubt that in the end our hard work to change Indonesia for the better will prevail.

There is one recent event which in my view have also changed Indonesia, and perhaps changed all of you, also.

None of us predicted it, none of us were ready for it, but it hit us like a brick wall.

I am talking about the earthquake and killer tsunami waves that destroyed communities in Aceh and North Sumatra on December 26, 2004.

Never before in the history of Indonesia have so many people perished in a matter of minutes. For those who survived, the emotional damage will stay with them for a very long time.

Indonesia has seen many natural disasters before, but the tsunami practically brought the whole country together like never before. After the tsunami, Aceh became seen not as a conflict area but as a disaster area. The whole of Indonesia wept, and came together. They donated what they can to the victims in Aceh and North Sumatra, through the Government, through the media, through local organizations and schools, through their work place. The rich, the poor, children, students, housewives, artists--everyone got into the act of caring and contributing. No other event has brought the whole country together like this.

7 weeks after the tsunami, we still have much to do. We have found many of the dead and buried them, but even as we gather here, rescuers are still finding the dead under the ruins. Over 550,000 homeless Acehnese are still in the emergency camps, and tens of thousands of tsunami orphans need to be looked after.

We are aiming that the current emergency relief phase will be completed by the end of March, after which we will move on to the phase of rehabilitation and reconstruction. We will do our best to ensure that the rebuilt community will be safer from the threats of future tsunamis.

But Aceh's rehabilitation and reconstruction will need to be carried out under a condition of maximum peace.

After the tsunami, the Acehnese are simply not interested in conflict. The real cause of the Acehnese is survival, reconstruction and healing.

I call on GAM at all levels, whereever they are, to terminate this conflict, to come to permanent peace with dignity, and to work together to rebuild Aceh under the framework special autonomy. This is what the Acehnese want, this is what the Indonesian Government is offering, and this is what the international community support unreservedly.

The time for peace—real peace, permanent peace--is now. Those who continue to espouse conflict represent not the interest of Acehnese but only themselves. They will be sidelined by the people of Aceh.

As we prepare for Aceh's reconstruction, the challenge before us now is NOT how to marshall resources, but how to manage them-- manage them effectively and properly.

With all the funds, resources and manpower, we must make sure that all the assistance are used in ways that empower the people of Aceh. We must make sure that the assistance is aimed at helping the Acehnese get back on their feet, to get their economy moving again, to give their livelihood back.

We must make sure that all the assistance is deployed in a coordinated, transparent and coherent manner.

We must make sure that all the international and national assistance fit into the Indonesian government's long-term Master Plan for Aceh's reconstruction.

We need to ensure that Aceh will be rebuilt in ways that respects its unique culture and rich Islamic heritage.

And we must ensure that the assistance will be deployed in ways that will lead to the strengthening of peace in that province.

The tsunami has also given way to a new phenomenon in international affairs.

It generated a tremendous amount of global goodwill and solidarity on a scale that is unprecedented.

It allowed military contingents from so many countries to work side-by-side with the Indonesian military, not to keep the peace between combatants, but to conduct humanitarian operations.

It allowed private citizens of various religions around the world to sent their volunteers and donations to help a distinctively Islamic society.

Perhaps because this is not about war, politics, conflict, the world's citizens were able to respond to it with a level of compassion that is rarely seen, allowing them to reach deep into their sense of humanity, spawning countless acts of kindness and selflessness, from Dili to Darwin, Beijing to London, Kuala Lumpur to Madrid, Singapore to Washington DC, Tokyo to Tehran.

When was the last time we saw this pervasive act of global kindness, compassion and solidarity?

We need to build on this global solidarity. What we all have done to help the tsunami victims around the Indian Ocean demonstrated the new heights of collaboration by the international community.

Let it be known years from now that this was a time when the community of nations joined forces with only one ideology binding them : humanity.

Let me now say a few words about Indonesia-Singapore relations. I know there is a great interest in Singapore towards Indonesia. Singaporeans read about events in my country daily in a special section on Indonesia in the Straits Times.

Let me begin by saying that I value my personal relations with Prime Minister Lee Hsien Loong, whom I respect as an intelligent, visionary leader with a common touch. PM Lee was one of the first foreign leaders to telephone me right after the Electoral Commission declared that I had won the Presidential elections. PM Lee also kindly attended my Presidential inauguration, the first Singapore leader to do so, and he was also one of the first foreign leaders to visit Indonesia after the inauguration. We talk frequently on the telephone, and it is a sign of our closeness that Prime Minister Lee sometimes called me on the phone with only 10 minutes notice. It's true...

I think the experience in the last few weeks has made relations between Indonesia and Singapore closer. It was Prime Minister Lee who called me in early January this year to suggest that ASEAN hold a Special Leaders Meeting on the Tsunami, which my Government gladly organized and hosted a few days later on January 6th.

That meeting not only demonstrated ASEAN's responsiveness to the worst natural disaster this region has ever seen, but also secured international commitment for the reconstruction of the stricken communities, and a commitment to establish a regional early warning system in the Indian Ocean.

Singapore was also quick to help us on the ground in Aceh when we needed it most. I remember well meeting the pilots of Singapore's Chinooks in Medan and Banda Aceh, and they were particularly helpful with logistical re-supply and medical evacuations from Meulaboh during critical times. Your Landing Ship Tanks (LST), in cooperation with the Indonesian navy, also helped to bridge the gap of supplies in Aceh's western coasts, and your Hercules C-130s were very instrumental to transport much needed supplies to Banda Aceh.

This experience of working together between the TNI and the Singapore Armed Forces bodes well for future cooperation, especially in Military Operations Other Than War, which I believe would give substance to the notion of an ASEAN Security Community.

But our cooperation on the Aceh tsunami tragedy is only part of our special relationship. The purpose of my visit here is to expand and deepen this important relationship.

In our talks yesterday, Prime Minister Lee and I have agreed to develop a new framework for bilateral cooperation. While continuing to actively deal with pending issues, we will move ahead to find new opportunities of cooperation in various areas of common interest. And I appreciate that Prime Minister Lee is sensitive to issues which my Government feels strongly about.

During this visit, we were able to make important headways, such as the signing of the Investment Guarantee Agreement, a commitment to discuss cooperation on tourism and air services, and to strengthen cooperation on fighting trans-national crimes, including on anti-terrorism and anti-corruption.

The bottom line is that our relations are steady and solid, and we are moving forward in dealing with pending issues. And I hope Singapore will continue to be part of our success, as you have always been.

I have come to the end of my remarks. I hope you take all the things I have said to you today not as a "lecture", but as a friend talking to another friend, well, hundreds of friends.

I thank you for listening.

Singapore, February 16, 2005

"Indonesia is a lot more stable and has better prospects than a few years back"—Emil Wolter, Polar Capital Partners Ltd, London.

(Singapore Business Review, May, 2005)

"Indonesia has never before allowed its citizens to choose their own mayors, governors and regents (the equivalent of a mayor in rural districts). Direct elections for these posts, which began this month, crown Indonesia's remarkable transition to democracy over the past six years. They might also improve the quality of government across the fissiparous archipelago."

(The Economist, 23 June 2005)

"Our gas development policy is driven by a vision to create an efficient, dynamic, transparent, environmentally friendly, competitive and world-class Indonesian gas industry which can support Indonesia's sustainable economy and promote greater prosperity for our people."

President Susilo Bambang Yudhoyono
Jakarta, January 18, 2005

"In the fight against trans-national crime and terrorism, we need to evolve an inclusive approach. We need to cultivate a new security culture which would allow all of us to cooperate with one another, irrespective of whether you are Russian, Chinese, Americans, Australians, Indians or Filipino."

President Susilo Bambang Yudhoyono
Denpasar, Bali, May 17, 2005

10

"Indonesia and Singapore : Strong Neighbors, Shared Future"

Remarks at a State Dinner tendered by
President of The Republic of Singapore

Singapore
February 16, 2005

♦ ♦ ♦ ♦ ♦

Your Excellency President Sellapan Rama Nathan,
Excellencies,
Distinguished Guests,
Ladies and Gentlemen,

First and foremost, allow me to express my heartfelt appreciation to Your Excellency, President of the Republic of Singapore, and Madame Nathan, for the warm and gracious hospitality that you have shown my wife and I, as well as the entire Indonesian delegation, during our stay here.

We gather here tonight to honor a strong, enduring relationship between the Republic of Indonesia and the Republic of Singapore. And we gather here as friends, partners, as neighbors, as family.

Singapore and Indonesia have always had close, special relations. But in the last few weeks, in the wake of the most catastrophic natural disaster in living memory, the fiber of that special friendship came to the fore.

As I expressed to you this morning, Mr. President, we in Indonesia are grateful for all the support and assistance that the Government and people of the Republic of Singapore have extended to us in the aftermath of the tsunami tragedy in Aceh and North Sumatra.

Singapore is among the first countries to lend her helping hands. Singapore Armed Forces, relief workers and medics arrived in Medan, Banda Aceh and then Meulaboh immediately after the tsunami. Your officers worked tirelessly and superbly with our TNI to save lives, to deliver supplies, to evacuate the injured.

Singapore also initiated the idea of the Special ASEAN Leaders Meeting on the Aftermath of the Earthquake and Tsunami, which was held in Jakarta on 6 January 2005,

And Prime Minister Lee Hsien Loong today informed me of Singapore's commitment to take part in Aceh's rehabilitation and reconstruction.

Clearly, the difficult tsunami experience has made us closer, and has made us even better friends.

The fact that our two countries are geographically bound together poses a special challenge and opportunity for us. The more our relations evolve, the more we must become better neighbors.

This is why it was an easy decision for me to decide that Singapore would be among the first destinations of my foreign bilateral visit since elected President.

I want this visit not only to highlight our special relations, but also to strengthen it and to expand it so that we can begin with a new era of bilateral relations.

In a sense, we already begun that new era when Prime Minister Lee Hsien Loong kindly attended my Presidential inauguration on October last year, the first Singapore leader to do so, and when he also became one of the first foreign leaders to visit me after the inauguration.

Our bilateral relations are full of undiscovered potentials. We have to strive harder to develop them.

And I think during this visit we have made some important movements forward. I am pleased that the Investment Guarantee Agreement (IGA) between Indonesia and Singapore will be signed tomorrow. By way of this agreement, we hope that trade and investment between our two countries will increase considerably.

We also appreciate the participation of Singapore's businessmen during the recently-held "Infrastructure Summit." Back-to-back with this Summit, a joint business mission involving Indonesian, Singaporean and Malaysian businessmen was also organized in Jakarta.

We are also actively discussing the promotion of cooperation in the fields of tourism and civil aviation.

And I very much appreciate the joint commitment made between Prime Minister Lee Hsien Loong and I today to instruct our officials to negotiate the Extradition Treaty expeditiously.

To promote cooperation between Indonesia and Singapore, it is important for our two countries to pursue and expedite the establishment of the Joint Cooperation Council (JCC). The JCC will provide us with a useful mechanism to broaden and deepen bilateral cooperation as well as to manage and address all on-going issues. This, in my view, would constitute a concrete step in our efforts to foster closer and deeper relations.

Indonesia and Singapore have rich and complex and challenging relations. We need to manage our bilateral relations rationally and objectively and in the spirit of friendship and good-neighborliness, to the satisfaction of both sides.

And we must always stay true to the ASEAN spirit and our tradition of good-neighborliness. I believe there is much that Singapore and Indonesia can do together to strengthen regional order, and to realize our objective for an ASEAN Community.

Finally, I am pleased to share with you that the series of meetings I had this morning has been productive and fruitful for deepening and expanding our bilateral relationship.

I therefore look forward to Singapore and Indonesia working even more closely, both at the bilateral level as well as within the framework of ASEAN unity.

With those brief remarks, may I now request every one present in this banquet to rise and join me for a toast to the health and success of His Excellency President Sellapan Rama Nathan and to the progress and prosperity of our two countries.

Thank you very much.

Singapore, February 16, 2005

"Indonesia is a fragile, new democracy. Endemic corruption, the abuse of government positions, human rights and legal impartiality are high on Dr. Yudhoyono's sweeping reform agenda...Only substantial new foreign investment can produce the economic growth needed to soak up Indonesia's huge pool of unemployed. Dr. Yudhoyono knows that unless his Government can make a real dent in poverty, democracy will remain vulnerable to the political spoilers and their old, dirty rules."

(The Sydney Morning Herald, 6 April 2005)

"I am an optimist who try to see an answer in every problem, unlike the pessimist who see problem in every answer."

President Susilo Bambang Yudhoyono
Jakarta, January 17, 2005

"As we build our legal system, we have to avoid a situation where there is much law, but little justice."

President Susilo Bambang Yudhoyono
Bali, May 4, 2005

11

Message
By
President Susilo Bambang
Yudhoyono
to the Kidnappers of Two
Indonesian Journalists in Iraq

Presidential Palace Jakarta
February 19, 2005

Editor's Note:

President Susilo Bambang Yudhoyono made this televised statement in the middle of the night from Istana Merdeka, after being awakened by Special Staff for International Affairs, Dino Patti Djalal, around midnight who relayed confirmation that the two Indonesian journalists were taken hostage. Upon hearing this bad news, the President immediately decided to make his televised appeal for their release there and then Budiyanto and Meutya Hafid were released by their kidnappers on February 21 2005. The President made his statement in Bahasa Indonesia, and below is the English translation.

◆ ◆ ◆ ◆ ◆

Assalammu'alaikum Warrahmatullahi Wabarakatuh

This morning I received a report informing that two Indonesian nationals and professional journalists, Mr. Budyanto and Ms. Meutia Hafid, were declared missing while performing their work in Iraq. Subsequently, the officials from the Indonesian Ministry of Foreign Affairs and other Governments, informed that our two journalists were very likely being kidnapped somewhere in Iraq.

We continue to seek information on the current whereabout and activities of these journalists, and about half an hour ago I received confirmation that the two journalists are taken hostage somewhere in Iraq.

I, Dr. Haji Susilo Bambang Yudhoyono, President of the Republic of Indonesia, hereby confirm that those two journalists are truly in Iraq in order to carry out their professional assignment. They are not in any way involved in politics or the conflict in Iraq. Prior to their current assignment, they covered humanitarian activity of the Indonesian workers in Malaysia, and then they reported on the tsunami disaster in Aceh, also from the humanitarian point of view. They have come to Iraq this time in order to cover the activity of our Iraqi brothers and sisters because as the world's largest Muslim country, Indonesians are certainly eager to know the conditions our brothers and sisters in Iraq.

Therefore, I strongly appeal for the release of those two innocent individuals who are merely doing their job so that they can safely return to Indonesia to join their family and friends back home. I communicated with the families of both journalists, and like all of us in Indonesia, their family is so concerned with their fate. I once again knock on your conscience and appeal for the release of our two journalists and their safe return to Indonesia.

I wish to thank and express my appreciation to those who have shown their goodwill and assistance in ensuring the safety and release of the two Indonesian nationals. May God bless them.

Wassalammu'alaikum warrahmatullahi wabarakatuh.

"...for the first time in years Indonesia has reason for some optimism. Since winning the country's first direct-election presidential campaign in September, Yudhoyono has won international praise for his crisis-management following the tsunami and his efforts to fight terrorism and the corruption that's rampant in Indonesia's political and business circles"—**Brian Bremner and Assif Shameen.**

(BusinessWeek Online, 4 July 2005)

"I knock on your conscience and appeal for the release of our two journalist and their safe return to Indonesia"

President Susilo Bambang Yudhoyono
Jakarta , February 19, 2005

"Remember: the use of soft power charms and disarms. Hard power, on the other hand, if it is used incorrectly, provokes resistance and, sometimes, resentment."

President Susilo Bambang Yudhoyono
Washington DC, USA , May 25, 2005

12

"On Globalization and Sustainable Development"

Speech at the Inaugural Opening of
Lake Toba Summit :
"Network of Regional Governments for
Sustainable Development"

Tiara Hotel-Medan, North Sumatra
March 10, 2005

♦ ♦ ♦ ♦ ♦

His Excellency and my good friend President Xanana Gusmao of Timor Leste,
Excellencies,
Ladies and Gentlemen,
Dear friends,

Let me begin by welcoming all of you to Medan.

I am so pleased to see so many distinguished leaders from Indonesia and from all over the world here in this first Summit meeting Network of Regional Governments for Sustainable Development.

Indonesia has always had strong interest in the concept and practice of sustainable development. We regard this meeting of regional governments and local authorities here as an important milestone to deepen international cooperation so that we can collectively reach the targets of The Millennium Developments Goals.

Our gathering here in Medan, North Sumatra, has a symbolic meaning.

As we all know, recently, the good people of North Sumatera experienced the wrath of mother earth. In the sunny morning of December 26 last year, a major earthquake and a succession of giant killer waves combined to produce a force of destruction on a scale never seen in living memory.

Communities that lived on the shores of Aceh and North Sumatra were wiped out, their homes washed away, flattened to the ground. In a matter of minutes, hundreds of thousands of people lost their lives, tens of thousand remain missing, over 550,000 have become homeless, and tens of thousands of children have become orphaned.

No doubt, all of you have seen footage of the tsunami on your television, but I assure you that what you see on the video is only a small sample of the widespread, untold horror that occurred on that fateful day of December 26.

It will require momentous efforts for them to rebuild their lives and achieve collective emotional healing.

The people of Aceh and North Sumatra never saw a tsunami before, but they also never saw the kind of response that the world showed them.

On December 28, from Banda Aceh, the provincial capital which suffered great destruction, I called on the world to show global solidarity for the tsunami victims, but even then I did not expect the international response that transpired.

Governments around the world contributed billions for tsunami victims around the Indian Ocean. Many sent their troops to Aceh to work with the Indonesian military to conduct emergency relief operations. Meanwhile, millions of citizens all over the world performed their own acts of solidarity. School children sent their saving for the tsunami victims. And so did housewives, workers, NGOs, companies big and small.

My good friend President Xanana Gusmao recently handed over through me voluntary donations from citizens of Timor Leste for Aceh obtained from house to house. And former President Clinton told me a few days ago when we met in Medan that one-third of the American households contributed to the tsunami victims.

Clearly, the tsunami experience has brought all of us, Governments and peoples of the world, closer together in ways that have never been seen before.

I would even go so far as saying that this global solidarity in response to the tsunami is a new trend in international relations. And it is something that we must continue to nurture.

I believe it is that spirit of togetherness that brings us together here today.

We are all gathered as part of a great journey for humanity, which was enshrined in the Millennium Declaration of 2000.

Our global challenges are enormous.

Consider the statistics.

It is estimated that 1 out of 5 persons living on this planet still live on less than US$ 1 per day.

About 800 million people in the developing world are suffering from malnutrition.

Some 10 million per year children have died of preventable diseases, which is about 30,000 children per day.

About 115 million school-aged children are not getting their education.

And 1 out of 5 people worldwide do not have access to clean water.

Against this backdrop, our quest for sustainable development becomes critical for the wellbeing, indeed survival, of humanity and also of mother earth.

We have all signed on to meet the targets of the Millennium Development Goals by 2015 or earlier, and we must keep our momentum to reach that goal.

I am particularly glad to see that this conference is focused on how regional governments and local authorities can help promote sustainable development.

Since 1999, we in Indonesia have embarked on a very ambitious decentralization program, because we know that our country cannot grow unless the provinces and the districts (kabupaten) also grow. Decentralization is part of our democratization and reformasi.

By decentralizing, we want to empower local Governments to take ownership of their own development paths. But we have to make sure that decentralization is about spreading out good governance and does not lead to decentralizing corruption.

We envision a dynamic Indonesia dotted from east to west and north to south by numerous growth centers – each having dynamism of its own, each running on its own steam.

Each of you will bring your own unique experience in local governance to this forum. But as you chart your future course, allow me to bring to your attention several challenges which you might want to address.

I think one key challenge is making people in the regions, in the provinces understand globalization. We have all heard the cliché "think globally, act locally". The problem is that few of us, if any, understand how globalization works. And for those who slightly understand it, even fewer would understand what to do about it, and how to make globalization work for us.

I have found this to be true for many of the provinces in Indonesia.

Just yesterday I was in the city of Tarakan in East Borneo, a city rich with oil deposits, and there I heard the local Government planning to be the next "little Singapore". A few weeks ago I was in the province of Riau where the Governor and local Parliament spoke about "going international".

And nearly every province I visited asked how they can attract foreign direct investment.

In each of these cases, you have local governments and local people who want to make globalization work for them, who want to reap its benefits, but are struggling with the means and methods to achieve it. We all are.

This conference is a great way to help them understand better.

Another challenge is helping the regional governments and local authorities figure out how to connect with the global world, the world beyond the national border.

In a world of ASEAN Free Trade Agreement, in a world of production "hubs and spokes", connectivity can be a critical tool for regions to leap forward. But connectivity can be a confusing thing also.

I grew up in a world of one channel television. Yes, one channel. If I did not like what was on television, I had no option but to turn it off. But today I live in a world where my television has over 100 channels. It's exciting, but it's also confusing.

Our world today is as complex and confusing as my 100 channels cable TV.

While we must be connected, we must also be careful what we are connected to. In a complex global world, we cannot be connected to everything. Connectivity requires selectivity and specialization. Each of us must decide what is important for us and what kind of connectivity is required for it.

I hope that the experience of taking part in this conference will sharpen your sense of how you want to define your connectivity.

A third challenge for the regions is how to develop our human capital.

When I was in school, my school teacher told me that we are blessed to live in a country where the soil is so fertile that all you have to do is drop a seed and moments later you will see it thrive and bloom.

Whether you administer a village of 100, a town of 100,000 or province of 10 million, and whether your area is endowed with rich minerals or zero natural resources, ultimately it is the human capital, the brain power, that will set your people free – free from ignorance, free from want.

It is therefore absolutely critical to invest in your people.

How do we invest in people? By total commitment to education, by promoting the health sector, by promoting an open society where creativity can thrive, by providing our people with the dignity of having jobs, by promoting equal opportunity and equality before the law.

Once you have this solid reservoir of human capital, your society will be assured of a more sustainable development.

A fourth challenge is how to recalibrate the definition of development.

Development of course means different things to different people. But development is more than just the absence of poverty or the protection of the environment.

We cannot have development if hatred thrives, if bigotry and prejudice rule, if ignorance prevails, if conflicts flare.

We now live in a world with rising ethnic and religious conflicts.

That is why we have to start defining development also as tolerance building. Which means we have to find ways to cherish diversity and to bolster tolerance and harmony. I am sure each of you have your own experience on how to promote tolerance.

All of these challenges have a common thread: governance. Governance—good governance—is the key to unlock the potentials of our society, of any society. In a way, "governance" is the ideology of the New Millennium.

The Sustainable Development Plan implementation recognizes that good governance within each country and at the international level is essential for sustainable development.

Sound environmental, social and economic policies, democratic institutions responsive to the need of the people, the rule of law, anti corruption measures, gender equality and enabling environment for investment and trade are the basis for sustainable development.

And that is why I take great pleasure in seeing all of you here today. You belong to a group with a name that is not so easy to the ear – NRG4SD – it sounds like a fancy computer model.

You have come a long way since the NRG4SD was formed during the Earth Summit (WSSD) in 2002 in Johannesburg, South Africa, as a follow-up to Agenda 21 during the Rio Summit of 1992.

And I know you will be totally relevant in the effort to achieve, by 2015, the targets set in the Millennium Development Goals.

I wish you all the best in your deliberations.

Thank you, and Horas !

Medan, North Sumatra, March 10, 2005

"I like Indonesia. The economy has good growth and companies have a positive earnings growth outlook"—Bruno Vanier, Edmond de Rothschild Asset Management, Paris.

(International Herald Tribune, 4 July 2005)

"There's a more businesslike attitude, of 'Let's get things done,'... Instead of going 30 kilometers per hour, you're going 90 now"—Cheong Kum Hong, Chief Investment Officer, Commerzbank Asset Management, Singapore.

(The New York Times, 17 February 2005)

"There are signs the new president of Indonesia is winning his war on corruption. Few signs provoke more trepidation than the three-meter monster that greets you when you enter Jakarta's drive's licensing maze. It is a flow chart that describes the 10-step process to get your license, known to Indonesians as a SIM. For the locals, and anyone who lived here, it is guaranteed to instill fear: 10 steps in any bureaucratic process mean either 10 long queues or 10 bribes...But now, suddenly, everything has changed...At the licensing centre at least, the message seems to be getting through. Although it's fast too early to claim success, other anecdotal evidence is emerging that the new leader's anti-corruption drive is beginning to work."—Matthew Moore

(The Age, Melbourne, 19 February 2005)

"Never, ever stop dreaming. Never stop imagining. Never stop thinking. Never stop wondering. Never stop being curious. Never stop asking questions. Never stop trying to search for answers.

This is the only way by which you will know more, and understand better, not just about science, but about life in general, and also about your own self."

President Susilo Bambang Yudhoyono
Jakarta, December 6, 2004

"Our nationalism is not an angry or arrogant one. We do not subscribe to narrow nationalism, ultra nationalism, or self-absorbed nationalism. We do not overestimate ourselves, and nor do we underestimate others. We treat big, medium and small-sized powers with equal respect.

Our ability to maintain this right kind of nationalism is important to our neighbors, to our region, and is a source of our authority and respect at the international arena."

President Susilo Bambang Yudhoyono
Jakarta, May 19, 2005

13

"Things to Remember as You Grow Up"

Remarks to Visiting
Jakarta International High School Students

Istana Negara, Jakarta
March 15, 2005

♦ ♦ ♦ ♦ ♦

Hello everybody.

I am very happy to welcome all of you to Istana Negara. It is a modest building but I assure you that the walls of this palace bear witness to a great number of historical events. I hope as you tour this premise later, you will get the chance to feel history. Which I do--everyday.

I am given to understand that you are at the 12th grade, which is a critical stage just before you enter university. It will be a big line to cross in your life, both in your life style and in your academic development.

So I hope you do not mind if I give certain advise that for my part have been useful to know.

At least, you can leave this palace with something to think about.

I have three advise for you.

The first thing is that you should always remember that you all are worth the same to begin with. Look at the person to your left. Look at the person to your right. Now, look at the person in front of you and behind you. You know what is the difference between you and them ?

Nothing.

You are all born with equal dignity as a human being. It is up to you what you to do with it.

You can use that dignity to make you a better person, to become a good friend, an honest person, someone who contributes to the well-being of others in society. Or you can neglect and abuse that dignity to become a corrupt person, a person who harms himself and harms others in society. It's up to you what you do with your own dignity. It's your choice. A poor person who loves his family and who earns an honest living has much more dignity than a rich person who abuses his family and earns a dishonest living. So use your dignity, your most precious asset, well.

The second thing I want you to remember is that you all have the same capacity to learn and grow. I read somewhere that if your brain remembers 10 information every second, 24 hours a day, every year for 100 years, you will only have used 10 % of your total brain capacity. Can you imagine that ?

Your capacity to learn, to grow is boundless. God is so great and generous with us humans. Yes, some of you may learn quicker than others, some may have greater IQ than others, but you all have the same capacity to learn and grow. Again, it is up to you what you do with your own brain capacity. You can ignore it and not learn anything so that what you know now will be no different than what you know 20 years from now. Or you can use your brain power to grow as a person, to study hard, to understand things better, to master new skills, to learn new language, to become an expert in something. The choise is yours.

That's why I have a favourite saying which I wish to quote for you: "20 years from now, it will not matter how well you danced, how your hair looked and what kind of brand names you wear on your body. What will matter is what kind of knowledge you manage to gain and how you applied them in your life." Looking back in my life, I feel that this is so true, and I am sure you will find it to be true also.

The last thing I want to tell you is simply this: stay focused in your life. You probably have heard this before from your parents or teachers, but that does not make it less true or less relevant.

You know, I grew up in a very different world from you. My world was very simple. Life was simple for me back then. I had no computer, no internet, no handphone, and my television had only 1 channel. The world was also easier to understand, and it moved with a speed that I could follow easily.

The world now, to me at least, is so fast, so confusing, so difficult to understand. The political, economic, social and technological environment has become so complex and so difficult to understand. I hardly know the latest fad and I hardly know if I am up to speed with events.

My answer to this is not necessarily to run as fast as the world is spinning. On the contrary, the antidote to that fast world resides in our ability maintain simplicity, and to maintain focus in what you want in life and how you want to achieve it. You can imagine yourself in a gigantic supermarket that has in stock every single product known to man : it may be exciting, but if you do not know what you want, you will simply be lost and overwhelmed. Being focused, and for me, keeping my simplicity, is the best prescription in this fast, confusing world. Simply put, it is an ability to say and tell yourself : know what you want, plan what you want and do what you want.

This is how I find my sense of purpose and direction, and this is how I find my stability, my peace with myself and with the world. This is how I find my balance.

So these are my food for thought I have for you today, for whatever its worth. As you travel farther in life, and you move on to your new adventures in life, and as you grow as a person, I am sure you will encounter things that will remind you of what I said to you this morning.

Have a great tour of the palace, and please send my best regards to your parents at home.

Thank you.

Jakarta, March 15, 2005

"*This is the first Indonesian government with a pro-business agenda*"—James Castle, Castle Group; Governor, American Chamber of Commerce in Indonesia.

(Singapore Business Review, May, 2005)

"*...not only have the Indonesians been expecting a series of domestic changes to be carried out by the new leader, but ASEAN neighbors are also closely watching Indonesia's ongoing transformation, which will undoubtedly affect the shape of intra-ASEAN relationship and beyond. Indonesia was active in international politics, particularly among developing and newly founded nations, through the Non-Aligned Movement during the Cold War and once recognized as the leader of ASEAN before the fall of President Suharto in 1998. Yudhoyono's self-portrayal as a sophisticated leader signals his eligibility to claim the status of ASEAN leader and bring back the country's glory days as a key regional player.*"—Pavin Chachavalpongpun.

(The Nation, Bangkok, 26 February 2005).

"Remember what Spiderman said in that movie : With great power, comes great responsibility."

President Susilo Bambang Yudhoyono
Jakarta, December 6, 2004

"The power of collaboration is the power to create, the power to build, the power to change."

President Susilo Bambang Yudhoyono
Jakarta, January 17, 2005

14

"It is not enough for Indonesia and Australia just to be neighbors"

Remarks at a State Dinner tendered by Governor General of Australia

Canberra, Australia
April 3, 2005

♦ ♦ ♦ ♦ ♦

His Excellency Governor General of Australia, Major General (Ret)
Michael Jeffrey,
His Excellency The Honorable John Howard, Prime Minister
Excellencies,
Distinguished Guests,
Ladies and Gentlemen,

On behalf of my delegation, allow me to express how honored and
happy we are to be here tonight with all of you. Your kindness,
your hospitality, your sincere welcome warms our hearts.

We come here on this day with broken hearts. Broken, the moment
we heard the news that an Australian Sea King helicopter crashed
in Nias yesterday while conducting humanitarian operations to help
earthquake victims. We are informed that of the 11 on board,
2 survived with injuries but the rest, 9 of them, did not make
it. I cannot find the words to express our sadness and profound
condolences for this horrible tragedy. My Government decided

last night that we would give the 11 Australian medals of honor--
the Satya Lencana Kebaktian Sosial--for their outstanding service
and ultimate sacrifice. And while this dinner is held to honor my
delegation, I would prefer that our dinner tonight is also to honor
the 11 Australians, particularly the 9 who gave their lives for the
good of humanity, which is a cause larger than life.

Ladies and gentlemen,

It took us 8 hours to fly from Jakarta to Canberra. But actually,
this is a journey many years in the making. This visit is certainly
long overdue.

In the history of our bilateral relations, only 2 Indonesian Presidents
had visited Australia : President Suharto went to Townsville in 1975,
and President Abdurrachman Wahid came to Canberra in 2001. The
time lag between their visits was too long.

That is why when I was sworn-in as Indonesia's sixth President in
October last year, I immediately decided that Australia would have
to be one of the FIRST countries that I would visit after my first 100
days in office. I wanted to make it very clear that having good,
stable relations with Australia is a priority for my Government.

I am therefore pleased to be the third Indonesian President to
visit Australia, and I hope to have more visits to Australia in the
future.

I think this visit will be regarded as historic, not because it is
long overdue, but because of what we intend to achieve out of

it. Tomorrow, after our talks, Prime Minister John Howard and I will declare the Comprehensive Partnership between Indonesia and Australia, effectively setting forth a new era of bilateral relations between Indonesia and Australia.

It will be a fitting tribute to how close we have become as neighbors recently. The outstanding way by which Australia offered its helping hand to Indonesia during the tsunami tragedy and during the Nias earthquake will be remembered as one of the finest moments in our relations. I will have more to say publicly on that tomorrow during the luncheon at the Great Hall of Parliament House.

My delegation will be in Australia for 4 days altogether, including an overnight stop on my way back from New Zealand. We will visit Canberra, Sidney and Darwin. I look forward to my discussions with Prime Minister John Howard tomorrow. I also hope to meet as many Australians as possible during my stay here.

When I depart Australia a few days from now, I expect to carry more than just fond memories about your beautiful country and the good friends that I meet here. My hope is that after this visit, there will be no more any lingering doubt as to the tremendous importance of Australia to Indonesia, of Indonesia's desire to strengthen our relations with Australia, and of the deepening bonds of friendship and cooperation between our Governments and peoples.

As I have said over and over to my Ministers : it is not enough Indonesia and Australia just to be neighbors. It is imperative for us to be strong partners.

On that note, let it be known that I have every confidence that my visit here will make Indonesia and Australia become strong partners.

Thank you.

Canberra, Australia, April 3, 2005

"Indonesia in 2005 should not be seen as a nation in crisis...The crisis has passed...And seven years into Indonesia's new democracy, Indonesians have surprised the naysayers and the analysts, and perhaps even themselves, and emerged as an increasingly self-confident, democratic nation...A culture of democracy has not only taken root in Indonesia, but begun to flourish, in ways often not seen in supposedly "mature" democracies...Despite the massive loss of life and destruction in Aceh, the Yudhoyono administration also demonstrated that it continues its overall Indonesia-wide development and reform agenda. In other words, I believe the government deserves accolades for not focusing solely on Aceh, at the expense of other pressing reform issues, particularly related to the economy. President Yudhoyono resisted some suggestions from the international community to postpone his much-promoted "infrastructure summit" and the annual Consultative Group on Indonesia (CGI) meeting, of which Indonesia was, for the first time, the Host this year. The overall effect: demonstration that this government is competent and professional at managing multiple issues and agendas."— Dr. Douglas E. Ramage, the Asia Foundation.

(Testimony at U.S. House of Representatives Committee on International Relation's Subcommittee on Asia and the Pacific's hearing on "Indonesia in Transition: Recent Developments and Implications for U.S. Policy", 10 March 2005, Washington D.C.)

"*Some of us can talk proudly of successful elections, or of great military victories, or about phenomenal rises in GDP, or about export growth, or about expanding and integrating markets, or about outstanding human development index. Still, these things do not erase an uneasy feeling which many of us feel about the present and future state of international and national security.*"

President Susilo Bambang Yudhoyono
Santiago-Chile, November 20, 2004

"When I was a young officer in the Indonesian army, I remember well reading with great admiration about Vietnam's ferocious struggle and military accomplishments. Vietnam is proof to the dictum that the best asset a nation can have is her spirit, her fighting spirit. We are now watching that fighting spirit of Vietnam being transformed and being used for a completely different undertaking: economic development."

President Susilo Bambang Yudhoyono
Hanoi-Vietnam, May 29, 2005

"I grew up in a world of one channel television. Yes, one channel. If I did not like what was on television, I had no option but to turn it off. But today I live in a world where my television has over 100 channels. It's exciting, but it's also confusing.
Our world today is as complex and confusing as my 100 channels cable TV."

President Susilo Bambang Yudhoyono
Medan, March 10, 2005

15

"A Comprehensive Partnership for Australia and Indonesia"

Speech at The Great Hall-Parliament House, Canberra

Canberra, Australia
April 4, 2005

♦ ♦ ♦ ♦ ♦

Thank you, The Honourable John Howard, Prime Minister.
Thank you, The Honourable Kim Beazley, Leader of the Opposition.

Thank you all for your warm welcome.

I am happy to be here, but I come with a heavy heart. I am utterly devastated by the helicopter crash in Nias which killed 9 and injured 2 of Australia's finest. Please accept, on behalf of the people and the Government of Indonesia, our deep condolences and profound sadness for this awful tragedy.

They died in glory : the glory of the ultimate sacrifice, the glory of a selfless act to help those who are suffering. There is no greater honor than that. And for that, the Indonesian Government will bestow upon the 11 Australians medals of honour—the Satya Lencana Kebaktian Sosial for their outstanding service and sacrifice.

It is a great honor for me to be here with all of you today. I am humbled by the presence of hundreds of distinguished Australian friends who fill this room. I do not know what you have been told, but Russel Crowe is NOT coming to this lunch.

My name is Susilo Bambang Yudhoyono.

I am the only child of parents who lived in a small village in Pacitan, East Java. After graduating from high school, I happily followed my father's footsteps into a military career. And for some reason, history intervened with my life and made me the sixth President of Indonesia.

History also made me the first Indonesian President to visit Australia since 2001. I have a long way to go to catch up with my good friend Prime Minister John Howard, who has visited Indonesia 11 times. And by the way, according to our top secret intelligence report, today is a big day for Prime Minister Howard. Today is the 37th Wedding Anniversary of John and Jannette Howard, so my wife and I would like to wish them a happy anniversary.

I come here today to bring you the warm greetings and message of friendship from the good people of Indonesia to the good people of Australia.

I also bring Indonesia's message of heartfelt thanks and gratitude, especially from the people of Aceh and North Sumatra, for the generous contribution and acts of compassion and solidarity shown by the people and Government of Australia immediately after the tsunami.

I salute the soldiers of the Australian Defense Forces and the Australian relief workers, who worked tirelessly side by side with the Indonesian military, during the emergency relief operations.

Every Australian in this room, and in the living rooms across Australia, who saw our hardship, felt our pain and acted upon it, has every reason to be proud for what you and your country have done for the tsunami victims.

It is humanity and solidarity at its best. Today, the people of Aceh and North Sumatra are starting to pick up the pieces of their shattered lives.

Many of the dead have been buried. The survivors and the sick are being looked after. Children are starting to go to school. People are again flocking to mosques for prayers. Families are being reunited. And the provincial Government is coming back to life.

It is true what they say : the greatest rage of nature is no match for the unbreakable will of the human spirit. The spirit to survive. The spirit to live, to love, to give, to overcome.

And let it be remembered that when we in Indonesia were down and out, and when we needed help most, you came and you stood by us.

It will require massive efforts for the Acehnese to get back on their feet. Ultimately, what will save the Acehnese is not just what was done in the first week of the disaster, but more importantly, what is done to help them rebuild their lives in the years to come.

For this purpose, Prime Minister John Howard and I have established the Australia-Indonesia Partnership for Reconstruction and Development (AIPRD), which is a bilateral scheme to help the reconstruction of Aceh, North Sumatra and other disaster areas in Indonesia. Once again, thank you, Australia.

Our tsunami experience unveils one important point : that the relations between Indonesia and Australia are getting stronger, closer, better.

And that is the very purpose of my visit to your great country : to affirm our special relations, and to make it even stronger.
Indonesia and Australia have been part of each other's history for ages.

In particular, Indonesians will not forget Australia's firm support for our struggle for independence in the late 1940's.

And over the years, our relations have experienced many twists and turns, highs and lows. We know from experience that our relations are so complex and unique that it can be pulled in so many different directions, and it can go right as often as it can go wrong. Which is why we have to handle it with the greatest care and counsel.

You will all notice that recently, we have begun to relate to each other differently.

We both suffered immensely from the devastating terrorist attacks in Bali on October 12th , 2002.

Two years later, on September 9ᵗʰ 2004, we were shocked, again, by a huge blast outside the gate of the Australian Embassy in Jakarta. A few months ago, the tsunami drew our Governments and peoples ever closer together.

And I am particularly honored that Prime Minister Howard graciously attended our Presidential inauguration on October 20 last year, the first Australian Prime Minister to do so in history.

And just 2 days ago, 9 Australians died and two injured in the line of duty after their Sea King helicopter crashed while trying to help earthquake victims in Nias.

So against this backdrop, this morning, Prime Minister Howard and I discussed the same question that was asked by all our predecessors.

That question is : where do we want to take this relationship ? What do we want to do with it ? And what kind of relationship do we want it to be ?

Same questions. But new answers.

I am convinced we can take this friendship between Indonesia and Australia far. Very far.

For we now live in geopolitical and geoeconomic environments that are different from the ones of the previous decades.

Indonesians looking south would now see the richest country in the southern hemisphere, one of the fastest growing economies in the OECD. A bastion of stability, progress, dynamism.

Indonesians looking south would also see a confident country down under which has reinvented herself successfully, with an open, tolerant society based on multi-culturalism.

Australians looking north would now see that along the equator spans the world's third largest democracy that is Indonesia—third, after India and the United States. In fact, Indonesia would be the world's second largest democracy, after India, if based on voting turn out.

Australians looking north would also see a country that is home to the world's largest muslim population—there are more muslims in Indonesia than in the entire Middle-East. It is also a wondrous place where Islam, democracy and modernity thrive together.

And Australians looking north would also see in Indonesia a bridge to East Asia.

You look at these facts and you just know that the relationship between Indonesia and Australia can be anything BUT ordinary. It is not enough for us to be just neighbors. We have to be strong partners.

Today, Prime Minister John Howard and I reviewed our relations and agreed to commit Indonesia and Australia to a Comprehensive Partnership.

By doing so, we are heralding a new era of Indonesia - Australia bilateral relations.

The Comprehensive Partnership is a logical consequence to a relationship that over the years has become so complex, so full of challenges, so full of promises.

The Comprehensive Partnership assumes that the security, prosperity, and stability of Indonesia and Australia are inter-connected.

It assumes that our countries are locked together not just by geography but by a common future, one that can be best harnessed if only we can closely work together for the long-term.

The Comprehensive Partnership will provide the broad framework for all our bilateral cooperation schemes and serve as the primary guide in directing the future of Indonesia-Australia relations that will cover arrangements in the fields of politics and security, economics, as well as socio-cultural affairs.

Through the Comprehensive Partnership, Australia and Indonesia are embarking upon a path that emphasises the importance of our commonalities rather than our differences, one that reflects the richness of our friendship. And this strong partnership between Indonesia and Australia is not only beneficial for ourselves, but can contribute to resolving regional and global issues.

The Comprehensive Partnership is a landmark development in the history of our relations, and the worst thing we can do to it is to take it for granted. In my view, we can help to bolster this Partnership in a number of ways.

First, it would have to build on the existing extensive cooperation and make them more coherent. Indonesia and Australia have teamed up on many great ventures in recent years. We worked together successfully to convene a series of regional conferences on key issues, on counter-terrorism, on people trafficking, on money laundering, and on inter-faith dialogue. These important initiatives are moving forward with practical measures and we should continue to support them.

Secondly, the Partnership would have to be substantiated by closer ties between our officials of all levels. Our leaders, our cabinet members, our politicians, our parliamentarians, our informal leaders -- they can all make this relationship come to life by reaching out to one another. I am glad that the Seventh Australia Indonesia Ministerial Forum in Canberra convened successfully.

Thirdly, the Partnership can only go far if it is substantiated with people-to-people links from all walks of life. Remember : it's all about the people. The Partnership would have to be both top down and bottom up. It would have to have direct relevance to the lives of our people, and it would have to bring our peoples closer, be they students, artists, journalists, tourists, scholars, workers. I am glad to see that thousands of Australians visit Indonesia to study, to work, to invest, and to have fun. Similarly, I am pleased to see some 25,000 Indonesians study in Australia. In fact, two of my Ministers are graduates of the Australian National University. And my younger son, Baskoro, also graduated from Curtin University in Perth a few weeks ago.

I am particularly delighted that Prime Minister Howard announced today that the Australian Government will provide some 600 scholarships to Indonesian students.

What a great investment in our peoples and in our common future. Once again, thank you, Prime Minister.

Fourthly, there are different ways to measure the results of our Comprehensive Partnership. We can look at the trade statistics, at the investment figures, at the tourism numbers. These are all important.

But I think the best way to measure the Partnership is in terms of how much trust and confidence develop out of it, how much goodwill it generates, how much we come to understand one another, and how much closer we become.

Ultimately, this is what we need to nurture for the long term.

Finally, the Comprehensive Partnership requires us to recalibrate our relationship. Yes, the tsunami tragedy has made us closer, but ultimately it is NOT agony that drives our Partnership, but the mutual optimism, the firm belief in our shared interests and our common future.

It will be a great learning process for both of us. We will need to learn from each other, to learn from the past, to draw from each other's strength. And we will need to constructively manage the complex set of issues—some easy, some difficult in our bilateral relations.

In this process of recalibration, I want you to see the Indonesia that I see every day. And I assure you that it is NOT the picture of Indonesia that sometimes--sometimes--are trivialized and treated as caricature in the media.

I hope you see beyond such snapshots and see a nation that, given our seemingly endless natural disasters, has been down on luck lately, but remains high in spirit and strong in will.

I hope you see a resilient people that continues to beat the odds, a nation that continues to bounce back even stronger no matter how hard and how many times we are hit.

I hope you see a vibrant democracy that continues to mature, a promising economy that continues to grow, a dynamic people that is eager to fulfill its potentials.

I hope you see why I am confident that Indonesia will SOON become a vast oasis of peace, progress and stability.

And with all this, I hope you see the enormous possibilities and opportunities that await Indonesia and Australia.

Just imagine the creative energy that can be unleashed by the connection between our two resourceful peoples.

Just imagine the vast area of democratic peace and cooperation that will be created between the largest archipelago on the equator and the great continent down under.

And just imagine the world of good that can be brought about between Indonesia and Australia as two fellow democracies.

I leave you with that thought, and I thank you.

Canberra, Australia, April 4, 2005

"As the world largest Islamic nation, Indonesia has a duty to contribute to the progressive development of global Muslim society. As a developing country with a long history of finding solutions to gargantuan economic challenges, Indonesia can contribute to the daunting challenge of eradicating poverty"— Michael Vatikiotis.

(International Herald Tribune, 14 April 2005)

"As the first Indonesian president to be elected through direct universal suffrage, and backed by a mandate from a considerable majority of Indonesian voters, President Susilo Bambang Yudhoyono is injecting new energy into the 10-member Association for Southeast Asian Nations. Furthermore, by demonstrating that democracy can take root in a moderate Muslim country, Yudhoyono has proven Western skeptics wrong and given a welcome boost to ASEAN's reputation as a region of stability, development and progress."—Eric Teo Chu Cheow

(The Japan Times, 27 November 2004. Reprinted by the Korea Herald, 30 November 2004).

"While you go out to take the risk in explorations, the Government can offer you a more open, relaxed and attractive policies that is much friendlier to investors."

President Susilo Bambang Yudhoyono
Jakarta, December 12, 2004

"I do not think there are too many countries out there that have gone through so much trials and tribulations, and have bounced back even stronger each time."

President Susilo Bambang Yudhoyono
Jakarta, January 24, 2005

16

"Indonesia's Business Opportunity"

Opening Remarks at a Breakfast Meeting with Australasia and The Australia Indonesia Business Council

Sydney, Australia
April 5, 2005

♦ ♦ ♦ ♦ ♦

Ladies and Gentlemen,

Let me begin by thanking The Asia Society Australasia Center and the Australia Indonesia Business Council for inviting me to speak here today.

I am pleased to meet all of you here in Sydney. I fondly remember visiting your beautiful city back in 2003 as Co-ordinating Minister for Politics and Security. Back then, I had a feeling that I would return to this city, though I certainly did not imagine that I would come as Indonesia's President.

The nice thing about being President, of course, is that when you are invited to give an address, no matter what topic they assign you, they usually let you speak about anything you want.

So today, I wish to speak to you about two subjects. First, the question of how Indonesia is doing, especially since the new political landscape that was created after the historic Parliamentary and Presidential elections last year.

The second subject is my favorite, that is, on the improved state of Indonesia - Australia relations, and how it can translate into greater business opportunities for you.

Let me start with the first subject : how is Indonesia doing ? Are things changing ? Are things changing for the better ?

The simple answer to that is "yes". Let me offer 3 points to support the proposition that Indonesia is moving forward steadily, but surely.

First, our political development and democratic transition is robust.

If you have not been to Indonesia lately, you will hardly recognize the political landscape.

Democracy is alive and kicking. Civil society is thriving, and so is freedom of speech and of the press. Political participation is strong. The Parliament is very active and independent. The relationship and responsibilities between the Presidency and the Legislature is much clearer than before. And for the first time, an Indonesian President is directly elected by the electorate. We are also seeing the return of political stability and certainty as the present political arrangement is expected to hold-up until the next elections in 2009.

And there is definitely a new "energy" since the historic elections of 2004. The great yearning for change, so predominant during the elections, now takes the form of huge expectations for my administration. These expectations drive me and my Government to do our best, but I must admit that these expectations at the beginning were too high. After my first 100 days, I think the people are developing more realistic expectations.

Secondly, our economy is steady, stable, growing and full of opportunities.

In 2004, Indonesia was able to maintain macroeconomic stability with inflation at 6.4 percent and growth at 5.1 percent.

This year, we expect growth to pick up to 5.5 percent, and with the right policies, we are convinced we will achieve our target for an average growth rate of 6.6 percent in the next five years. Per capita income is now higher than prior to the crisis at over $1000/ capita.

We are also managing our fiscal situation with debt levels coming down and the deficit under control. My decision on March 1, to raise the price 29% certain oil products was politically difficult but economically necessary for our long-term growth. With the fiscal situation vastly improved, Indonesia now has one of the smallest deficits in Asia, with budget deficit outcomes being below forecast in recent years. Debt levels have gone down rapidly and are expected to continue to do so.

The debt to GDP ratio has been successfully reduced from 99% in 2000 to 53% in 2004. It is predicted that by the end of 2005 the debt to GDP in 2004 will decline to 48%. This is considered very good even by OECD standard.

By the end of 2004, the sign of investment recovery are evident with the import of capital goods increasing by 44 percent, investment rising by 11 percent, and for the first time since the crisis, we are seeing net capital inflows.

I happily note that confidence in Indonesia is growing, with upgrades being undertaken by various Rating Agencies, booming stock market, increases in the pledge by donors at the recent CGI (Consultative Group on Indonesia) meeting in January. For example :
◆ Moody's upgraded Indonesia two-notch in 2003 to B2, once in June and other in September.
◆ S&P upgraded Indonesia three-notches in 2003 and 2004 to B+ (in May 2003, October 2003 and December 2004)
◆ And Fitch upgraded long term local and foreign currency sovereign rating from B+ to BB- with positive outlook (January 2005)

So the signposts are good, and I have every confidence that we will stay on track towards growth.

Thirdly, we are holding up well despite being the Government with arguably the worst luck for getting one bad break after another. The hardest part of my Presidency is dealing with the unknowns, and there have been too many of them. The earthquake in Nabire, the earthquake in Alor, the massive tsunami in Aceh and North Sumatra, the flood in South Sumatra, the earthquake in Nias.

I think there is a quality of resilience and endurance about Indonesia that is simply remarkable. And each tragedy seems to make us even stronger as a nation.

I suppose the bottom line is that Indonesia is transforming rapidly— not just changing, but transforming.

And as Indonesia is fast transforming, Indonesia - Australia relations are also undergoing transformation.

This is the third day of my visit in Australia, and everything I have seen so far convinced me even more that Indonesia and Australia are headed for stronger, closer, better relations.

Yesterday, Prime Minister Howard and I announced a Comprehensive Partnership that promises a new era of bilateral relations between Indonesia and Australia. This Partnership promises to strengthen what is already one of Indonesia's most elaborate relations with any country.

This Comprehensive Partnership affects you, the business community, because ultimately what fuels this partnership is the people. The more people interact, the more students exchange, the more businessmen connect, the stronger the partnership.

I believe that we are ready to embark on a broader, deeper and mutually advantageous relationship based on not just G-G relations, but most importantly B-B (business-to-business).

After all, this has proved to be the more resilient part of our links. Our bilateral relations may have its ups and downs, but the economic and business relations between our two countries generally have not been affected by them.

Just look at our trade.

Trade between our two countries have continued grow, with two way trade reaching A$ 8.49 billion. Indonesia is Australia's 10th largest markets, with Australian exports rising to A$ 4.23 billion, while Indonesian exports to Australia reached A$ 4.26 billion.

Meanwhile, approved Australian investment in Indonesia reached $ 3.9 billion making it the 7th largest investor. A number of Australian companies have significant investments and a long history of involvement in the Indonesian mining and energy sector. Australian businesses have also entered into the agro-based sectors and the financial, health and education sectors.

But please excuse me for saying this, for I think our business links can do better. Much better.

There are plenty of new investment opportunities that have not been fully harnessed. For example, the Joint Working Group on Agriculture and Food industry recently identified the following opportunities in Indonesian food and agriculture industries for Australian businesses : growth potential for cheese production, good prospects for business alliances in the high growth beverage sector, downstream processing of beef, bakery and cereal production, and new and novel food ingredients.

There are also opportunities in infrastructure development, which is a top priority for my Government's economic program. In January this year, we held a major infrastructure summit in Jakarta, after which 91 projects worth $22.4 billion, out of the total of $156 billion, will be tendered in 2005.

20 projects have been announced in Tranche I in March, and the remainder in June. These include toll roads, electricity, gas, transportations and telecommunication projects. The government has a plan of mutually beneficial public-private sector partnership in infrastructure investment for the commercially viable sectors. For those sectors that are not attractive for private investment, the government will use its own resources.

In persuading you to take part in Indonesia's infrastructure development opportunities, I am of course aware of the issues that are of concern to foreign investors. Bureaucratic bottlenecks, completing needed policy and regulatory reforms, and the risk management framework--yes, we are working hard on this.

The government is also working hard to improve the general investment climate and reduce the costs of doing business in Indonesia. Firstly, the government is currently reviewing the investment law to ensure national treatment and provide clear guidelines.

Second, we reviewing the approval, registration and licensing procedures with the objective of streamlining and providing transparency. We hope to achieve these improvements beginning this year.

Third, we are committed to addressing key issues already identified by the business sector as burdening the costs of doing business. The labor regulations related to retrenchment, outsourcing and contract labor, and wage setting are being reviewed with the objective of finding a better balance between the need to protect workers on the one hand, and overburdening employees and contributing to an inflexible labor market, on the other hand.

We are also undertaking a comprehensive review in order to reduce the number, cost and time to process exports and imports, and reducing the time and administration costs at the tax and customs departments.

On the issue of decentralization, we are reviewing the various overlapping regulations between the central government and local governments with the focus on improving legal certainty and efficiency.

Fourth, we know that the issue of legal certainty is of important concern for investors. We are doing a number of things to address this.

We are reviewing and amending laws and regulations, harmonizing rules and regulations, establishing new courts and improving the management of courts.

Finally, my government has and will continue to take a firm stance against corruption. We have enacted the necessary laws and regulations and we have also taken action in a growing number of corruption cases of government and non government officials.

There is also the acceleration of the action-oriented program to address illegal logging which has resulted in the seizure of tons of illegal logs and the arrests and prosecution of those allegedly involved.

So there you have it. A new President. A new Parliament. A new Indonesia. An exciting new bilateral relations between Indonesia and Australia. And a whole set of new business opportunities for you.

My only hope is that you take advantage of all this. And that is why I am here today : to PERSONALLY convince you that if you invest your money with us, you WILL grow with us, and your investment WILL be in good hands and good prospects.

I am convinced that Indonesia is well on its way to an exciting new era of growth, dynamism and progress for Indonesia.

Be part of it. Profit from it. Join us in investing in Indonesia's future.

I thank you, and I look forward to our discussions.

Sydney, Australia, April 5, 2005

"Indonesia gave a visionary leader a huge mandate last September. Now, they are hoping Yudhoyono's next 1,000 days in office will not only be less tumultuous than the tsunami-hit first 100 days but will see some of that vision translate into reality" —Assif Shameen

(Asia Inc, February 2005)

"My Government attaches great importance to two key areas that will dramatically improve and enlarge our pool of human capital: investment and education. History teaches us that if you develop these two areas—investment and education-- everything will fall into place, everything will grow."

President Susilo Bambang Yudhoyono
Tokyo, June 2, 2005

"Indonesia has never engaged in a military pact with a foreign country, and there will be no change in this policy. This also means that we will continue our policy of not allowing any foreign military bases on Indonesian territory. Indonesia does not have a country which we consider a threat or an enemy."

President Susilo Bambang Yudhoyono
Jakarta, May 19, 2005

17

"On Indonesia–New Zealand Relations"

Speech at the State Dinner hosted by
Prime Minister of New Zealand

Wellington, New Zealand
April 6, 2005

♦ ♦ ♦ ♦ ♦

The Right Honorable Helen Clark,
Prime Minister of New Zealand,
Mr. Gerry Brownlee MP, Deputy Leader of the Opposition,

Thank you Prime Minister Helen Clark, thank you Deputy Leader of the Opposition Mr. Gerry Brownlee, for your kind words.

Honored Guests,
Ladies and gentlemen,

My name is Susilo Bambang Yudhoyono.

Just in case you are wondering : yes, it's true, I am the man from Indonesia who brought you the sunshine today.

I have more sunshine to give you tomorrow, and also the day after. And if you are all nice to me, I will leave you with some extra sunshine even after I depart Wellington on Thursday.

My delegation and I are honored to meet all of you here in this beautiful Parliament building. We arrived in Wellington this morning, and I have been so touched by the warmth of your welcome shown to me, my wife and my delegation here.

When I think of New Zealand from now on, I will think of fresh air, beautiful landscapes and good food, but most of all, I will think of the gentle warmth and kind souls of the Kiwis here.

I am here today to fulfill the invitation by my good friend The Honorable Prime Minister Helen Clark to visit New Zealand—as I also invited her to visit Indonesia--and to honor my promise to her that I would visit New Zealand sooner rather than later.

I hope you will take it as a clear sign that my Government is eager to strengthen relations with New Zealand early on.

I have met Prime Minister Helen Clark three times before : in Santiago, Chile, during the APEC Summit last year, in Vientiane, Laos, at the ASEAN Summit, and in Jakarta at the Special ASEAN Leaders Meeting on the Tsunami on January 6 this year.

In each of these meetings, I have found a connection with Prime Minister Helen Clark which grew stronger at each meeting. We understand each other well and we both know what to do with this relationship : that is, to strengthen it.

I am especially glad that our fourth meeting is taking place in New Zealand.

I find it particularly significant that I am the first President to visit New Zealand since 2001, and the third President to do so in the history of Indonesia - New Zealand relations.

Today, Prime Minister Helen Clark and I held very productive meetings, as I expected. We discussed many topics and saw eye-to-eye on many issues. We agreed that our relations are good and stable, but we also agreed that it is still way below its potentials.

One of the key themes in our discussions is that we must do more to encourage people-to-people contacts between Indonesians and New Zealanders.

I say this because despite the good relations between our Governments, our peoples still do not know much about each other, they have not mutually engaged in a substantial way, and because of that, they do not understand one another as well as they should.

The relationship between our countries can come to life very substantially if we have more exchanges of parliamentarians, business actors, students, tourists, artists, journalists, experts.

But I think the tsunami experience has also had a deep impact on our relations. For the first time, the tsunami exposed New Zealanders to Indonesia's pain. And for the first time, New Zealanders related to Indonesia in an emotional way, and responded in solidarity. This is something new in our relations. And we need to build on this.

I would end my remark here, but I would be a bad President if I did not make an attempt to make a little sales pitch about my country.

On this, there is only one point that needs to be said: I believe in my heart and soul that Indonesia is on the verge of a great transformation—not just change, but transformation.

We have passed a huge test of history by conducting one of the most complex elections anywhere in the world, and did so in a peaceful and orderly way.

Those elections reaffirmed Indonesia's status as the world's third largest democracy, and second largest in term of voting turn-out. There are twice as many voters in Indonesia as there are sheep in the whole of New Zealand—my Ambassador reported to me that you have 60 million sheep. I hope you are not thinking of giving them the right to vote.

And as that democracy connects with governance, we will see Indonesia becoming not just the world's third largest democracy that we are today, but also becoming a vibrant democracy, a stable democracy, a peaceful democracy, a strong democracy.

But Indonesia will become much more than that. We are heading towards better, bigger things.

We will become a thriving, open, free, tolerant, multicultural society.

We will become a huge market of 220 million, connected to the AFTA, with rising purchasing power and greater productivity.

We will become a nation whereby democracy, Islam and modernity flourish together.

We will become a vast oasis of peace, growth and stability along the equator.

We will become an outward-looking nation that will be the anchor for peace and stability in the region, and a voice for peace and justice in world affairs.

And that Indonesia will be New Zealand's friend. That Indonesia will be New Zealand's partner. That Indonesia will stand and grow together with New Zealand in peace and prosperity.

That is why I believe Indonesia and New Zealand have a promising future together.

And that is why I am here today : to begin our path together with a clearer sense of purpose.

I thank you.

Wellington, New Zealand, April 6, 2005

> *"The political transitions in both Indonesia and the United States provide an opportunity to fine tune our bilateral relationship with a large moderate, and influential country that can be an anchor of stability in Southeast Asia and a symbol of compatibility of moderate Islam with democracy and modernization"* — J. Stapleton Roy, former US Ambassador to Singapore, China, and Indonesia.
>
> (Asia Program Special Report, no. 127, January 2005 (Woodrow Wilson International Centre for Scholars)

"Do not be shy to share your know-how and new and advanced technology with your local partners."

President Susilo Bambang Yudhoyono
Jakarta, December 12, 2004

PHOTO BY ABROR

"Connectivity is a source of diplomatic empowerment."
President Susilo Bambang Yudhoyono

Jakarta, May 19, 2005

18

"Marilah kita bersama menatap ke depan"

Pidato di Hadapan Parlemen Nasional Republik
Demokratik Timor Leste

Dili, Timor Leste
9 April 2005

◆ ◆ ◆ ◆ ◆

Bismillahirrahmanirrahim,
Yang terhormat Saudara Ketua, dan para anggota Parlemen
Nasional, Republik Demokratik Timor Leste,
Hadirin yang saya muliakan,
Salam sejahtera bagi kita semua,

Mengawali pidato ini, marilah kita bersama-sama memanjatkan puji dan syukur ke hadirat Tuhan Yang Maha Kuasa, karena hari ini kita dapat bertemu, dalam suasana penuh keakraban dan persaudaraan. Suasana pertemuan seperti ini, mudah-mudahan dapat terus kita pelihara dan kita kembangkan, di masa-masa yang akan datang. Suasana seperti itu, sangat penting artinya, untuk membina hubungan baik yang permanen, antara kita, sebagai dua bangsa yang merdeka dan berdaulat.

Hadirin yang saya muliakan,

Saya ingin menggunakan kesempatan yang membahagiakan ini, untuk menyampaikan ucapan terima kasih dan penghargaan yang setinggi-tingginya, kepada Ketua Parlemen Nasional Timor Leste, dan seluruh anggota Parlemen yang saya hormati. Ucapan terima kasih itu, saya sampaikan pula kepada Pemerintah dan rakyat Timor Leste, atas segala keramah-tamahan dan sambutan yang hangat kepada saya, dan seluruh anggota delegasi Indonesia, sejak kedatangan kami ke Dili, tengah hari kemarin. Segala keramah-tamahan dan kehangatan itu, telah menghapus rasa lelah kami, setelah beberapa hari melakukan kunjungan kenegaraan ke Australia dan Selandia Baru.

Ucapan terima kasih dan penghargaan yang setinggi-tingginya, saya sampaikan pula atas segala perhatian dan bantuan, yang telah diberikan oleh Pemerintah dan rakyat Timor Leste, ketika kami sedang berjuang keras mengatasi keadaan, akibat terjadinya gempa dan gelombang tsunami di Aceh dan Sumatera Utara. Presiden Xanana Gusmao sendiri telah datang ke negeri kami, untuk menyampaikan rasa duka dari saudara-saudara kami di Timor Leste, serta memberikan bantuan melalui Operasi Cinta Kasih yang telah dilakukan. Kehadiran beliau, pada saat kami sedang berduka, benar-benar menunjukkan rasa persahabatan dan persaudaraan yang tulus. Sahabat yang baik, adalah sahabat yang datang di kala kita senang dan gembira. Sahabat sejati adalah sahabat yang datang, di kala kita sedih dan berduka.

Saudara Ketua,
Para anggota Parlemen Nasional,
Hadirin yang saya muliakan,

Pertemuan kita di Dili hari ini, berlangsung masih dalam suasana duka, atas wafatnya Sri Paus Johannes Paulus II. Kami bersama-sama dengan seluruh umat Katolik Timor Leste, ikut berduka di hari berkabung nasional yang baru saja berakhir kemarin. Bagi kami bangsa Indonesia, Sri Paus adalah tokoh dunia yang sangat kami hormati. Beliau telah memberikan keteladanan dalam memimpin dan menghargai dunia yang penuh kemajemukan. Sepanjang pengabdiannya, beliau tidak pernah berhenti menganjurkan dialog dan kerjasama antarumat beragama. Cita-cita beliau untuk membangun tata dunia yang damai dan harmonis, di mana komunitas umat beragama hidup berdampingan secara damai dan saling menghargai, adalah sejalan dengan prinsip-prinsip, yang dianut dalam falsafah bernegara bangsa kami. Kami percaya, cita-cita Sri Paus yang mulia itu, akan dilanjutkan oleh pengganti beliau.

Hadirin yang saya muliakan,

Kunjungan saya ke Timur Leste, merupakan kunjungan kenegaraan yang pertama kali saya lakukan. Sejak saya dilantik menjadi Presiden Republik Indonesia yang ke-enam, pada tanggal 20 Oktober 2004 yang lalu, saya telah memprioritaskan kunjungan kenegaraan ke negeri ini. Di hati bangsa kami, bangsa Timor Leste adalah saudara yang sangat dekat. Kita adalah dua bangsa dan dua negara yang bertetangga dan berbatasan.

Kami ingin sekali melihat bangsa Timor Leste memperoleh kemajuan dan kejayaan, sejak berdirinya negara ini, beberapa tahun yang lalu. Kami telah betekad untuk membangun kerjasama dan saling membantu, agar kedua bangsa dapat bangkit bersama, menatap hari depan yang gemilang. Saya sependapat dengan pandangan Perdana Manteri Mari Alkatiri, bahwa hubungan kedua negara akan dibina atas dasar pandangan ke depan, bukan pandangan yang menoleh ke belakang. Pandangan ini beliau kemukakan dalam pembicaraan bilateral kami kemarin.

Untuk itu, kita telah memiliki sejumlah agenda bersama. Sebagian dari agenda itu telah kita lakukan. Sebagiannya lagi masih dalam proses pengerjaan dan penyelesaian. Di samping itu, ada pula sejumlah agenda yang tengah kita bahas bersama, untuk kita laksanakan di masa-masa yang akan datang. Semakin banyak agenda bersama yang kita sepakati, akan semakin erat pula hubungan kerjasama kedua negara kita. Saya melihat dan meyakini, semangat dan keinginan untuk meningkatkan kerjasama itu, demikian besar, di antara pemimpin pemerintahan kedua negara.

Memang masih ada sejumlah persoalan yang tersisa yang belum sepenuhnya dapat kita tuntaskan. Masalah-masalah yang tersisa itu antara lain adalah masalah pengungsi, masalah aset, pembayaran hak-hak mantan pegawai negeri sipil, polisi dan tentara Indonesia di Timor Leste. Kita juga belum sepenuhnya menuntaskan masalah keamanan bersama di wilayah perbatasan. Namun kita harus bersyukur dan mengakui, bahwa sebagian besar dari masalah-masalah itu telah kita selesaikan.

Pada tahun 1999, jumlah pengungsi di Timor Barat berjumlah 285.000 orang. Kini jumlah yang masih tersisa adalah sekitar 16.000 orang. Saya yakin, masalah ini akan dapat diselesaikan dengan cara yang tepat dan bijak. Masalah aset akan terus kita rundingkan, dengan mempertimbangkan tingkat kemajuan ekonomi yang nantinya tentu akan dicapai oleh rakyat Timor Leste. Kami juga memahami diperlukannya penyusunan perangkat hukum nasional Timur Leste, yang mengatur masalah itu. Pembayaran hak-hak mantan pegawai negeri sipil, polisi dan tentara, juga akan terus diupayakan penyelesaiannya.

Mengenai masalah perbatasan, kita sesungguhnya telah mencapai berbagai kemajuan yang penting. Kita telah mampu menyelesaikan 96 persen masalah perbatasan darat antara kedua negara. Kesepakatan sementara mengenai perbatasan darat itu, telah ditanda-tangani oleh Menteri Luar Negeri kedua negara di Dili, pada tanggal 8 April 2005 kemarin. Saya percaya, sisanya yang empat persen, akan dapat diselesaikan dalam waktu dekat ini. Selanjutnya, kedua negara akan memasuki perundingan untuk menentukan batas laut kedua negara. Dengan demikian, nantinya masalah perbatasan antara kedua negara, baik batas darat maupun laut, dapat kita rampungkan.

Sementara itu, Pemerintah Indonesia juga telah membantu kelancaran hubungan jalur laut antara Okusi dengan Dili. Demikian pula pembukaan jalur hubungan darat, yang menghubungkan Okusi dengan wilayah Timor Leste lainnya, yang akan segera dilakukan dalam waktu yang tidak terlalu lama. Kedua Negara, kini tengah mempersiapkan pos-pos keamanan dan imigrasi di tapal batas masing-masing, untuk mempermudah kelancaran hubungan melalui jalur darat ini. Di lain pihak, Pemerintah Indonesia, berterima kasih atas inisiatif Pemerintah Timor Leste, untuk memberikan kemudahan kunjungan setiap warganegara Indonesia ke Negara ini, dalam melakukan ziarah ke makam sanak-saudaranya, yang ada di wilayah negara ini.

Pemerintah Indonesia juga menyambut baik keinginan Pemerintah Timor Leste, untuk membuka Konsulat di Denpasar dan Kupang. Pemerintah Indonesia juga tengah mengkaji pembukaan konsulatnya di wilayah Timor Leste. Dengan dibukanya konsulat-konsulat ini, kita harapkan, hubungan kerjasama antara kedua negara akan semakin erat lagi di tahun-tahun mendatang.

Saudara Ketua,
Para anggota Parlemen Nasional Timor Leste,
Hadirin yang saya muliakan,

Sebagai komitmen yang nyata dari Pemerintah Indonesia untuk membantu kemajuan Timor Leste, kami akan meneruskan program beasiswa, kepada mahasiswa-mahasiswa Timor Leste yang belajar di Indonesia. Dalam rangka meningkatkan sumberdaya manusia di bidang administrasi dan pengelolaan pemerintahan, Pemerintah kami juga menawarkan kesempatan pendidikan dan latihan di bidang bea-cukai dan perpajakan, serta pertanian dan kesehatan. Dalam waktu dekat, Pemerintah Indonesia akan memberikan kesempatan kepada 100 orang anggota Kepolisian Timor Leste, untuk mendapatkan pendidikan, di berbagai pusat pendidikan dan pelatihan Kepolisian Negara Republik Indonesia.

Dalam upaya meningkatkan hubungan internasional, Pemerintah Indonesia juga telah mengundang Pemerintah Timor Leste, menjadi peserta Konferensi Tingkat Tinggi Asia Afrika. Konferensi ini akan diselenggarakan di Jakarta mulai tanggal 22 April yang akan datang. Acara ini, kemudian akan dilanjutkan dengan Peringatan 50 tahun Konferensi Asia Afrika yang pertama, yang akan diselenggarakan di Bandung. Kehadiran pemimpin Timor Leste dalam forum internasional ini, kiranya dapat dimanfaatkan untuk mendorong kerjasama yang erat, antara Timor Leste dengan negara-negara di kawasan Asia dan Afrika.

Sebagaimana telah kita ketahui bersama, Indonesia juga telah mengundang Timur Leste, dalam dialog segitiga antara Republik Indonesia, Timur Leste dan Australia. Kita sedang menjajaki kerjasama ekonomi dan perdagangan antara Australia Utara, Timor Leste dan propinsi Indonesia yang berdekatan letaknya, seperti Nusa Tenggara Barat, Nusa Tenggara Timur dan Bali.

Indonesia juga secara aktif mengajak Timor Leste, untuk turut serta dalam Forum Dialog 6 negara di kawasan Pasifik Barat Daya. Demikian pula keikut-sertaan Timor Leste dalam ASEAN Regional Forum. Mudah-mudahan pertemuan para Menteri Luar Negeri negara-negara ASEAN di Cebu, Philipina, minggu depan ini, akan menyepakati keikutsertaan Timor Leste dalam Forum itu.

Komitmen dukungan Indonesia kepada Timor Leste dalam berbagai forum internasional ini, benar-benar merupakan dukungan yang tulus. Seperti telah saya katakan di awal pidato ini, kami ingin melihat bangsa dan negara Timor Leste, dapat memainkan peranan yang penting dalam percaturan antarabangsa. Dukungan kerjasama internasional ini, akan terus kami tingkatkan, di masa-masa yang akan datang.

Sementara itu, kita juga telah mencatat banyak kemajuan dalam hubungan perdagangan. Pemerintah Indonesia akan terus membantu penyediaan bahan bakar minyak, atas dasar saling menguntungkan bagi kedua negara. Hubungan perdagangan di kawasan perbatasan, baik formal maupun tradisional, sebagaimana yang selama ini telah berjalan, akan terus kita tingkatkan.

Dengan selesainya perundingan masalah perbatasan darat nantinya, kedua negara dapat segera membuka kesempatan penduduk di kawasan perbatasan, untuk memasuki wilayah kedaulatan kedua negara, dengan menggunakan pas pelintas batas. Langkah ini akan meningkatkan lagi hubungan kultural dan perdagangan, antar penduduk di kawasan perbatasan.

Hadirin yang saya hormati,

Setelah kunjungan kenegaraan saya kali ini, saya berharap, akan lebih banyak lagi kunjungan para pemimpin dari kedua negara kita. Saya sangat menghargai kunjungan yang beberapa kali telah dilakukan oleh Presiden Xanana Gusmao dan Perdana Menteri Mari Alkatiri ke negeri kami. Demikian pula kunjungan para menteri dan pejabat lainnya. Saya pun berharap, Saudara Ketua dan para anggota Perlemen Timor Leste, dapat berkunjung pula ke negara kami.

Saya yakin, perkenalan, persahabatan dan kedekatan pribadi dari pemimpin kedua negara, akan sangat membantu membangun kerjasama kedua negara. Hubungan baik antar pribadi itu, dapat menembus hambatan-hambatan yang bersifat formal dan protokoler. Saya yakin pula, hubungan pribadi yang erat antara pemimpin kedua negara, akan semakin mendorong peningkatan hubungan persahabatan dan persaudaraan, antara rakyat kedua negara.

Akhirnya, izinkanlah saya menggunakan kesempatan ini, untuk sekali lagi menyampaikan rasa hormat dan penghargaan yang setinggi-tingginya, kepada para Pemimpin dan rakyat Timor Leste, atas penerimaan yang baik dan penuh keramah-tamahan kepada saya dan seluruh anggota Delegasi Indonesia. Semoga apa yang telah diberikan akan menjadi amal-kebaikan, dan diterima oleh Tuhan Yang Maha Kuasa. Semoga pula, semua kebaikan itu, akan dapat meningkatkan hubungan baik kedua bangsa dan negara, sebagaimana yang telah menjadi harapan kita bersama.

Demikianlah pidato saya. Atas segala perhatian dan kesempatan yang telah diberikan oleh Saudara Ketua, dan seluruh anggota Parlemen Nasional Timor Leste, saya sampaikan ucapan terima kasih yang tulus.

Salam sejahtera untuk kita semua

Dili, Timor Leste, 9 April 2005

"Damning reports about the damage done to Indonesia's forests by illegal logging are nothing new. Nor are government promises to do something about it. In February, for instance, a group called the Environmental Investigation Agency (EIA) alleged that $600m-worth of timber was being smuggled from Indonesia to China every month, with the active help of the army and police. Susilo Bambang Yudhoyono, Indonesia's president, duly pledged a crackdown in March. But Operation Sustainable Forest, as the resultant campaign is known, does stand out from its many predecessors in one respect: it appears to be yielding some results."

(The Economist, 5 May 2005)

"You know, our media is intensely focusing on the first 100 days of my Government. Well, I wish I could say to them : It's not the first 100 days that are difficult. It is the whole 5 years."

President Susilo Bambang Yudhoyono
Jakarta, January 19, 2005

"Which is why in today's international context, the real challenge of Asia-Africa is not about developing the power to confront, but the power to connect."

President Susilo Bambang Yudhoyono
Jakarta, April 22, 2005

19

"Reinvigorating Asia Africa Business Ties"

Speech at The Asian-African Business Summit 2005

Mulia Hotel, Jakarta
April 21, 2005

♦ ♦ ♦ ♦ ♦

Mr. Chairman,
Distinguished Speakers and
Participants to this Important Business Summit,

It is indeed a great pleasure for me to join this distinguished gathering of the captains of business and industry of Asia and Africa.

I would like to thank and give my highest appreciation to the Chamber of Commerce and Industry of Indonesia, hosts and organizers of this very important Asian-African Business Summit.

This forum adds a crucial dimension to the Asian-African Summit that we will launch tomorrow morning. The concerns and issues on your agenda truly reflect the "Spirit" of the Asian-African Conference held in Bandung in 1955, the "Bandung Spirit".

In Bandung 50 years ago, the first generation of Asian and African leaders gave voice to the yearnings of the peoples of our two great continents. So loud and clear was that voice that the world listened.

The sense of kinship and solidarity that was kindled among these leaders and their peoples came to be known as the Bandung Spirit. Inspired by that Spirit, the nations of Asia and Africa have worked closely together through the decades.

In doing so, we Asians and Africans helped transform the political landscape of the world. We helped bring about the demise of colonialism and the eradication of apartheid and various other forms of prejudice. Together with like-minded nations from other regions, we founded the Non-aligned Movement, a global force that is well and alive today.

But we did not put the Bandung Spirit to work in the socioeconomic and cultural fields. No mechanism, no process was established for concrete cooperation in the economic field between the Asian and African nations. Thus, only half the vision of the Bandung Conference has been served.

But the Asian-African Summit 2005 will rectify that oversight. At the Summit, we will make up for five decades of lost opportunities to harness the Bandung Spirit for the socioeconomic welfare of the Asian and African peoples by establishing a New Asian-African Strategic Partnership.

This partnership will focus not only on political solidarity and sociocultural relations but also economic cooperation.

The Partnership will entail three tiers of interaction: the intergovernmental level, the level of subregional organizations and the people-to-people level. Of course transnational cooperation and transactions among businessmen and entrepreneurs such as those of you in this room today, will be a major part of people-to-people interaction.

The Partnership will take into account the vast diversity of Asian and African nations and build on existing regional and subregional initiatives to promote a wide range of dialogues, including dialogue between government and business, and most importantly between business and business.

Today's Forum is the first of such a dialogue – and of course we hope the first of many more to come --- which will yield concrete follow up measures and action plans --- and at the end of the day in mutually beneficial business for both sides.

Since you are all tough-minded businessmen, I know what your first question about this Partnership is: Will it work?

My answer is: YES. It will work because all of us will make it work. When I say "all of us" I mean not only governments but also the rest of society, including the academia, the mass media, the non-governmental organizations and civil society, as well as the business community.

The business sector plays a vital role in that Partnership because, with your resources and your skills, you can help government and the rest of society address the stark realities, the challenges and opportunities that define our time.

You may ask yourselves, just what is the potential for such a Partnership? And what are the main elements?

First let me reflect on the potential for the partnership given the current miraculous developments in the two regions and the potential complementarities.

The dynamism of the Asian region and the rebound of a number of the Asian countries after the crisis is well known. What has been largely unnoticed is the steady integration of the economies of Asia. Driven by increased intra regional investment flows and business networks, integration of trade in Asia has taken place even without there being a formal regional trade agreement.

In recent years, such integration gained momentum through the various initiatives and engagements of ASEAN, such as the AFTA, the first phase of a free trade area agreement between China and ASEAN. We also see the negotiations between ASEAN and a number of dialogue partners including India, Japan, Australia and New Zealand; as well as the ASEAN plus Three process. The pace is even more rapid today, with most of the Asian economies eagerly negotiating free trade arrangements with one another.

In Africa, we also see increased reforms being undertaken to improve its economic prospects and what is remarkable is the degree of political integration that the continent has achieved in so short a time. Africa does have a set of formal mechanisms for cooperation in the politico-security field as well as in the economic field. Asia can learn much from Africa's experience in formal continent-wide integration.

I also believe there is a convergence of trends in our two regions with regard to a growing desire by our peoples for greater democratic space, good governance and accountability of governments. This will in turn translate also into stronger economic relations between our two regions.

I strongly believe that achieving good governance is key to the growth of investments and the economy of the countries in Asia and Africa.

What could possibly become the "miracle" of future decades is the current remarkable growth of the economic cooperation between Asia and Africa. For instance, whilst the absolute level of trade between the two regions is still low, between 1980 and 2004, the proportion of African exports destined for Asia more than tripled from four to 15 percent.

At the same time, ASEAN countries, China, Korea and India are becoming important investors in African countries, using various modes of delivering investment.

Today, this surprising but welcome development is taking place with little or no involvement of governments. Imagine what could happen once the new Asian-African Strategic Partnership starts working : we can expect a sharper rise in economic relations between the two continents.

I do not wish to be rhetorical at this Business Summit, so I would like to urge all of us to be realistic in identifying the way forward. Let us together come up with action plans to elaborate on how this can be achieved. For instance given the small volumes of trade we can think of ways to pool exports and imports through various gateways into our respective regions, including the potential for links between the different regional agreements that already exist in Asia (e.g. AFTA) and Africa (e.g. Southern African Development Community). We can also consider how to make the General System of Tariff Preferences (GSTP) between developing countries be more effective.

We must also focus on trade and investment facilitation programs which focuses on the smooth and ease flow of goods, services, people and investment between our two regions. This could of course include how we can improve more direct and effective transportation links between our two regions.

Then there is the issue of information exchange, promotion of trade and business opportunities and how government-private sector or business-business networks can improve this.

The task of governments is to facilitate businesses, so let us work together to formulate a set of concrete steps in all these areas.

Ladies and Gentlemen, I do hope that you will provide the Asia-Africa Summit with some clear recommendations and action plans that we can follow up to truly realize the other half of the Bandung Vision.

Indeed, we have so much to gain from the cooperation of others in facing these global challenges. Indonesia has always been an advocate of North-South engagement, and an even more ardent proponent of South-South cooperation—especially between and among Asian and African countries under the banner of the Bandung Spirit.

In the days to come, with the New Asian-African Strategic Partnership in operation, the countries of both continents can work more effectively together to help build a more equitable world financial and economic architecture.

We can also have a bigger voice in the reform of multilateral institutions, including the United Nations, the World Bank and the World Trade Organization. We should also jointly call for the commitment of developed countries for achievement of the Millennium Development Goals in the countries in Asia and Africa by 2015 by delivering their promise of increased aid commitment and debt relief and/or cancellation.

Through coordinating our policies and our procedures, we can support and impart new momentum to the positive socioeconomic and political developments taking place in our continents. Thus, we can radically alter the pattern of global trade and investment flows, making the Indian Ocean an exceptionally busy two-way street of economic cooperation.

Ladies and gentlemen,

This being a Business Summit and me being a "salesman" President, please allow me to say a few words about economic development and prospects in Indonesia.

Indonesia has bounced back from the crapping economic crisis that devastated our nation in 1997.

Indonesia today has come a long way in pursuing democratic consolidation and the tasks of reforms--"reformasi". Last year, we completed the most complex free and fair elections anywhere in the world, with a voting turning that is the world's largest after India.

The economic rewards of our reforms are evident. Growth has been picking up surely and steadily. Growth was 5.1 percent in 2004 and we expect it to be 5.5% this year. My government hopes to achieve an average of 6.6% growth in the next five years. Purchasing power has also returned back to pre crisis levels at $1030 per capita and with a population of 220 million, the potential for the Indonesian market is self evident. Investment recovery is also happening with investments rising by 11 percent, and for the first time since the crisis we are seeing net capital inflows.

We have also been able to manage our fiscal situation with debt levels coming down, the deficit under control and we have also under taken the difficult but necessary decision to raise fuel prices by 29 percent on March 1, 2005 in line with the rising world price of oil.

My Government's development strategy is based on what I call the Triple Track.

- The first track is to achieve sustainable higher economic growth through a combination of strong exports and increased investments, both domestic and foreign.
- The second track is to stimulate the performance of the real sectors to create more employment.
- And the third track is to promote the development of the rural economy and agriculture to alleviate poverty.

The Triple Track Strategy is essentially pro-growth, pro-jobs, pro-poor.

With this Triple Track Strategy, we intend to reach our economic targets at the end of our term. By 2009, we aim to reduce the unemployment rate from 9.5 percent to 5.1 percent, and we seek to cut the poverty rate in half to 8.1 percent.

What is worth noting is the important role that small and medium enterprises play in our economy, and the strong policy support that government extends to undersized economic players.

We have also a fairly successful microcredit sector and we are willing to share with other Asian and African countries our experience in this important field of finance.

And of course, that is what I hope to see the result from this Business Summit and from the Asia Africa Summit tomorrow : greater interlinkages between the Indonesian economy and the Asia-African economic dynamism, boosted by the active support of the private sector.

For at the end of the day, governments can only encourage economic activity. Businessmen and industrialists are the ones who put together start-up companies, joint ventures, mergers and acquisitions, or trade and financing arrangements.

We must therefore increase and strengthen dialogue between governments and private business sectors all over Asia and Africa. So much information that private business needs is in the hands of government. Dialogue can make access to such information so much easier. The Partnership can create venues for that dialogue.

Governments can play a matchmaking and facilitating role between transnationals and local suppliers, while transnationals can inform governments what kind of policy support will strengthen these links.

Governments and transnationals working together on a regional or intercontinental framework can devise arrangements that allow economies of scale work for small suppliers. That kind of teamwork can also address problems like the small size of domestic markets, high costs of capital imports and imported technology, and inadequacy of infrastructures.

It has been proven that big corporations can profit very substantially by re-engineering their products and services to fit the requirements and the pocketbooks of the poor. Working together, governments, big business and small enterprises can also find ways by which they can help the poor create wealth.

The business sector should not underestimate the government's need and appreciation for information. I believe the time is ripe for the business sector to advocate for more enlightened government economic policies.

And I think that once the New Asian-African Strategic Partnership is established, it will be worthwhile for corporations and business organizations to test the commitment of governments to dialogue. If both sides have the goodwill and the determination to address the realities of our time, and if both prepare well for dialogue, I am certain that the process will be enlightening and useful.

I like to imagine that what we are witnessing today may be the beginning of an era of dialogue in Asia and Africa—between and among continents, regions and subregions; between and among all stakeholders in development.

That would be the best thing that ever happened to the Bandung Spirit and to the peoples of Asia and Africa.

Jakarta, May 21, 2005

" Yudhoyono has won international praise for his response to the tsunami and his blunt talk about the country's problems, including terrorism and human right abuses by the military. But what really has the markets smoking is a five-year, $145 billion spending plan he unveiled in January to upgrade Indonesia's creaky infrastructure—everything from a $178 million airport extension in Jakarta to a $1.5 billion gas pipeline. Cash-strapped Indonesia can ill afford such a massive public spending program, but Yudhoyono says foreign investors will contribute at least $90 billion, then lease the facilities out to cover the costs and make a profit."—Brian Bremner and Assif Shameen.

(BusinessWeek, 4 July 2005)

"If there is disconnect between democracy and governance, you will have a dysfunctional democracy. The world is full of examples of democracies becoming unstable, democracies in decay, democracies in regression, democracies ruined by conflict and poverty. We do not intend to go that route."

President Susilo Bambang Yudhoyono
Jakarta, January 24, 2005

"Indonesian muslims can live in peace and harmony with non-muslims, as our forefathers have done for centuries."

President Susilo Bambang Yudhoyono
Jakarta, September 7, 2004

20

"Let Us Build A New Strategic Partnership between Asia and Africa"

Opening Remarks at The Opening of
The Asia-Africa Summit 2005

Jakarta Convention Center, Jakarta
April 22, 2005

♦ ♦ ♦ ♦ ♦

Bismillahirrahmanirrahim
Majesties, Royal Highnesses,
Excellencies Leaders of Asian-African Nations,
Your Excellency UN Secretary-General Kofi Annan,
Ladies and Gentlemen,

At long last, at long last, we are all gathered here.

It took fifty long years for this conference to happen, but Asia and Africa have finally assembled here again.

Today, the sons and daughters of Asia and Africa stand together in this Hall as equals. And we stand tall, proud and free.

Let us therefore begin by giving a big applause, to honor the first generation of Asian and African leaders who started it all in Bandung in 1955.

What they did was truly remarkable. At a volatile time when the new world was searching for order, they awakened the collective spirit of Asia and Africa, they set forth a new course, and they ignited a new sense of solidarity and activism that transformed our two great continents. In short, what they did was no less than to change the world, and shaped the second half of the 20th century.

Alhamdulillah, the gathering which in 1955 began with 29 countries— 3 from Africa, 26 from Asia--now have grown into a large conference of 106 independent countries.

But we do not come here to reminisce, nor to bask in self-romanticization. Nor are we here to exchange pleasantries, or to lament our problems.

We come here because we need to ask hard questions and find real answers about how Asia and Africa can adapt and respond to the challenges of today's world.

We must ask: Why did it take 50 years—a lifetime—for Asia and Africa to reconvene after the success of the first Summit in 1955 ?

We must ask: Does the Bandung Spirit mean the same in 2005 as it did in 1955 ? If the Bandung spirit has served us well over the years, how can we adapt that spirit to today's circumstances ?

And we must ask: now that Asia-Africa is reconvened in great numbers and with robust confidence, how can we make it relevant ? Relevant to us, and relevant to the world.

The sad fact of history is that, while the Bandung Spirit lived on after 1955, the Asia-Africa process stumbled. The last time we heard of the "Asia-Africa" conference was in 1965, when the attempt to reconvene the second Asian African Summit in Algiers faltered.

What we need to remember here is that "Asia-Africa" faltered NOT for lack of spirit, but for lack of process, for lack of planning, and perhaps—perhaps--for lack of prudence.

But for those who question whether the Bandung Spirit is still relevant, I would say that the case for Asia-Africa solidarity today is even more compelling than it was 50 years ago. Let us not forget: as we entered the new millennium, Asia-Africa remains the missing link, in the worldwide structure of inter-regional relations.

- Across the Atlantic Ocean, there is the formal alliance between Europe and North America.
- Across the Pacific Ocean, there is the formal linkage between Asia and the Americas, through APEC and the ASEAN Regional Forum.
- But across the Indian Ocean, none existed between Asia and Africa, despite the success story of the first Asia-Africa Summit in 1955.

Our meeting here today is therefore an inauguration of that new bridge across the Indian Ocean, that new bridge between the wonderful worlds of Asia and Africa.

Indeed, the international environment today is much more conducive, for the coming together of Asia and Africa.

Asia and Africa are no longer burdened by the Cold War, which in 1955 pulled the Asian and African participants in Bandung in different directions.

Asia and Africa are now much more accustomed and open to each other. We have developed better skills of cooperation and interactions. And we are much more integrated into the world economy than 50 years ago. And of course, television, radio, internet, fast airplanes, trade, sports and tourism have brought our peoples closer.

Asia and Africa are also now home to important regional and sub-regional organizations, as well as to the proliferation of bilateral and multilateral ties.

And beyond Asia-Africa, in contrast with 1955, we now see a world much more sympathetic to our problems, and eager to work and engage us.

Which is why in today's international context, the real challenge of Asia-Africa is not about developing the power to confront, but the power to connect.

Asia-Africa must connect with itself, but it must also connect with other international and regional groupings.

Thus, we can do much more with Asia-Africa in 2005 compared to 1955.

Just think about it : 106 countries now grace the continents of Asia and Africa, comprising more than one-half of the membership of the United

Nations, encompassing an area that is almost half of the world. We speak for 4.6 billion people, or 73 percent of the world's population. Our combined Gross Domestic Product amounts to $9.3 trillion.

But being too impressed with demographics or economic statistics, will not get us very far.

The renewed Asia-Africa process that we are trying to nurture will matter only if we can make it relevant to the problems and opportunities of Asia-Africa.

And the problems of Asia and Africa are plenty.

But the most persistent among them is the enduring fight against poverty.

Africa is the only continent where poverty is on the rise, where 40 percent of all Sub-Saharan people live on less than a dollar a day. Asia also has vast pockets of poverty, where people living in extreme poverty, outnumber those in Africa by several hundred millions.

And of course, Asia and Africa's problems do not stop there.

25 million Africans, and 7,5 million Asians, are victims of the HIV / AIDS epidemic. Millions of our peoples do not have access to clean water, proper education, energy, healthcare.

Environmental degradation is pervasive. Armed conflicts of various kinds kill our people, and distort our national development.

Terrorism and trans-national crimes are on the rise. Corruption retards our national growth. And the people of Palestine, after all these years, are still deprived of the independent and sovereign State, which is rightfully theirs.

And that is why today, in 2005, we have to sound a different battle cry. In 1955, the battle cry of the day was "Freedom", which made perfect sense given the persistence of colonialism back then. But now that Asia and Africa are free, we must take on the next phase of that battle for human dignity.

That battle is called: the quest for good governance. And the struggle for good governance is not necessarily easier than the struggle for freedom.

If Asia and Africa can learn anything from the past 5 decades, it is that the success or failure of governance, explains the success and failure of states. It also explains the success or failure of peace, the success or failure of development, the success or failure of nation-building.

Good governance is what will fulfill the promise of freedom that our fathers struggled for. And good governance is what will truly "liberate" Asia and Africa, and unleash our true potentials. The vision of Asia-Africa therefore, should be a vision that enhances good governance.

But the worst thing you can do to a great vision is to deprive it of practical detail.

Thus, as we reaffirm our faith in the Bandung Spirit, now we must care to give it flesh and form.

Excellencies,
Ladies and Gentlemen,

Let us now therefore build a Strategic Partnership, that will bind our two continents in a vibrant, pragmatic and forward-looking way.

That partnership should cover evenly three broad areas of cooperation: political solidarity, economic cooperation, and socio-cultural relations.

It should promote human resources development, enhance capacity building, and technical cooperation, to create a constructive environment for the region.

That partnership should promote rich interaction at three levels : at the intergovernmental level, at the level of sub-regional organizations, and at the level of people-to-people contact. That is why for that partnership to work, it will demand the active involvement of the business sector, the academia, civil society and the mass media.

The operation of that Strategic Partnership should be based on, and guided by, a wide range of agreed principles that the nations of Asia and Africa passionately believe in. Foremost of these principles are the Dasa Sila of Bandung, laid down by the Asian-African Conference of 1955.

And as a practical measure, the mechanics of our cooperation must give allowances to the immense diversity of our social and economic systems and levels of development.

We should never be inward-looking. We should be non-exclusive, and be willing to cooperate with all stakeholders. In particular, Asia-Africa must be at the forefront of the global cooperation, to reach the objectives of the Millenium Development Goals by 2015.

The Strategic Partnership should also serve as an instrument for the promotion of a just, democratic, accountable and harmonious society. Thus, we can strengthen the process of our own nation-building and state-building, as well as social integration.

Moreover, we must take it upon ourselves to promote and protect human rights and fundamental freedoms. Not the least of these is the most basic of human rights—the right to live! No Asian or African should die, because he or she is too poor to live.

And in the various multilateral forums where our interests are at stake, we should coordinate our moves, and speak with one strong and clear voice. Acting as one community, we can make sure that even the smallest among us will not be marginalized.

I am glad that through this Summit, Asia and Africa remains unyielding in supporting our Palestinian brothers and sisters in their epic struggle to gain their independent, sovereign state, where they can be assured freedom, justice and peace.

So these, brothers and sisters, are the principles that form the hallmark of the Strategic Partnership, which will lead us to our true destiny.

You know, in 1955, Indonesia's founding father and first President, Sukarno, declared in Bandung that "Asia-Africa would unleash the moral force of nations, in favor of peace."

I believe that in 2005, Asia-Africa can be, and must be, more than a "moral force". Much more.

Through this Strategic Partnership, Asia-Africa can be transformed, no longer just as a geographical expression, but as a true geopolitical and geo-economic reality.

I believe that, if we revive and adapt the Bandung Spirit in our hearts, and make this Partnership work for us, the story of Asia-Africa in the 21st century, can be very different from its 20th century past.

Asia-Africa will be a non-exclusive concert of nations living in peace and harmony, bonded in partnership and conscious of its historic and cultural roots.

And Insya Allah, it will be one big caring society, where our peoples will live in comfort and dignity, free from fear of violence, oppression and injustice. We will all be free from the clutches of poverty, and at liberty to rise to our fullest potential.

That will be the ultimate freedom.

I look forward to working, and sweating, with all of you to achieve that Strategic Partnership, and to write the future history of Asia-Africa.

Thank you.

Jakarta, April 22, 2005

"Why is so much money going into Indonesia's property market? It has been one of the better performing sectors of the economy in recent years. In Jakarta, shopping malls enjoy 90 per cent occupancy levels and more are being built. Developers are going for residential property which over the long term is thought to offer the greatest potential for growth."

(The Business Times, 18 June 2005)

"In Aceh Province in Indonesia, 2,000 schools and 200,000 homes must be constructed. Even the United States would have a difficult time getting a million people back into their houses in a year or two."—William J. Clinton

(The New York Times, 22 June 2005)

"We believe the investment case for Indonesia should evolve from one being undervalued to that of growth, as the economy gears up for structural recovery"

(Deutsche Bank Indonesia Strategy Report, 13 May 2005)

"And given the disparity in the levels of development between the provinces, my Government is committed to pursue a policy of 'infrastructure for all', that is, to allocate investments in infrastructure in the more developed regions as well as in the less developed areas."

President Susilo Bambang Yudhoyono
Jakarta, January 17, 2005

"But if we succeed in making history at all, it will be because we succeed in elevating the Bandung spirit to the level of strategic partnership. We hope that this strategic partnership will give Asia and Africa the bridge of cooperation that has been missing all these years."

President Susilo Bambang Yudhoyono
Jakarta, April 22, 2005

21

"A Meeting Place of The Minds"

Remarks at a State Dinner In Honor of Heads of Delegation to The Asia-Africa Summit 2005

Presidential Palace, Jakarta
April 22, 2005

♦ ♦ ♦ ♦ ♦

Bismillahirrahmanirrahim

Majesties, Royal Highnesses,
Excellencies Leaders of Asian-African Nations,
Ladies and Gentlemen,

It is a great honor for my wife and I to once again welcome all of you to Indonesia and to this modest palace, which is called, appropriately of course, the "Freedom Palace".

The walls of this Palace are silent witnesses to many great stories in the long history Indonesia, but I think from now on tales will be told about the evening of 22 April 2005 when representatives from 106 countries throughout Asia and Africa and the Secretary General of the United Nations dined together in peace and friendship.

Today, we all worked very hard in our productive discussions about the future of Asia-Africa. That's why I told my wife that I am having a few friends over for dinner tonight.

Despite our busy schedule during the Summit, I hope that you are able to see more of my country. And I hope that you like what you see.

For we Indonesians take pride in the changes that have taken place in our country—that is why we make it a point to call it the New Indonesia. It has indeed undergone much change.

And when I talk about change, it is not so much in the physical landscape of a country but in the soul of a nation.

Seven years ago, the Indonesian economy was devastated by the Asian financial crisis. The economic debacle led to social and political turmoil. The only way the nation could save itself was through vigorous and far-reaching reforms that had to be carried out in all aspects of our national life.

So we began our "reformasi" and our democratic transition.

It is a difficult undertaking, especially when dealing with a country of 220 million comprising of hundreds of ethnic groups, but the results have been worthwhile.

Our economy has bounced back, internal conflicts are being contained or resolved, political reforms are moving forward, and stability is returning to Indonesia.

And last year, we held three national elections in a span of six months, what is described by some as the most ambitious and complex free and fair elections anywhere in the world.

So that is the change that I speak of.

I hope you forgive my very obvious attempt to make a sales pitch about my country, but I am told this is one of the advantages of being the host of this large Conference.

The other advantage, of course, is the great learning experience -and also a humbling experience—that comes from hearing the great speeches, wise thoughts and new ideas from the best sons and daughters of Asia and Africa. We have always wanted to see this Asia-Africa conference become a meeting place of the minds, and I think we have achieved that in good measure today.

Asia-Africa is a household name in Indonesia. We learn about Asia-Africa at school, from our parents and from history books. The Asia Africa Conference was not only an everlasting achievement of our independent and active foreign policy, it is also a healthy expression of our inter nationalism. It is therefore a great personal honor for me to be involved in this 21st century effort to reawaken Asia-Africa cooperation and to rediscover Asia-Africa solidarity.

Indeed, though this meeting of the minds today, we discovered many things. We discovered that the Bandung spirit is very much alive. We discovered that many of our problems are the same. We discovered we have many opportunities to grow together. We discovered there is a strong collective will to build on Asia-Africa cooperation.

But if we succeed in making history at all, it will be because we succeed in elevating the Bandung spirit to the level of strategic partnership. We hope that this strategic partnership will give Asia and Africa the bridge of cooperation that has been missing all these years.

But as a retired general, I must tell you that I know a thing or two about bridges. There are different kinds of bridges. There is the stable bridge, the shaky bridge, the temporary bridge, the solid bridge. Our strategic partnership has to be a durable, it has to be solid and it has to perform its obvious function: to bridge.

Our key challenge now is to pool our resources and marshall our collective efforts to construct a solid edifice of that Asia-Africa strategic partnership.
Once again, thank you for coming, it is a great pleasure to see all of you here tonight and do enjoy the evening.

I thank you.

Jakarta, April 22, 2005

"*The government accepted $5.48 billion of foreign direct investment in the first five months of 2005, the Investment Coordinating Board said last month. That was almost double the amount a year earlier.*"

(International Herald Tribune, 4 July 2005)

"Let me state for the record how much I appreciate all the good work of President Megawati Soekarnoputri and her Cabinet. I intend to build on my predecessor's accomplishment to bring greater prosperity for Indonesia."

President Susilo Bambang Yudhoyono
Jakarta, January 19, 2005

"The hardest part of my Presidency is dealing with the unknowns, and there have been too many of them. The earthquake in Nabire, the earthquake in Alor, the massive tsunami in Aceh and North Sumatra, the flood in South Sumatra, the earthquake in Nias."

President Susilo Bambang Yudhoyono
Sydney, Australia, April 5, 2005

22

"Practical Task for
Asia - Africa"

Speech at The Closing of
The Asia-Africa Summit 2005

Jakarta Convention Center, Jakarta
April 23, 2005

♦ ♦ ♦ ♦ ♦

Bismillahirrahmanirrahim

Majesties, Royal Highnesses,
Excellencies Leaders of Asian and African Nations,
UN Secretary-General Kofi Annan
Ladies and Gentlemen,

We have just concluded extensive deliberations on how we can work together to promote Asia-Africa solidarity and cooperation for the long-term.

We have heard many views and ideas and proposals, and reviewed many issues, that confront Asia and Africa. We have had a productive two-day meeting in an atmosphere of trust and renewed partnership.

As a result of the Summit, we have adopted two outcomes:

1. The Declaration on the New Asian-African Strategic Partnership (NAASP), and
2. The Joint Asian-African Leaders' Statement on Tsunami, Earthquake and Other Natural Disasters.

In addition, our Ministers have also adopted a series of action plan as part and parcel of the Leaders' Declaration. These are contained in the "Joint Ministerial Statement, on the New Asian-African Strategic Partnership Plan of Action".

The most important legacy of this conference is the establishment of a New Asian-African Strategic Partnership. The Declaration on the New Asian-African Strategic Partnership is a milestone in the history of our movement. Through this Partnership, we will create in the years ahead, a legacy of socio-economic and cultural development, to future generations of Asians and Africans.

The New Asian-African Strategic Partnership covers three areas of partnership, namely political solidarity, economic cooperation and socio-cultural relations. We envision an Asian-African region at peace with itself and with the world at large, where our people can live in stability, prosperity, dignity and free from the fear of violence, oppression and injustice.

We have also reaffirmed that the Spirit of Bandung, which is the spirit of solidarity, friendship and cooperation, continues to be a solid, relevant and effective foundation for fostering better relations among us as well as for resolving global issues of common concern.

In the process of our nation and state building, progress in the social and economic realms need to be further strengthened. Here we highlight the importance of working together to address globalization, poverty and underdevelopment.

Our partnership shall also strive for greater multilateralism, and for a central role of the United Nations in global affairs.

Despite the political advances reached by the peoples of Asia and Africa, the Palestinian people continue to be deprived of their right to independence. Therefore, we remain steadfast in our support to the Palestinian people and to the creation of a viable and sovereign Palestinian state, in accordance with the relevant UN resolutions.

We also highlight the importance of dialogue among civilizations to promote a culture of peace and tolerance among religions and culture.

The Strategic Partnership highlights the need to address issues of common concern, such as armed conflict, weapons of mass destruction, transnational organized crime and terrorism.

Our strategic partnership also emphasizes the need to promote practical cooperation in areas such as trade, industry, investment, finance, tourism, information and communication technology, energy, health, transportation, agriculture, water resources and fisheries.

We are determined to prevent conflict and resolve disputes by peaceful means.

We also emphasized on the importance of promoting of human resources development, enhanced capacity building and technical cooperation.

And we also addressed the need for joint efforts to mitigate natural disasters, such as tsunami, earthquakes and other natural disasters.

I would like to add that, in pursuing our goals, we underlined the important role of all stake holders, and the need to have enhanced interaction among governments, among sub-regional organizations, and through people-to-people contacts.

We have also decided to have an institutionalized process, through convening a Summit meeting every four years, a Ministerial Meeting every two years, as well as Sectoral Ministerial and Technical meetings when deemed necessary.

So we have achieved much in the last two days. Not only have we reaffirmed our commitment to the Bandung Spirit, we have also adapted it to the needs of our times, and we have given it concrete practical contents. And most importantly, we have established a mechanism, to ensure the continuity of the Asia-Africa process.

Through the operation of this Partnership, we will uphold the enduring values and principles bannered by the Dasa Sila Bandung, or Ten Principles of Bandung, and engraved in the Charter of the United Nations.

Tomorrow, in Bandung, we will observe in simple rites the Golden Jubilee of the Asian-African Conference of 1955.

We will thus pay homage to the first generation of Asian and African Leaders who, fifty years ago, warned the world of the irresistible tide of Asian and African nationalism and the demise of colonial regimes.

We will also reenact the historic walk of these early Statesmen from the Savoy Homan Hotel to the Gedung Merdeka—a reflection of our fervent and humble wish to follow in their footsteps.

We will also plant a garden of Asian and African trees which represent the investment of our resources and best creative energies for the welfare of our future generations.

And we will formally sign the Declaration of the New Asian-African Strategic Partnership, which is our ticket to a brighter future for our nations.

It is here today and yesterday, however, that we accomplished the substantive work that gives meaning to what we will do tomorrow. And I am personally delighted that we have accomplished so much during the past two days.

I therefore wish to thank all of you for your active participation and contributions. It has been an honor and privilege working closely with Leaders of such broad mind and far-reaching foresight.

I would like to express our gratitude to UN Secretary General His Excellency Kofi Annan for joining us in this important endeavor and for his valuable guidance.

I would also like to thank my Co-chair, His Excellency Thabo Mbeki, for his invaluable contributions as well as for the cooperation and support of the South African Government that ensured the success of this Asian-African Summit 2005.
And to all the Ministers and senior officials from all over Asia and Africa who have worked so hard in preparing this meeting in the last few months, please accept our appreciation.

With great satisfaction and gratitude, I now declare this Summit closed.

I thank you.

Jakarta, April 23, 2005

"Whatever happens, the aftermath of the tsunami will affect Indonesian economics and politics for years to come. That represents both a burden and an opportunity for Yudhoyono's government."—Assif Shameen.

(BusinessWeek, 24 January 2005)

"My Government is a firm believer in the notion that 'growth' and 'equity' must go together. And my Government is equally determined to see to it 'prosperity' and 'poverty' should not be allowed to go hand-in-hand."

President Susilo Bambang Yudhoyono
Jakarta, January 19, 2005

"I think the best way to measure the Partnership is in terms of how much trust and confidence develop out of it, how much goodwill it generates, how much we come to understand one another, and how much closer we become."

President Susilo Bambang Yudhoyono
Canberra-Australia, April 4, 2005

23

"Celebrating 50 years of Asia-Africa Spirit"

Statement at The Observance of The Golden Jubilee
of The Asian-African Conference

Gedung Merdeka, Bandung
April 24, 2005

♦ ♦ ♦ ♦ ♦

Majesties and Royal Highnesses,
Excellencies
Your Excellency Secretary-General Kofi Annan,
Ladies and Gentlemen,

We meet today in a place made sacred by history.

Fifty years ago, within these walls, the first generation of leaders of the two great continents of Asia and Africa came together and held the first Asian African Conference.

Here, they carried out a truly heroic deed. They gave voice to the voiceless. Through them, spoke the hundreds of millions who populated Asia and Africa, and who had, until then, languished in silence.

They spoke of their yearning for freedom, which could not be denied. They expressed their hunger for peace, without which there could be no freedom.

They made this clear: what they wanted was true peace, not the peace between all-powerful master and helpless slave, nor the peace of the graveyard that comes after violent conflict.

It must be a peace born of goodwill between equals.

They affirmed that all nations, all human beings are equals by virtue of their humanity. And all have an equal right to live— not just to survive—but to live in freedom, which is the most fundamental of human rights. This is the essence of the Dasa Sila Bandung, which they laid down as a code of ethics for international relations.

To help achieve peace, they would work in concert to bring back the gift of reason to a global landscape unreasonably divided into power blocs. They would therefore uphold and promote the principles and ideals engraved in the Charter of the United Nations.

That desire for peace was the seed that would eventually sprout into the Non-aligned Movement, the greatest movement for peace that the world has ever seen.

They also spoke of their desire for economic and social development, without which there could be no human dignity. They would work closely together to redeem themselves from poverty, ignorance and prejudice.

This determination to work together, this deep sense of kinship among Asian and African nations came to be known as the Bandung Spirit. I like to think, however, that this Spirit was already developing long before Bandung gave it a name.

Since ancient times, there has been a great deal of cultural and commercial contact between our continents. The immensity of the Indian Ocean has never been an impassable barrier. It has always been a busy highway.

Time and again, adventurers, missionaries, traders, envoys and exiles from one continent crossed over to the other. They did so at a frequency that was amazing—since they did not have the benefit of modern technology.

But the first major demonstration of the spirit of Asian-African solidarity and kinship would not take place until the middle of the 20th century.

That was in 1949 in New Delhi where Conference of Asian and African Nations gave notice to the world that they were all solidly behind the Republic of Indonesia in its revolutionary struggle for independence and sovereignty.

As early as 1947, several African and Middle Eastern as well as Asian countries had been individually supporting the Indonesian revolution. But they all came out in force together for Indonesia in 1949.

That crucial demonstration of Asian-African solidarity helped ensure the survival of our young Republic. Indonesia may therefore be regarded as the first child of Asian-African solidarity.

Indonesia seized a historic opportunity to hosting the Asian-African Conference in Bandung in 1955. That was when the spirit of Asian-African solidarity assumed a proper name and a reference point.

Participants and sympathetic observers went so far as to call Bandung the Peace Capital of Asia-Africa. Humbly we in Indonesia accept that designation for this highland city. We do so in honor of the statesmen who labored here fifty years ago in the name of Peace.

Since that time, too, the Bandung Spirit has been a guidance and a rallying cry for generations of Asian and African leaders. It was this same Spirit that inspired us yesterday in Jakarta to establish a New Asian-African Strategic Partnership.

Through that partnership we would pool together the vast resources and the tremendous creative energies of Asia and Africa to solve some of the most persistent problems of development we are facing.

Through that partnership we would contribute significantly to the ultimate conquest of poverty as a constant torment of the human condition.

And through that partnership we would advance the cause of peace, equitable prosperity and social justice.

One day all of us who are gathered here will be judged by history. That judgment will not be based on what we say here nor on what we said in the Summit we just held.

History will judge us on the basis of what we do in the days, months and years ahead—whether we are faithful to the Bandung Spirit or we betray it through failure of political nerve.

We will be judged on how dedicated we are to our Strategic Partnership, on whether we can make it work to ensure a better life for our children's children.

Let us therefore work together so that we will deserve the kindness of history.

Bandung, April 24, 2005

"In Indonesia, posititivity is awaking. Thanks to President Yudhoyono, we believe investors are starting to feel optimistic for the first time in a long while"—A Report by Morgan Stanley.

(Singapore Business Review, May, 2005)

"Indonesia, with its oil, gas, gold, fertile soil and relatively well-educated population, should be one of the economic powerhouses of Southeast Asia."—Tim Johnston

(The Times, 21 October 2004)

"But if we succeed in making history at all, it will be because we succeed in elevating the Bandung spirit to the level of strategic partnership. We hope that this strategic partnership will give Asia and Africa the bridge of cooperation that has been missing all these years."

President Susilo Bambang Yudhoyono
Jakarta, April 22, 2005

"Now that Asia and Africa are free, we must take on the next phase of that battle for human dignity.
That battle is called: the quest for good governance. And the struggle for good governance is not necessarily easier than the struggle for freedom."

President Susilo Bambang Yudhoyono
Jakarta, April 22, 2005

"In fact, whereas Vice-President Hatta in 1948 used the metaphor "rowing between two reefs", today, as we have safely passed the two reefs, I would use the metaphor "navigating a turbulent ocean" to describe the challenge faced by Indonesia's foreign policy."

President Susilo Bambang Yudhoyono
Jakarta, May 19, 2005

24

"Providing Our Citizens Equal Access to Justice"

Keynote Speech at the Opening Ceremony of
The 15th Annual Meeting and Conference of
The Inter-Pacific BAR Association

Nusa Dua, Bali
May 4, 2005

♦ ♦ ♦ ♦ ♦

Bismillahirrahmanirrahim,
Assalamu'alaikum warahmatullahi wabarakatuh,
Excellencies,
Distinguished participants,

Before I say my words of welcome, let me begin by saying that I have never seen so many lawyers in my life. I wish to commend and congratulate the Inter-Pacific Bar Association, not just for organizing this important conference but for having successfully gathered so many lawyers in one room !

You know, when I served in Bosnia some years ago as a UN peace-keeper, we used to collect a lot of jokes: military jokes, lawyer jokes. And the best ones were always lawyer jokes. But this is one occasion where I will restrain myself from telling any lawyer jokes. Not because I do not want to, but because my own lawyer warned me not to !

That said, I am very pleased to welcome all of you here in Bali for the Opening Ceremony of the 15th Annual Meeting and Conference of the Inter-Pacific Bar Association.

Bali is truly a wondrous place—they call it "the island of the gods"— and everytime I visit this place I always discover something new. I am very sure that you will be enchanted by the mystical charm of this island.

But apart from enjoying the fresh air and scenic landscape, I hope you will also feel a more powerful force : the force of a country in the midst of tremendous transformation.

Not just change : transformation !

This is the country where we have just completed the most ambitious and most complex free and fair elections anywhere in the world. The only thing more incredible than the complexity of our elections was the fact that they were conducted peacefully and orderly. Today, Indonesia would count as the world's second largest democracy if based on the number of voting turn-out.

This is also the country which was swept by the "reformasi" movement. This movement grew from popular demands for the eradication of collusion, corruption and nepotism.

It led to wide-ranging reforms -- political reform, constitutional reform, economic reform, military reform, bureaucratic reform, legal reform, social reform.

Today, we are still carrying the banner of "reformasi" and we have come a long way in pursuing these reforms over the last 8 years.

But I tell you this : at the heart of all these reforms is legal reform. It is an easy concept but a monumental undertaking. Unless we succeed with legal reforms, our transformation will only be artificial.

And I believe this is what binds all of us together in this conference : the belief in the supremacy of the rule of law as the basic organizing concept for our society.

The Asia Pacific region is home to many, many political systems with different history, different peoples, and different traditions. But whether you come from Vietnam or Brunei, China or Indonesia, Japan or Malaysia, we all subscribe to the principle of statehood where our citizens are equal before the law. And we all believe in delivering justice for all.

Rule of law of course is a very simple concept, but it has many fundamental consequences.

If we commit to the rule of law and build our nation upon its foundation, our democracy will become stronger.

If we persist with the rule of law, our capacity for governance will grow.

If we faithfully practice and protect the rule of law, we will be able to generate a climate of trust, confidence and predictability which is necessary to attract resources and promote economic development.

And if we promote rule of law, we will be ensured of social progress and dynamism.

You see, I truly believe that the best way for a country to grow is to produce a system whereby its citizens can have equal access to justice. By doing this, we are not only promoting equality, we are also advancing equal opportunity.

So I hope you realize that, as lawyers in your respective society, you are important agents of change. You will change people's lives, and you will change your country in a way that is very fundamental and far-reaching.

But I have a little word of caution for you. I grew up being a soldier, and I am not a lawyer. But I know that there is much that you can do with the law. You can do a tremendous amount of good with it. But you can also use the law to produce tremendous damage, if exercised irresponsibly. As we build our legal system, we have to avoid a situation where there is much law, but little justice. There is a Chinese proverb which reminds us: "Though the sword of justice is sharp, it will not slain the innocent."

That's why I think it is important to follow not just the letter of the law, but also to observe the ethics and morality. We may belong to different professions, but in the end, our success is judged by our ability in promoting justice and advancing human dignity.

I also think that by promoting the kinds of interaction that take place in this Conference, you are also perfecting the technology for peace. What you do is so important to bridge between peoples and professions, and to promote understanding between peoples of this region.

By strengthening the rule of law throughout this region, and by cementing the legal communities, you will contribute one way or another in making the Asia Pacific region more just, more prosperous and more peaceful.

I wish you all the best in your deliberations. By pronouncing Bismi llahirrahmanirrahim, I hereby declare this meeting and conference officially open.

I thank you.

Wassalamu'alaikum warahmatullahi wabarakatuh.

Bali, May 4, 2005

> *"Indonesia exemplifies to the world how Islam can play a positive and healthy role in a society...The government of President Susilo Bambang Yudhoyono offers the best opportunity in well over a decade to deepen cooperation along a broad front for the purpose of locking in democracy for all the people within a united Indonesia"*—Ambassador (Ret) Alphonse F. La Porta.
>
> (Testimony at U.S. House of Representatives Committee on International Relation's Subcommittee on Asia and the Pacific's hearing on "Indonesia in Transition: Recent Developments and Implications for U.S. Policy", 10 March 2005, Washington D.C.)

"We Indonesians always talk proudly about our national identity, but do not forget that there is also such a thing as "international identity"—how we project ourselves to the outside world, and how we are perceived by the international community."

President Susilo Bambang Yudhoyono
Jakarta, May 19, 2005

"I believe that in 2005, Asia-Africa can be, and must be, more than a "moral force". Much more.
Through this Strategic Partnership, Asia-Africa can be transformed, no longer just as a geographical expression, but as a true geopolitical and geo-economic reality."

President Susilo Bambang Yudhoyono
Jakarta, April 22, 2005

25

"Terorism : A New Fight for ASEAN"

Keynote Speech at The Opening Ceremony of
The 25th Asian Chiefs of Police Conference
(ASEANAPOL)

Denpasar, Bali
May 17, 2005

◆ ◆ ◆ ◆ ◆

Bismilahirrahmanirrahiim
Assalamualaikum warahmatullahi wabarakatuh

Distinguished heads of delegation,
Distinguished guests,
Excellencies,
Ladies and gentlemen,

Before anything else, I am informed that today is the happy occasion of the 25th anniversary of ASEANAPOL. So please accept my congratulations and happy anniversary to all ASEAN Police Forces. We are pleased to celebrate your achievements, and we commend your meritorious service to your nation and to our region.

You know, I too have been married for almost 25 years, and I know from personal experience that any human association that can last as long 25 years must be doing something right.

I am honored to welcome all of you to this important conference of the 25th ASEAN Chiefs of Police (ASEANAPOL) here in Bali.

You have chosen the appropriate place to hold this importance Conference. For it was here in this peaceful island of Bali that mad terrorists committed unspeakable crimes by indiscriminately blowing up two crowded nightclubs in Kuta. That tragedy happened on October 12, 2002, and I think most Indonesians still remember where they were when they first heard about this horrible attack.

The emotional scar from that fateful evening will remain with us for a long time. But the Bali bomb was also a turning point for Indonesia's counter-terrorism efforts.

It ended the debate whether Indonesia was a terrorist target.

It confirmed that a network of terrorist groups were actively operating in our country.

It sparked a swift response that led to the capture of the Bali bombers and their associates.

And most importantly, it put Indonesia firmly on the frontline in the global efforts to fight terrorism.

But what I find to be particularly extraordinary was how the Balinese responded to this rude assault on their peaceful lives. The Balinese did not resort to violent acts. They did not go around seeking vengeance with hatred. Instead, they resorted to prayers to seek solace from their Creator. And they bounced back quickly to reclaim Bali's famous reputation as a peaceful, welcoming paradise, the top tourist destination in the world.

The way the Balinese coped with the tragedy revealed the true character of the Balinese people as a deeply spiritual people imbued with great strength of the mind.

The most important lesson from Bali bomb, however, can be summarized in two words : international cooperation. I remember well the skeptical general public and media pundits who thought that the Government will never be able to crack this case and catch the terrorists. Which is why we commend the talented Police General I Made Mangku Pastika, who is with us today, for leading a highly effective investigation of the Bali bomb.

But with all the talents in his team, General Pastika was also able to count on the support from fellow policemen with a wide array of expertise, from Australian Federal Police, FBI, BKA of Germany, Scotland Yard, Swedish Police, French Police, Dutch Police, Japan National Police Agency, Philippine National Police, ICPO-Interpol and others.

As a result of that international cooperation, most of the Bali bombers are now behind bars, and while some of them are still running, we know who they are.

It was also due to that international cooperation that we were able to uncover the network of terrorist groups in the region.

And that is why you are all here today: to pool resources, to share experiences, to exchange know-how, and to strengthen cooperation that would enable all of us to fight trans-national crimes in all its forms, thus preventing them from harming our citizens.

In some ways, this fight is something rather new for ASEAN. When ASEAN was founded in 1967, Governments in this region faced different sources of threat. Back then, our security, our safety, were endangered by what we now call "conventional" threats or "traditional" threats: armed rebels, ethnic conflicts, military attack, invasion, inter-state warfare, cold war rivalry, nuclear war.

But today, we face a very different world where, apart from the persistence of some traditional threats, we are also haunted by "non-traditional security threats". Terrorism, financial crises, forest fires, drug trafficking, people trafficking, money laundering, economic crimes, cyber crime, diseases, natural disasters.

In many cases, these non-traditional security threats are not only more real, they are also more destructive and more damaging to the lives of our citizens.

Think of what the Bali bomb did to the Bali economy and the larger Indonesian economy.

Think of what SARS did and what AIDS is doing to our generation.

Think of what the giant tsunami killer waves did to the communities around the Indian Ocean.

Each of these threats created far-reaching damages that could exceed the damage done by an invading army.

Indeed, our security paradigm has changed. During the Cold War, governments ensured their national security by keeping intelligence from each other. Today, in the post-Cold War world, or in the post-September 11 era or in post-Bali bomb era, we can ensure our common security only by sharing our intelligence with one another.

In the past, many of us engaged in exclusive security arrangements to protect our country. Today, in the fight against trans-national crime and terrorism, we need to evolve an inclusive approach. We need to cultivate a new security culture which would allow all of us to cooperate with one another, irrespective of whether you are Russian, Chinese, Americans, Australians, Indians or Filipinos.

In the past, our knowledge on security required us to know about grand alliance systems, about non-alignment, about strategic straits, nuclear-free zones, aircraft carriers and weapons system. We still need to know these things, but today, our knowledge on security also requires us to know names and aliases of terrorists such as Dr. Azahari and Noordin Mohamad Top, to know the habits of groups such as Al Qaeda, to know their source of finance, and to know the workings of their sleeper cells and recruiting system.

Ultimately, our success in fighting trans-national crimes depends on a number of variables. It requires us to maintain our political will and stamina to sustain what is sure to be a long-term fight. It necessitates us to allocate appropriate resources to fight these threats. It demands us to develop better networking between our law enforcement agents. It requires us to keep up with technological developments. It requires us to improve the mechanisms by which we coordinate our police, our intelligence, and our immigration and customs officials. And it necessitates us to think outside the box, and to be as adaptive and creative as the terrorists and criminals on the other side of the law.

In the final analysis, the fight against trans-national crimes, especially terrorism, requires us to take comprehensive measures. Military measures alone will not end it, and neither will mere diplomatic and intelligence cooperation. We need to ensure greater law enforcement cooperation, and we also need to address the roots and causes of terrorism.

So as you gather and deliberate on the long list of security issues before you, I hope you know how much your work and collaboration will affect the lives of our peoples. And I hope you know that the peoples of this region are counting on you.

You know, it is generally thought that peace and stability requires the fancy work of statesmen, diplomats and military generals who work to develop peace and promote confidence-building measures.

But as we crossed into the 21st century, it is quite obvious that peace and security in our region will also much depend on the work of the police officers in this region. Simply put, when it comes to protecting our citizens, you are all at the frontline.

I wish you all the best in your deliberations, and by saying Bismilahirrahmanirrahim, I take great pleasure in declaring this conference open.

I thank you.

Wassalamualaikum warahmatullah wabarakatuh

Denpasar – Bali, May 17, 2005

"With her moderate outlook, Indonesia can and should be an active promoter of peace between religions and nations, in particular in a conflict where religion plays a role, as it does in the Middle East, between Israel and the Palestinians."—Emmanuel Shahaf.

(The Jakarta Post, 17 May 2005)

"But being too impressed with demographics or economic statistics, will not get us very far.
The renewed Asia-Africa process that we are trying to nurture will matter only if we can make it relevant to the problems and opportunities of Asia-Africa."

President Susilo Bambang Yudhoyono

Jakarta, April 22, 2005

"There is no use having an independent mind and freedom of action if we end-up making the wrong turns or become marginalized. And there is no sense for us to be different, just for the sake of being different, or to be active just for its own sake. Our independence and activism must therefore be combined with a constructive mindset so that we can attain our national objectives."

President Susilo Bambang Yudhoyono
Jakarta, May 19, 2005

26

"An Independent and Active Foreign Policy for The 21st Century"

Keynote Speech delivered for a Special Event organized by the Indonesian Council on World Affairs: "Indonesia and the World"

Shangrila Hotel, Jakarta
May 19, 2005

♦ ♦ ♦ ♦ ♦

Bismillahirrahmanirrahiim

Assalamualaikum warahmatullahi wabarakatuh

Mr. Chairman,
Your Excellencies,
Distinguished guests,
Ladies and Gentlemen,

A few weeks ago, I received an invitation from ICWA to give what would be my "first foreign policy speech", as President of Indonesia.

I received that invitation with mixed feelings, of relief and anxiety.

Relief, because by inviting me to speak about "Indonesia and the world", ICWA was practically giving me the hint, that I could speak about anything I want. Which is perfectly alright by me.

And anxious, because the topic of "Indonesia and the world" is so large, that while I might know where to begin, I would not know how to end it. I hope the next time ICWA picks a more narrow topic, like the "meaning of life", or "Indonesia and the universe", they would still consider me as a speaker.

Having said that, let me start by commending ICWA for the outstanding job they have done in promoting public understanding of Indonesia's foreign policy. I am honored to be invited here to address this distinguished gathering.

What I will NOT do today is give an overview of Indonesia's foreign policy. There is already a rich body of literature which chronicles Indonesia's diplomatic relations.

And Foreign Minister Hasan Wirayuda has done excellent annual reviews of our foreign policy at the beginning of the year.

Today, I wish to speak about a foreign policy concept that is of fundamental interest to Indonesians. I am referring to the independent and active foreign policy. I will discuss what I think are the elements of that principle, and then relate it to specific foreign policy issues.

Some 57 years ago, in 1948, Vice-President Mohammad Hatta made a speech titled "Mendayung di antara dua karang" or "rowing between two reefs". The reefs that Vice President Hatta referred to in his historic speech were the growing antagonism between two opposing Eastern Communist and Western Capitalist Blocks.

Vice-President Hatta argued strongly that Indonesia must avoid choosing sides between the two blocks. Vice President Hatta was not advocating a policy of neutrality, but he passionately reasoned that Indonesia must strive to be a "subject, not an object" in international affairs, where we determine our own path.

This thinking was then coined as "independent and active foreign policy", and it became one of Muhammad Hatta's most important legacies.

Over the years, governments have come and go, Indonesia has had six Presidents, and our political system has undergone major changes, but "independent and active" remains the primary foreign policy principle for Indonesia.

What I find striking is that in the past 5 decades or so, this basic policy has shown a remarkable degree of resilience and adaptability.

The questions have to be asked : What are the elements of an independent and active foreign policy? And what does it mean to be independent and active today, 57 years after Muhammad Hatta made his famous speech?

We need to ask these questions, because the world we live in today is radically different than the one faced by our forefathers.

Our forefathers did not know the terms and phenomena such as, globalization, interdependence, governance, the internet, cyberworld, CNN, NGOs, sophisticated international terrorist networks--all the things which are part of our present day world.

In fact, whereas Vice-President Hatta in 1948 used the metaphor "rowing between two reefs", today, as we have safely passed the two reefs, I would use the metaphor "navigating a turbulent ocean" to describe the challenge faced by Indonesia's foreign policy.

My purpose today is to go deeper into the concept of "independent and active foreign policy", which has served us so well since the beginning of our Republic, and to sketch how it can better serve Indonesia's national interests in the coming years.

It is not an attempt to rewrite the book, but simply to add more pages to it.

So what are the conceptual properties of independent and active foreign policy?

Well, to begin with, as always, it entails "independence of judgment" and "freedom of action". But I would also add the necessity of a **constructive approach** in the conduct of foreign policy.

Being independent-minded and having freedom of action is indeed critical. But there is no use having an independent mind and freedom of action if we end-up making the wrong turns or become marginalized. And there is no sense for us to be different, just for the sake of being different, or to be active just for its own sake. Our independence and activism must therefore be combined with a constructive mindset so that we can attain our national objectives.

A constructive approach may mean many things.

It denotes an ability to turn adversary into friend, and to turn friend into partner.

It means having the diplomatic, intellectual and emotional capacity to respond to complex foreign policy issues.

It also means putting to rest a siege mentality, wild conspiracy theories, excessive suspicion, an overly defensive attitude, or the fear that the world is out to get us.

In short, constructivism helps us to use our independence and activism to be a peace-maker, confidence-builder, problem-solver, bridge-builder.

This way, our independent and active policy becomes relevant-- relevant to our national interests, relevant to our people, relevant to the international community.

Secondly, independent and active means that we will NOT enter into any military alliances. Indonesia has never engaged in a military pact with a foreign country, and there will be no change in this policy. This also means that we will continue our policy of not allowing any foreign military bases on Indonesian territory. Indonesia does not have a country which we consider a threat or an enemy.

It is also imperative for Indonesia to develop a strategic posture that is non-threatening to its neighbors and to the region. Indeed,

Indonesia must evolve a strategic posture that strengthens peace and stability, regionally and internationally.

Third, an independent and active foreign policy is all about **connectivity**.

Our ability to connect with the wider world is critical to the performance of our independent and active foreign policy. Our connectivity determines our influence and capacity to shape the international order.

Connectivity is a source of diplomatic empowerment.

Remember: in 1955, during a volatile international situation, we connected with Asia and Africa through the Bandung Conference, and sparked a whole new movement, which elevated the role of the developing world in international affairs.

In 1967, when we needed stability for our development, we connected with countries in Southeast Asia to form ASEAN, and changed the face of this region forever.

Connectivity serves our independent and active policy in many ways.

It compels Indonesia to have an active and healthy engagement with its neighbors, with the major powers and emerging powers, with the regions of the world, and with international institutions and a whole range of non-state actors.

It calls on us to find ways to plug into the globalized world.

It obliges us to closely tune-in to regional and international issues which affect us. And it necessitates us to link-up with an array of international actors, including business actors, NGOs and individuals.

It must be remembered, however, that in the very complex world of today, it is impossible to be connected to everything, and to be engaged with every international issue. We must develop the right kind and the right degree of connectivity, one that is consistent with our national objectives, and with our resources.

Fourth, "independent and active" should project Indonesia's **international identity**.

We Indonesians always talk proudly about our national identity, but do not forget that there is also such a thing as "international identity"—how we project ourselves to the outside world, and how we are perceived by the international community.

International identity defines a country's role, place and standing in the world community.

We should be a country that has a solid national identity, but also a strong international identity.

Our international identity must be rooted in a strong sense of who we are. We cannot be all things to all people. We must know who we are and what we believe in, and project them in our foreign policy.

The bottom line is this. We are a proud nation who cherish our independence and national unity. We are the fourth most populous nation in the world. We are home to the world's largest muslim population. We are the world's third largest democracy. We are also a country where democracy, Islam and modernity go hand-in-hand. We will stay our course with ASEAN as the cornerstone of our foreign policy. And our heart is always with the developing world, to which we belong.

These are the things that define who we are, and what we do in community of nations.

We are also proud of our diplomatic heritage. Indonesia convened the historic Asian-African Conference in 1955. We are a founding member of the Non-Aligned Movement. We are a founding member of ASEAN. We are at the forefront of North-South Dialogue. We were at the forefront of the international law of the sea diplomacy. We helped the peace settlement in Cambodia and in the Southern Philippines. We are helping to manage potential conflicts in the South China Sea. We helped design the ASEAN Security Community. We have always been active in shaping regional order. And recently, we hosted the historic second Asian-African Summit in Jakarta.

This long history of intense and creative diplomatic activism shapes our international identity.

Fifth, independent and active foreign policy should **reflect our true brand of nationalism**. Nationalism is of course on the rise in Indonesia, a trend that we also see in many other countries. But our nationalism is not an angry or arrogant one. We do not subscribe to narrow nationalism, ultra nationalism, or self-absorbed nationalism. We do not overestimate ourselves, and nor do we underestimate others. We treat big, medium and small-sized powers with equal respect.

Remember: what makes Indonesia great and relevant is that we have a brand of nationalism that is open, confident, moderate, tolerant and outward looking. And as our nation grows, we must make sure that we strengthen this brand of nationalism.

Our ability to maintain this right kind of nationalism is important to our neighbors, to our region, and is a source of our authority and respect at the international arena.
So this brand of nationalism—the open, moderate, tolerant and outward-looking nationalism--must be at the root of our internationalism.

So these are the elements of independent and active foreign policy, which we have implemented with remarkable consistency throughout the years. It is hardly an exhaustive list, and the able members of ICWA may want to dig deeper into them.

Ladies and Gentlemen,

Let me now move on to the challenges we are facing in implementing our independent and active principle. Of these challenges, the challenge of security is often the first that comes to mind.

In this enlightened age, weapons of mass destruction, including nuclear, biological and chemical weapons, continue to proliferate.

We have to live with the reality or threat of armed conflict not only between states but within states. That is why the trade in small arms and light weapons is so rampant.

As if these were not enough, we have to confront threats of terrorism and other transnational crimes, massive illegal migration, epidemics and degradation of the environment.

Then there is the challenge of development, which is basically the problem of poverty.

Some 1.1 billion human beings, most of them in Asia and Africa, live on just about a dollar a day. Every day some 20,000 of them die, because they are too poor to live. Those who survive are attended by the pangs of hunger, and the crippling effects of ignorance and disease.

Poverty is so widespread in the developing world, because of the crushing impact of the debt burden, the inability of poor countries to access export markets, the steady spread of epidemics, the implosion of cities, and the degradation of the environment. These are threats spawned by the imbalances and inequities of international economic relations.

Not all the challenges of the world situation today are totally unwelcome. There is the challenge of democracy.

All over the world, people are seized with a desire to take their destiny in their own hands, to personally choose who will govern them, and to take part in the decision-making processes that affect their lives.

If a government can accommodate the desire of its people to claim their basic rights, the results can be exceedingly positive for the country itself, for its region and for the world at large. This is precisely what happened in Indonesia and several other Asian countries in recent times. Earlier, it happened in South Africa. It is now beginning to happen in the Middle East and elsewhere.

These challenges clamour for an effective response—for action.

Indonesia is addressing these challenges in all the appropriate multilateral forums, through bilateral arrangements, and through individual national initiatives. The foremost multilateral forum through which we address these challenges is, of course, the United Nations.

We are aware that the UN Secretary-General, in his report, "In Larger Freedom: Toward Development, Security and Humanright For All ", has presented a carefully formulated package of proposals in the interrelated fields of development, security and human rights, as well as for UN reform.

We agree with the basic thrust of the report—that we cannot have security without development, nor can we have development without security, nor can we have both of them without respect for human rights. We share the Secretary-General's view that, at the global level we can effectively tackle these basic challenges only through a reformed and revitalized United Nations.

In this context, we have always urged that the composition and procedures of the Security Council be reformed—to make the

Council more democratic and representative of the present world constellation.

We have always stood for the immediate implementation of the Monterey consensus, and for the completion of the Doha round of trade negotiations in a way that will favor development.

In the same context, we appeal to our developed partners to relieve the developing world of the debt burden and to allocate 0.7 percent of their gross domestic product for official development aid.

We look forward to the reform of the UN Human Rights Commission. In the meantime, as Chairman of that Commission, we are striving as much as we can during our tenure to advance all human rights all over the world.

We will continue to wage an advocacy for non-proliferation of all weapons of mass destruction and for disarmament. We keenly anticipate the conclusion of a convention on terrorism.

We are carefully studying the package of proposals presented by the Secretary-General and in September, we will seek and work for collective action in response to these proposals.

At the inter-regional level, we are actively involved in the development of the New Asian-African Strategic Partnership. With our Asian-African partners, we are developing concrete projects to address the basic challenges facing the countries of the two continents. One major initiative will be the development of a disaster early warning and response system in the Indian Ocean area. This Partnership can also help in the quest for peace in the Middle East, and help bring about a state of Palestine living in peace with its neighbors within secure, internationally recognized borders.

The individual countries in this Partnership may be poor, but our combined economic power can be enormous, if wisely consolidated and infused with synergy.

At the regional and sub-regional level, the mainstay of our foreign relations is our involvement with ASEAN.   With the rest of the ASEAN family, we are now building an ASEAN Community that rests on the pillars of a Security Community, an Economic Community, and a Socio-cultural Community.   In building this Community, we in ASEAN are taking full responsibility for our own security.   We will also complete our integration into a single free trade and investment area.

It is Indonesia's hope that in the process, ASEAN will develop and nurture common values, particularly those that promote human dignity and freedom.   The cause of democracy and human rights will thereby be advanced in this part of the world.

Apart from that, a larger integration process will be launched at the East Asia Summit in Kuala Lumpur later this year.   This Summit will gain significance by virtue of the expected participation not only of ASEAN and its Northeast Asian neighbors—China, Japan and South Korea—but also of India, Australia and New Zealand.

ASEAN, however, should remain in the driver's seat, and should continue to be the centre of gravity of the integration process.

There is as yet no clear-cut architecture of the East Asia grouping that will result from this Summit. But it is possible to anticipate the development of an East Asia community by 2012.

ASEAN-China, ASEAN-Japan and ASEAN-India free trade areas will be in place by 2010, and today Australia and New Zealand are seeking intensified economic engagement with ASEAN.

It is just a matter of time, before the separate arrangements are welded together, to form one immense and powerful economic unit. When that community comes into existence, it will comprise about half of the world's population and include the second largest economy, and the two most dynamic of the great economies in the world today.

In all these developments, you can expect Indonesia to be playing an active and catalytic role. Our capability to bring nations together, so that they can interact with significant results, has been proven in the Asian-African Summit.

At the same time, we will remain actively engaged with Europe, Latin America, and the rest of the Pacific region.

Ladies and gentlemen,

Let me conclude by saying this: those of you who have been in this country would feel that there is a new energy in Indonesia since the end of last year. I hope you would also notice the same energy in our foreign policy. Foreign policy has a critical role in my administration, and I hope all the Indonesian diplomats who are in this room know that I have high hopes for them and that I am counting on your creativity and contribution.

After all, we have today an Indonesia that is capable and eager to actively engage the international community in the common task of building a better world.

Let me end my speech on that optimism.
Thank you.

Wassalamualaikum Warrahmatullahi Wabarakatuh

Jakarta, May 19, 2005

"Many investors and Indonesian consumers are betting Yudhoyono will reach his goal of lifting gross domestic product growth in the world's fourth largest country to 7.2 percent in 2009. After his election, the Jakarta Composite Index rose 40 percent to a record 1152 on March 22 before falling back to 1142 on March 23. That compares with a 4 percent rise in the Standard & Poor's 500 Index in that period. GDP jumped 6.7 percent in the final quarter of 2004 -- the most in nine years -- from a year earlier as Indonesians bought more products ranging from cars and motorcycles to clove cigarettes."—William Mellor.

(Bloomberg News, 24 March 2005)

"This is a key challenge for the next five years, namely how to accelerate sustainable economic growth by consolidating micro-reform while maintaining macro-economic stabilization."

President Susilo Bambang Yudhoyono
Jakarta, January 19, 2005

27

"A Message from Nada to Maggie"

Speech at The Asia-Pacific American Heritage Event

White House-Washington DC, USA
May 25, 2005

♦ ♦ ♦ ♦ ♦

President Bush,
Distinguished guests,
Ladies and gentlemen,

Thank you, Mr. President, for inviting me to join you here today.

I stand before you here to deliver a message of thanks from a grateful nation half way around the world.

My country, Indonesia, suffered most from the horrible tsunami last December. Some 200,000 people were killed in a matter of minutes, and over 500,000 survivors lost their homes.

When I arrived in Aceh the day after the tsunami, almost everything close to the sea had been destroyed, flattened to the ground, swept by the waves.

Nothing had ever prepared us for something like this. Nothing.

It was under these circumstances that we experienced an incredible display of global solidarity immediately after the tsunami.

And it was during this desperate time that American servicemen came and helped.

The USS Abraham Lincoln arrived with its much-needed helicopters to help deliver food and supplies to survivors that could not be reached by land. And USS hospital ship Mercy provided medical care to the injured and the sick at a time when we were all worried that more people would die from diseases than from the tsunami.

I remember my heart almost sank one day when I heard that a US Seahawk helicopter had crashed. But I was glad to hear directly from Ambassador Lynn Pascoe that the crews were alright, even though their Seahawks had to make an emergency landing on a paddy field. And not surprisingly, the crews were itching to get back into action to save lives.

America has every reason to be proud for what your Government, your citizens and your volunteers have done for the tsunami victims.

This was a time for valor and selfless sacrifice. The tsunami produced a lot of heroes. Heroes who saved lives. Heroes who gave hope to those who are suffering. And Americans were among these heroes. You all should be proud of that.

The funds that have been collected from millions of Americans will be very helpful to help the Acehnese rebuild their lives.

But I want you to know what really mattered was that they all came from the heart.

What really mattered was that each of you reached not so much into your pocket as into the new depth of your conscience, compassion and solidarity.

What really mattered was that you saw the pain of others and tried to help.

And with all our tears, words and deeds, what we all did together was to prove that the greatest wrath of nature was no match for the greater force that is the human spirit.

I said something earlier about reaching out. Let me read you a letter from Maggie, a 3rd grader from K-4 elementary in Charlevoix, Michigan, which through some good fortune I managed to obtain from Americorps.

Maggie was writing to a tsunami kid she did not know. This is what Maggie wrote :

"Dear friend,

Hi, my name is Maggie. I am sorry what happened in your country. I have heard some things about it. I hope your family and friends are okay. In church, I pray for you and your country. In school, we are raising money for your country. We have a loose change bucket and kids bring money in. Also, we are making tsunami bracelets to raise money too. I have made you one. I hope you like it. I will continue praying you and your country in church. Your friend, Maggie."

I faxed Maggie's letter to Aceh to be passed on to an Acehnese youngster, and a few days later, I received a response letter from Nada Luthfiyyah, a young girl from Banda Aceh. This is what Nada looks like (showing a photo of Nada). Nada wrote to Maggie, and I translate into English :

"My good friend, Hello friend. My name is Nada Luthfiyyah. I was so happy and my heart was touched to receive the letter you sent us. My family—my dad, mom, older brother and younger brother have disappeared, and now I live with my cousin. I hope you are healthy and well where you are. I am so glad you are paying attention to us here. I hope to receive your bracelet in the coming days because I want to wear it on my arm to remind me that I have new friend. Your friend, Nada".

I have asked my Ambassador, Sumadi, to personally deliver Nada's letter and photo to Maggie in Charlevoix, Michigan.

These two letters are extraordinary both in the words they conveyed and in the fact that two youngster from entirely different backgrounds made a connection.

An American girl who prays at church, collect loose change and make bracelets for tsunami kids two oceans away.

An Indonesian muslim girl who lost all her family and wants to kill the pain and is eager just to be a kid again, just like Maggie.

I think the world would be a better place if all of us start to have connections and conversations the way Maggie and Nada did.

I thank you.

Washington DC, May 25, 2005

"*For the past few years, most news reports from Indonesia have featured terrorist, regional insurgencies, and human rights violations. They portray a government that is dealing ineffectively with these problems and an economy that is falling further behind its Asian neighbors. Developments beneath the surface, however, lead to a more hopeful view: Indonesia—the world's fourth most populous country and the largest by far with a Muslim majority—is undergoing a profound political transition. Over the past five years, its democratic system has been overhauled quietly but brilliantly, and the foundations for a better system of governance have been put in place...Thanks to the brilliance of the recent political restructuring, the odds are good that Indonesia's transformation will proceed smoothly...The current experiment is now six years old, and it has a better record. But if the next government is unable to deliver more employment opportunities and to reduce corruption and senseless violence, Indonesia's political transition could stall and slip into reverse—a prospect that should be equally troubling to Indonesia's people and to the rest of the world.*"
—Lex Rieffel.

(Foreign Affairs, September/October 2004)

PHOTO BY ANUNG

"We cannot have development if hatred thrives, if bigotry and prejudice rule, if ignorance prevails, if conflicts flare."

President Susilo Bambang Yudhoyono
Medan, March 10, 2005

"When was the last time we saw this pervasive act of global kindness, compassion and solidarity?"

President Susilo Bambang Yudhoyono
Singapore, February 16, 2005

28

"Indonesia and America in A Changing World"

Keynote Speech at the Gala Dinner tendered by
The United States and Indonesia Society (USINDO)

Mandarin Oriental Hotel-Washington DC, USA
May 25, 2005

◆ ◆ ◆ ◆ ◆

Bismillahirrahmanirrahim

Thank you, Senator Kitt Bond, for your kind introduction, and thank you for your friendship for Indonesia. If you could kindly print me a copy of that very generous introduction ...

My first order of business is to invite all of you to give a big hand to honor Ambassador Al Laporta, Ambassador Ed Masters, Aleen Masters of USINDO, for the great work they have done all these years to get Indonesia and America closer.

The best badge of honor you can proudly wear is our great admiration and utmost respect for your tremendous contribution to the peoples of Indonesia and America.

I also commend the US-ASEAN Business Council—Matt Daley, Walter Lohman, Bob Heinz and colleagues—for their dedication and tireless work to promote business ties between America and ASEAN.

I am pleased to see all of you here tonight. Just in case some of you thought you came to the wrong reception, let me confirm that my name is Susilo Bambang Yudhoyono. I feel it necessary to say my name because a few months ago, I was introduced by someone as President Yoko Ono.

I come from a small village called Pacitan, in East Java. After graduating from high school, I joined the military, got married, earned a graduate Degree in the United States, led a peace keeping unit in Bosnia, got my 4 star, became a Minister, left the Government, joined the elections, and became Indonesia's sixth President last year. That is the short version, of course; the long version is actually much more complicated than that.

You know, this is my second keynote address for USINDO. I will never forget my first USINDO keynote address in 2003. Of all the 365 days that were available in the year for me to speak, USINDO managed to pick the one evening where the mighty hurricane Isabelle shut down Washington, DC. And I don't know how they did it, but USINDO managed to get a full hall of people who braved hurricane Isabelle. There was a moment when I suspected that they dressed up hotel staff in tuxedos to attend my keynote address.

I think USINDO is trying to make it up for me tonight by selecting a warm, lovely summer evening for me to speak before an even larger audience. And let me tell you, Al, that it's ...working!

I must admit, however, that tonight I see a force that is much stronger, much more powerful than hurricane Isabel. That force is the radiant spirit of friendship and goodwill that warms our evening tonight.

It is with that spirit that I come to this great country of yours.

And it is that spirit, that force, that drives the relations between America and Indonesia.

Today, I met with President Bush to discuss how to strengthen our bilateral relations. We agreed that our relations are stable and strong. I think we emerged from that meeting with an understanding that this relationship is too important to be taken for granted, and too promising to be taken lightly.

Ladies and Gentlemen,

I am sure you have noticed that something has happened to the relations between Indonesia and America recently.

There has been an incredibly deep emotional connection between America and Indonesia since the tsunami. Mainstream America became visually and emotionally exposed to Indonesia's tremendous agony. President Clinton told me that one third of the American households contributed to the tsunami victims, a display of solidarity that is perhaps unheard of in US history.

And on the ground in Aceh, the US military and the Indonesian military worked together day and night to find the dead and bury them, while saving the survivors. I was amazed to learn that the crews of USS Abraham Lincoln flew 2,800 missions in Aceh and Nias to deliver food, medicine, water to tsunami survivors. I was also moved to hear the devotion of the doctors and nurses on board USNS Mercy who performed over 19,000 medical procedures for tsunami victims in Aceh and Nias.

Which is why when the USS Lincoln and USNS Mercy ended their humanitarian mission in Aceh and Nias, they left behind thankful patients, tearful friends, and a grateful nation. You should all be proud of what America has done to help the tsunami victims.

The tsunami ordeal sparked global solidarity, but it also gave the world an insight into true face of Indonesia.

Look, I know that Indonesia has suffered from an image problem in the last few years. The financial crises, capital flight, political instability, ethnic conflict, the East Timor mayhem in 1999, separatist rebellions, the Bali bomb, the Marriot bomb, forest fires. All these events shaped international perception towards Indonesia.

But they no longer paint an accurate picture of what the present Indonesia is all about.

I have come tonight to present you with a sketch of Indonesia's profiles, as I see them from my office. These profiles, I think, reflect the real portrait of today's Indonesia.

The first of these is what I call the profile of courage.

These days, you see it all around the country, as we embrace and sweat for change.

But I saw it most clearly during the despair of the tsunami, when the whole of Indonesia wept, and came together.

The rich, the poor, children, students, housewives, artists--everyone got into the act of caring and contributing. No other event has brought the whole country together like this.

And in Aceh, courage was the common currency. I saw the ultimate sacrifice in our soldiers who drowned while trying to save the people. And I saw courage in the eyes of the soldiers I met at Meulaboh, who remained in their post to rescue the people, even as they found out that their family had perished. I saw the undying spirit in a young girl I met in Nias, who lost her entire family but told me the only thing she wanted to do was, to go back to school so she can be children again. I saw compassion in the thousands of volunteers who went to Aceh and Nias to bury the dead, risking infectious diseases.

And I saw an incredible will to survive in an Acehnese kid named Martunis, only 7 years old, who survived the tsunami after being adrift for 21 days in the open sea. He taught himself to eat instant noodles, and survived on just a few bottles of mineral water that floated by him in the water. He was found on January 15th. Because Martunis was wearing a replica of famous soccer player Rui Costa, the Portuguese national players are now looking after his rehabilitation.

In short, the tsunami has produced thousands of nameless heroes. It reaffirms the dictum that Indonesia is always at its best in the moment of our greatest despair.

This profile of courage, compassion and solidarity is what I want you to remember about the true face of Indonesia.
Then there is the profile of a democratic Indonesia.

Last year, we held one of the most ambitious, and most complex elections anywhere in the world. Over a period of 9 months, 3 rounds of elections were held: one Parliamentary round, and two Presidential rounds. What I find to be remarkable is that, it seemed like Indonesians cannot get enough of elections : in each of the three elections, voters turned out exceeded 110 million, making it a total of over 350 million voters for the whole year. Forgive me for saying this, but that is a larger voting turn-out than in the US.

We held the free and fair elections in our terms, in our own way, with our own resources. No one can dispute that, the Indonesian people have full ownership of our democracy.

I think the 2004 elections changed Indonesia for good.

It showed that Indonesians were not afraid of change.

It brought about new style and new standard of campaigning, which by consequence modernized Indonesian politics. It showed that Indonesia can pass through the second free and fair multi-party elections and secured a peaceful transfer of Government, which is a benchmark for democratic maturity.

It changed the political landscape, for the first time installing a President with a strong popular mandate, chosen not by political party but directly by the voters.

And most importantly, it produced widespread hope among Indonesians.

And those of you with business plans in Indonesia will be pleased to know that the overall result of the 2004 elections is a political order with greater stability, durability and predictability.

That is the face of democratic Indonesia.

And that is why, the relations between Indonesia and America today is different than before. Ours is now a unique relationship between two democracies, between the world's two largest democracies, between the world's oldest democracy and a younger democracy.

Ladies and Gentlemen,

I wish to tell you another face of Indonesia.

I call it the profile of change. My good friend Adam Schwarz, who came into my office a few weeks ago, called it a "new energy" in Indonesia.
Whatever you call it, many would tell you that Indonesia feels differently now.

A heat of change is upon us.

There are so many anecdotes that tell this story of change.

You see it in the corruption investigations of one of Indonesia's largest state-owned Bank, Bank Mandiri, or in the investigation of the Electoral Commission's shady procurement practice. You see it in declining smuggling activities at our ports. You see it in the fact that, for the first time, over 400 hundred people from many different elements have been detained for illegal logging. You see it in the fact that 37 officials—including Governors, mayors, regents and members of Parliament--are under investigation or being tried for corruption. You see it in the way we investigate the suspicious death of human rights activist, Munir.

My favourite story is of a provincial Government official who immediately cancelled his order of 9 expensive Mercedes Benz after I was sworn-in as President—a wise move, I must say.

Daily and weekly, you read stories in the media that tell you that Indonesia is back on its feet, that we are trying to do the right things.

We are undergoing a sweeping process of change and creative reconstruction. Some of them are relatively easy, others are painful.

And if you go by the numbers, I think we are on the right track. The rupiah is stable. The economy grew by 6, 4 % in the last quarter, despite the tsunami. We have one of the lowest budget deficits in Asia. Our stock market peaked to over 1.000. And for the first time, we are seeing net capital inflows. If you don't believe me, ask the rating agencies—S&P, Moody, Fitch—who have given Indonesia higher marks recently.

Finally, there is the profile of internationalism.

It means that Indonesia is no longer preoccupied with just domestic affairs, and the cliché about Indonesia being inward-looking no longer applies to us.

Indonesia is now an outward-looking country very much eager to shape regional and international order, and intent on having our voice heard.

It is a sign of our new internationalism that for the first time in Indonesia's history, my Presidential inauguration in October last year was attended by foreign leaders and special envoys, from Australia, Brunei Darussalam, China, Japan, Malaysia, Singapore, Timor Leste, Thailand.

In the last 6 months, we have actively projected Indonesia's new internationalism. At the ASEAN Summit, we strongly pushed for the ASEAN Security Community, and we are now at the forefront of the efforts to convene the "East Asia Summit".

After the tsunami, we called for global solidarity to help the tsunami victims around the Indian Ocean, and in early January, we held a tsunami summit in Jakarta attended by ASEAN leaders, leaders of tsunami-hit countries and donor countries, the UN Secretary-General, President of the World Bank.

And a few weeks ago, we hosted the Asian-African Summit in Jakarta attended by 106 countries, where a New Strategic Partnership was declared between Asian and African countries, to work for peace and prosperity.

The point is clear: internationalism will be very much part of Indonesia's dynamism in the next 5 years.

So these are the faces of Indonesia, which I see and hope you will remember. It is a profile of courage in facing the wrath of tsunami. It is profile of a vibrant democracy. It is the profile of change. And it is a profile of internationalism, in the pursuit of our independent and active foreign policy.

The total sum is a country in transformation. Not just a changing—but transforming.

You know, in 2001, my favorite columnist, Thomas Friedman, called Indonesia (along with Russia), "a messy state, too big to fail, too messy to work".

Well, if Thomas Friedman were to revisit Indonesia today, I would show him that Indonesia now is not "messy state", but a "fully-functioning democracy".

Ladies and Gentlemen,
Dear friends,

I have come here to America to strengthen our bilateral relations, but also because I believe that Indonesia and America have a very good opportunity to work together, to promote international peace and prosperity. Indonesia's independent and active foreign policy requires us to have a stable, strong, constructive and broad-based engagement with America.

I should like to share a few thoughts on a question, that many of my American friends have asked me: what should be America's role in the world? How should America engage the world?

Well, let me say this. The United States wields enormous power and influence in world affairs. It is referred to as the only remaining superpower in the world, the only country able to project its power anywhere around the globe. The United States has the world's largest economy, has the world's largest defense budget, has world's largest spending on intelligence, and has the world's largest diplomatic machinery. It also has nuclear weapons and is a permanent member of the UN Security Council. And its sense of nationalism today, particularly since 9-11, is highest than it has ever been.

The usage of America's enormous power, therefore, is a matter of great interest to the rest of the world.

The present and future world order will be determined by how America uses that enormous power at her disposal, and, more importantly, how she shares and allocate her resources to promote peace and prosperity.

America's enormous power is a source of security to some, and insecurity for others.

That is why, I think it is important for the US to project and emphasize more of its soft power. The US has no shortage of soft power: in terms of culture, values, sports, entertainment, business, education, science and technology, living standard, media, the US

has tremendous appeal to the international community. Remember:
the use of soft power charms and disarms. Hard power, on the other
hand, if it is used incorrectly, provokes resistance and, sometimes,
resentment.

America's engagement with the world has strongly emphasized
democracy, but perhaps there is a more important theme:
Governance. Governance, in my view, is the ideology of the 21st
century.

With governance, democracy thrives; without it, democracy fails.
If the world is to change for the better, it will require more than
the expansion of democracies, it requires the greater employment
of governance.

America's engagement with the world should also stress on
tolerance-- not just freedom, but also tolerance.

I would venture to say that in some cases, tolerance is more
important than freedom. It is tolerance that sets us free.
It is through tolerance that we can attain genuine peace.
It is tolerance that protects freedom, harness diversity
and delivers progress. It is tolerance that makes openness
manageable. In fact, I would even venture to say, that in the
affairs between states and within state, the real division is
those who embrace tolerance and inclusion, and those who
do not.

And when it comes to tolerance, no one has a monopoly. Whether
you are big, medium or small, we all can learn from one another.

We in Indonesia would also like to see the flowering of multilateralism on the international scene—so that we may see the grandeur of American leadership. For a leader does not work alone. A leader works with and through others. We would like to see America leading a multilateral global partnership, for peace and development.

In particular, the international community expects America to lead in the efforts to meet the Millenium Development Goals, which includes the goal to half the number of people living in poverty by 2015. The Millenium Development Goals has a unique uniting value, because it is not determined individually by a particular power, rather it is set collectively and democratically, by the community of nations.

I think, I also speak for the international community in expressing the hope, that the United States will remain open to students from all over the world.

I know, it is the natural instinct of Americans to want to change the world. What I would like to tell you is that the best way for America to change the world is to share your knowledge with the world. Remember: this is coming from a President, who graduated from Webster University in Kansas.

The United States is still the number one choice for Indonesian students who want to study abroad. And I am glad that today President Bush affirmed his desire to see more Indonesian students studying in America.

My final advise to America relates to something that my father taught me and a well-known virtue of Asian cultures. It is called: patience.

Everything about the American culture is super fast—just like globalization, just like the ATM machine. But the world is a big supermarket, where everyone runs on different speed. The world also has different clocks.

In such a world, patience, combined with perseverance, can be just the key to unlock the many problems of our world.
So be brave, America, but also be patient.

So these are my two-cents worth of advise to America.

If they are worth anything, it is because they come from the heart, and they come from a friend.

Ladies and gentlemen,

I have now come to the end of my remarks. Or perhaps more accurately, I have now completely run out of things to say to you.

I appreciate seeing all of you here tonight, and I speak on behalf of my people to thank you all for your friendship and goodwill for Indonesia.

Have a good evening, and God bless you all.

Thank you.

Washington DC, May 25, 2005

"Fifty years after international acknowledgement of its independence, Indonesia's nationalism is most likely to be expressed through attempts to reassert a regional diplomatic role. Such a leading role was diminished by the impact of economic adversity and political turmoil. To reclaim such a role, Indonesia would need to demonstrate substantive evidence of economic recovery, which requires an inter-dependence with the global economy and its institutions"—Michael Leifer.

(Michael Leifer (ed) Asian Nationalism (London: Routledge, 2000).

"Despite the growing uneasiness in the market, we believe that the country fundamentals remain well intact. In fact, we believe in the general perception that as risk aversion deteriorates (higher rates and slower exports), Indonesia being a high-yield country, should be most exposed.

(Deutsche Bank Indonesia Strategy Report, 13 May 2005)

"There are some things that cannot be measured by numbers and statistics. Employment may rise, inflation may go down, and the GDP may go up, but none of these things mean much if the nation as a whole becomes insecure, if conflicts persist, if it loses its fiber, if it loses its sense of identity."

President Susilo Bambang Yudhoyono
Singapore, February 16, 2005

"We have all heard the cliché "think globally, act locally".
The problem is that few of us, if any, understand how
globalization works. And for those who slightly understand
it, even fewer would understand what to do about it, and
how to make globalization work for us."

President Susilo Bambang Yudhoyono
Medan, March 10, 2005

29

"Rebuilding Aceh"

Keynote Speech before
The American Chamber of Commerce

Washington DC, USA
May 26, 2005

♦ ♦ ♦ ♦ ♦

Mr. Chairman,
Excellencies,
Distinguished Members of the American Chamber of Commerce,
Ladies and Gentlemen,

I am delighted and honored to be in the midst of so many true friends of Indonesia. But as I address you there is a part of me that keeps saying: "I wish I did not have to stand here and make a speech."

And the reason is: I have been told that a President always looks wiser when he is sitting down with his mouth shut.

But today I must stand up before you and speak. I want to seize this occasion to deliver to you an important message, a message of thanks from the people of Indonesia.

We appreciate all that the Government and people of the United States have done to help us in the hour of our greatest need. That was when tragedy in the form of earthquake and tsunami struck in our part of the world last December.

It was the day after Christmas, a bright Sunday morning when the earthquake and tsunami struck. Mothers, children, fishermen and small traders were on the beaches going through their morning routine. Vacationers were also on the beaches in large numbers.

In an instant, trillions of tons of seawater poured in, crushing and drowning the life out of all creatures caught in its wash and destroying all structures that stood in its way.

The catastrophe was unprecedented in its geographical scope, its fury reaching as far as the eastern coasts of Africa. Its destructive intensity can only be gauged by the sizes of the population it devastated.

The total death toll in several Asian and African countries reached some 200,000. As you all know, Indonesia suffered by far the greatest loss. In Aceh and Nias alone, the known death toll was about 120,000 with another 100,000 still missing.

What pains us deeply is the vast number of children who died in that tragedy. Even the children who survived must face a life without the loving care of parents who perished in the disaster.

Ladies and Gentlemen,

The response to this unprecedented catastrophe was also unprecedented. The governments concerned, the world community and international institutions, civic spirited organizations and even individuals promptly went into vigorous action.

Many of them were on the site of the tragedy within hours.

Millions of individuals all over the world dug deep into their pockets to contribute to the fund for Aceh. Others used their credit cards. But they all acted out of compassion and solidarity for the suffering of their fellow humankind.

We gratefully count the United States and the American people as among those who immediately responded with money and logistical resources, and sent rescue teams and relief workers.

With the help of friends from all over the world, including our American friends, we managed to complete all rescue and emergency relief work ahead of the expected time frame.

A good number of food stalls and small shops in Aceh and Nias are back in business. Schools are open. Mosques and churches are receiving their faithful. And we are now in the midst of reconstruction and rehabilitation work.

So the hard part begins.

In Aceh, whole districts of urban centres, entire towns and villages were leveled. At one time, all economic activity and all government administration and public services ground to a halt.

Apart from the horrendous loss of lives, the losses in public and private properties easily amounted to $5 billion, or the entire gross domestic product of Aceh.

A devastated environment had to be regenerated so that it can once again be a source of human livelihood. Not only houses but entire communities had to be reconstructed from scratch. Thousands of small businesses had to be restarted.

Admittedly some communities were impatient with the pace of reconstruction. We understand how they feel.

But we also had to take time to plan and to ensure not only coordination of our efforts but their relevance to the actual needs of the people. We especially had to plan for transparency, particularly in the disbursement of donated funds.

My administration worked double-time to devise a Master Plan for the rehabilitation and reconstruction of Aceh. We also put in place a Rehabilitation and Reconstruction Implementation Agency or BAPEL to carry out the strategy of the Plan with concrete programmes for the devastated communities.

We made sure that the programmes reflect the needs and sensitivities of the communities, rather than the priorities of the donors or the Government.

In the preparation of the Master Plan, which was supervised by our National Planning Agency, working groups in Jakarta linked with parallel working groups in Aceh, which represented the communities and their leaders.

These went through a workshop process that gained from valuable inputs from the World Bank, the Asia Development Bank, Australia, Japan and the United States. The result is a matching of community needs with reconstruction projects, based on the perceptions of the community members themselves.

Because donors are concerned about governance and accountability for funds, timely information on the status of programmes and disbursements will be regularly posted on the website e-Aceh based at the National Planning Agency.

We are determined that not a single cent will be lost on the way to the tsunami victims. We have a duty to use all funds entrusted to us wisely, effectively and responsibly. This is my personal commitment to you.

Keeping an eye on the flow of money will be an independent Advisory Board including eminent persons and government ministers reporting directly to the President.

Also on the watch will be a Supervisory Board made up of technical experts, community representatives and donor representatives.

Reporting directly to the President, the Supervisory Board will be responsible for governance oversight, audit, monitoring and the handling of complaints.

The five-pillar strategy of the Master Plan covers (1) restoring purely public infrastructures such as roads and schools; (2) restoring public facilities in support of private activities, such as markets;

(3) stimulating the local economy by, for instance, creating jobs; (4) restoring the capacities of local governments; and (5) securing the communities against possible future disasters.

Ladies and Gentlemen,

We have given the leadership of the BAPEL to Dr. Kuntoro Mangkusubroto, who brings to the position exactly what we need— a practical mind and a clean record of devoted public service.

With BAPEL in place, we can now accelerate rehabilitation and reconstruction work. And there are now a number of reliable mechanisms available for the private sector to channel contributions to the reconstruction of Aceh.

There is, for instance, the Multi-donor Trust Fund (MDTF) established and managed jointly by the Government of Indonesia and the World Bank.

By joining the Fund, a private firm can combine with others in order to pursue larger programmes with greater reach and impact. Within the Fund, it would be so much easier to achieve coordination and to keep track of the use of resources.

Or a private firm may choose to set up its own foundation with its own private trust for Aceh, in accordance with laws and regulations. The management costs will be higher, but there might be greater satisfaction on the part of the donor.

There are also other ways in between these two contrasting options.

For instance, a private firm can contribute funds to an existing project of international or bilateral donors.

It can provide parallel funding to an NGO so that this NGO can work with a donor that already has a project.

Two or more private firms can join forces and set up their own trust fund for the purpose of carrying out a project.

Or a private firm can simply extend a grant to an NGO or strike up a management contract with a consulting firm to implement a separate project under its own oversight and management control.

We will not impose a rigid blueprint on donors. So long as the project is within the purview of the Master Plan and all aspects of it are transparent and monitored so that it is coordinated with other efforts within the Plan, we will welcome it.

Indeed, it is absolutely essential that there be coordination between the donor and the government, and among the donors themselves.

It must be said that it is not enough to simply raise a large amount of money. It is just as important that we are coordinated, for otherwise there will be bottlenecks. And, then, money will not flow efficiently to where it is urgently needed. This we must avoid.

I must also stress that the Master Plan is not a rigid and dogmatic blueprint. It is a dynamic and living statement of intentions and commitment of resources. It will necessarily change as we make progress and we learn from our experiences in the field. And I am sure that there will be much to learn.

As we monitor activities in the field, we evaluate, and as a result of our evaluation we may have to make adjustments in the Plan.

As I said, this is not the easy part. There is no easy part in the work of reconstruction and rehabilitation.

But at stake is the future of the people of Aceh. They have suffered much, and lost much. Many of them have lost everything but their lives. They have, however, shown amazing endurance and courage, and a great will to live and move on to rebuild their shattered lives.

They do not want to live on charity forever.

I have no doubt that, with your help, it is only matter of time before Aceh makes a full recovery. And I like to think that, in the Acehnese, we are looking at a trait that is common to all of us Indonesians. We are resilient.

Seven years ago, all of Indonesia was in the clutches of the Asian financial crisis. And we were in the midst of a political tumult.

But we have since bounced back. Today we are consolidating our economic recovery as foreign direct investors once again are demonstrating their confidence in the Indonesian economy.

Last year's gross domestic product growth of 5.3 percent, the highest since the Asian financial crisis of 1997-98, was led by rising exports and a surge in foreign investments. In the first quarter of this year, we surprised even ourselves with a 6.35 percent growth.

And our democratic consolidation has come a long way.

We have amended our constitution so that a system of democratic check-and-balance among the three branches of government can be put in place.

We have empowered the regions and provinces and given them a fairer share of government revenues.
The military establishment is out of politics and getting out of business. We will only have professional soldiers.

Ladies and Gentlemen,

As President, I received my mandate directly from the Indonesian people in a free, honest and peaceful electoral process. Next month, we will hold local elections all over the country and thus further consolidate our democratization.

We have made considerable gains in governance and we are consolidating them. We are striving to improve our human rights record. We are cutting red tape in the bureaucracies.

A growing number of high officials are being brought to court on charges of corruption. In Indonesia, the days of impunity among the crooked are over.

The eradication of corruption is basic to our national development strategy: to create a climate in which investors feel confident and comfortable so that jobs can be created for the millions of our unemployed.

At the same time, we are maintaining economic stability as basis for growth. The rupiah is stable, inflation is kept manageable and the budget deficit is being steadily reduced. We will have a balanced budget by 2009.

Our major socioeconomic initiatives are in agriculture and rural development—a sector that promises tremendous growth. We have set aside a fund of $1.9 billion to help the most vulnerable segments of our society cope with the ongoing energy crunch.

Ours is an economy that promises abundant reward for the enterprising investor.

I therefore invite you to come to Indonesia to see for yourselves the many opportunities that we are opening up for investors.

Once again, thank you for taking the time to see me today, and I look forward to our discussions.

Washington DC, May 26, 2005

> *"Whatever happens, the aftermath of the tsunami will affect Indonesian economics and politics for years to come. That represents both a burden and an opportunity for Yudhoyono's government."*—Assif Shameen.
>
> (BusinessWeek, 24 January 2005).

PHOTO BY ANUNG

> "The challenge of change is to bring out the best in Indonesia. Our independence, our diversity, our tolerance, our simplicity, our openness, our love of family and community, our passion for unity and harmony, our rich spirituality, our neighborliness."
>
> President Susilo Bambang Yudhoyono
> Singapore, February 16, 2005

"Whether you administer a village of 100, a town of 100,000 or province of 10 million, and whether your area is endowed with rich minerals or zero natural resources, ultimately it is the human capital, the brain power, that will set your people free – free from ignorance, free from want."

President Susilo Bambang Yudhoyono
Medan, March 10, 2005

30

"Indonesia and Vietnam : Old Friends, New Challenges"

Keynote Speech at The Business Forum
Indonesia-Vietnam

Hanoi, Vietnam
May 29, 2005

◆ ◆ ◆ ◆ ◆

Bismillahirrahmanirrahim
Excellencies, Ladies and Gentlemen

I am very honored to be here today to meet all of you.

I thank the Vietnam Chamber of Commerce for arranging this Business Forum, and for giving me the chance to share some thoughts on how we can expand economic and business relations between our two countries.

Let me first tell you why I am here in your great country. I have come here for a simple purpose : to strengthen and elevate the relations between our two nations.

I have always believed that Indonesia and Vietnam share the right ingredients for a strong relationship. Indonesia and Vietnam are known to be very independent-minded countries in the community of nations. Indonesia and Vietnam were born out of a great revolutionary struggle. We are now countries in the midst of rapid reforms. And never forget that we have always had close historical bonds, especially when times were difficult for Vietnam. And we have similar views on many regional and international issues. So, you see, there is natural chemistry between us.

Vietnam has many admirers in Indonesia, including in me. When I was a young officer in the Indonesian army, I remember well reading with great admiration about Vietnam's ferocious struggle and military accomplishments. Vietnam is proof to the dictum that the best asset a nation can have is her spirit, her fighting spirit. We are now watching that fighting spirit of Vietnam being transformed and being used for a completely different undertaking: economic development. And we are certain that in this great challenge, too, Vietnam will prevail impressively.

I am here in Vietnam because I have always felt that there is a historical kinship that can go much farther if we both care to develop it.

Before I share my thoughts and ideas on how we can revitalize our partnership, let me take a few minutes to explain to you the current situation in Indonesia and the forthcoming plans for reform and change.

As you may well know, Indonesia has undergone a number of dramatic changes in the last eight years. Indonesia has weathered the crisis and experienced subsequent periods of slow growth. Much had to be done in the aftermath of the crisis to restore macroeconomic stability, the financial system, economic institutions and processes of governance.

Indonesia has achieved a number of milestones and progress. In 2004, Indonesia successfully completed a process of peaceful legislative elections and we held our first direct elections for the office of the President and Vice President. That elections gave us a big leap in our efforts to solidify our national reforms which began in 1997. I understand that Vietnam also has a similar "doi moi" program.

Our revitalization program involves a "triple track approach" which comprises of three objectives. First, achieving sustainable higher economic growth through a combination of strong investment and exports. Second, to stimulate the real sector to create jobs. Third, to promote development in the rural and agricultural economy since a large percentage of our population still rely on their livelihood from the agriculture sector.

With this program we hope to achieve an average growth rate of 6.6%, and to cut in half unemployment and poverty rates in the next five years.
After seven months in office, there is much good news.

In 2004, growth was 5.1% but in the first quarter of 2005, growth has picked up significantly to 6.4%, investment growth at 15% and export growth at 13.4%. This is a clear sign of early approval of the efforts of the new government in the first 7 months of being in office. With these trends, we are optimistic to achieve our initial target of 5.5% or even higher at close to 6%. The credit rating of

Indonesia has also improved with upgrades of our ratings by various rating agencies such as Fitch and Moodys.

Our per capita income has also now resumed back to its pre-crisis level at $1030/capita. The recovery in consumer purchasing power is evident with robust growth being experienced by our retail sector. For instance, motor cycle and motor vehicle sales jumped by 34% and 39% respectively in the first quarter of 2005 compared to the same period last year.

Given rising international oil prices, we have also undertaken the necessary and painful adjustment by raising domestic fuel price to better target subsidies and to improve the efficiency of the use of fuel. In general, we are working on improving our fiscal policy through improving the policy, streamlining administration and intensification of tax collection. All distortions in the tax system, luxury taxes and rationalization of tax regulations are being reviewed under the draft new tax law.

Of course, to maintain growth we know we have to increase investment, especially in infrastructure. Since January, my Government has submitted several draft laws and government regulations to complete regulatory framework for private participation in infrastructure development.

Other priorities in improving the investment climate relate to improving the labor regulations to make the labor market more flexible, passing the new investment law and streamlining the licensing process, and addressing issues of greater transparency and good governance.

Given the importance of maintaining competitiveness, the government has also focused on policies that will reduce the high cost of doing business. This includes ensuring that we have a functioning, efficient and transparent system for our customs office. I have undertaken regular site visits and are preparing a number of measures to improve the efficiency of our customs office by simplifying procedures, improving coordination, and strengthening systems.

My Government also puts a strong emphasis on putting in systems, cross and check balances to ensure good governance, because we strongly believe that this will be an important pillar to revitalizing our economy.

Let me now turn to the question before us: how can we revitalize Indonesia-Vietnam economic relations?

Just as Indonesia represents an important market of 220 million people with growing purchasing power, so does Vietnam – the second largest ASEAN country with its population of 82 milion and per capita income of US$600/capita --represent business opportunities for Indonesia. Total trade between Indonesia and Vietnam in 2004 was $1 billion. In 2004, Indonesian exports to Vietnam increased by 28%, reaching $601 million, whilst Indonesian imports from Vietnam increased only slightly to reach $415 million.

Given the size of our respective trade and market size, there is much more potential to increase the economic partnership between our two countries.

Given our population size and increasing purchasing power, there is a great potential to expand two-way flow of tourists. There is also the synergy between Indonesian investments in Vietnam and increased trade, as some of these investments are not only motivated by the current and potential market in Vietnam, but also by the wider Indochina market and to also take advantage of the ASEAN Free Trade Area. We see this in the various interests in consumer products, paper and pulp, and other wood based products.

We also believe that Indonesian businessmen can play a role in your infrastructure and oil and gas development by providing necessary equipment, pipes and services such as construction, oil and gas related services.

We can also provide various agriculture equipment to support your agriculture development. Given our expertise and experience in the forest and wood based production and the demand in Vietnam, there is the potential to develop win-win cooperation in this area.

I understand that our two sides have already begun to address the issues as to how to revitalize the economic relations between our two countries. My Minister of Trade was here a month ago with a group of Indonesian business representatives and I believe constructive talks were held at the government level as well as between the government and business representatives on both sides to find ways and means to increase economic and trade cooperation between our two sides.

In fact, we are already seeing the results today. I welcome the signing of 7 MOUs between Indonesian and Vietnam businesses to cooperate together to sell and market Indonesian products in your market, which will be signed at this Business Forum. These include a variety of our products such as beverages, cosmetics, pharmaceutical products and rattan furniture, as well as tourism.

I also welcome the quick response from both Chambers of Commerce to address the issues and potential opportunities which arose from the talks a month ago. I applaud the signing of an MOU between the Vietnam Chamber of Commerce and Industry and the Indonesian Chamber of Commerce and Industry at this Business Forum. The Chambers of Commerce on both sides have a lot of work to identify issues and opportunities for enhancing trade and investment.

I am also encouraged that the Indonesian business people and professionals here have recently formed an Indonesian Business Association (IBA) in Vietnam. IBA together with the Chambers of Commerce can also contribute to enhancing trade and investment between our two countries.

I assure you that my Government is committed to ensuring that we can facilitate the resolution of any problems, as well as promoting new opportunities.

There are also areas of cooperation for mutual benefit that both sides can explore. Given that Indonesia and Vietnam account for 60% of robusta coffee production, we can cooperate together to improve the quality of our coffee and explore other ways to cooperate.

I understand that there is already a Technical agreement between our two coffee associations, which has been followed up last month by Agreed Minutes on Cooperation on Robusta Coffee between our two governments. As already mentioned, I am sure we can find other areas of cooperation of mutual interest, such as agriculture development, infrastructure and oil and gas development, and the wood based sector.

Finally, Indonesia also looks forward to a strong partnership with Vietnam to address issues of mutual interest in the context of ASEAN economic cooperation. Indonesia also fully supports Vietnam's accession to the WTO because we see this as an important component of your "Doi Moi" program.

Ladies and Gentlemen,

In closing, let me thank the organizers of this Business Forum and hope that this is a good beginning to revitalize our economic partnership. Let me assure you that my Government will do our best to support this partnership.

Xien Camon (sin kamen – thank you).

Hanoi, May 29, 2005

"...the economy is ticking along nicely. It grew by 5.1% last year, the fastest rate since the Asian financial crisis of 1997. Investment, which had been lagging badly, is also rising to cater to a consumer boom. The budget deficit came in at a manageable 1.3% of GDP last year, and will be lower this year, thanks in part to the reduction in subsidies."

(The Economist, 5 March 2005)

"We have to make sure that decentralization is about spreading out good governance and does not lead to decentralizing corruption."

President Susilo Bambang Yudhoyono
Medan, March 10, 2005

"It is not enough Indonesia and Australia just to be neighbors. It is imperative for us to be strong partners."

President Susilo Bambang Yudhoyono
Canberra-Australia, April 3, 2005

31

"Aceh : 6 Months after the Tsunami"

Remarks for The World Report Conference, 25th Year
Anniversary of CNN at Atlanta, June 1, 2005
(Via teleconference from Tokyo, Japan)

Tokyo, Japan

♦ ♦ ♦ ♦ ♦

Bismillahirrahmanirrahiim,

Excellencies,
Conference Delegates,
Ladies and Gentlemen,

I regret that circumstances are obliging me to address you from half way across the globe, but I know we all speak with one heart. The tsunami has connected and united all of us.

I speak to you representing Indonesia, a nation which has suffered the most from the tsunami of December 26 last year. In a matter of minutes, over 200 thousand Indonesians lost their lives, and over half a million became homeless. It was definitely the worst catastrophe in the long-history of my nation.

In the days and weeks after this horrific tsunami, my Government was absolutely consumed with the rescue and relief efforts in areas which had become totally paralyzed. I arrived in Aceh the day after the tsunami--the worst day of my life--and we did everything we could to mobilize all our national resources for the emergency relief operation--the national and regional governments, the military, the police and all other agencies.

And we learned many lessons. We learned that our national disaster management system was inadequate to deal with the enormous scale of the devastation. We are now trying to improve our disaster management system to deal with future catastrophes, including the establishment of an early-warning system for the Indian Ocean. And we certainly learned a lot about many coordination issues as we pursued rescue and relief efforts under a condition of extreme duress.

And of course, given the magnitude of the situation, we learned very quickly that we could not do this on our own.

Indonesia deeply appreciates the immediate response of the world in the wake of the tsunami last December.

At the greatest hour of need, the global community mobilized rapidly, and contributed significantly to help us save lives. We are amazed and humbled by the world's response to our tragedy.

I would also like to especially thank the media for your diligent reporting on the disaster, enabling everyone all over the world to see and share our pain.

And if you could go to Aceh and Nias, you would hear the people themselves tell you how grateful they are that the world cares. You would see simple but sincere signs and banners on display, proclaiming their gratitude to various countries and organizations.

The Indonesian Government has allocated a substantial portion of our national budget for the reconstruction of Aceh and Nias. For this year's budget, we have earmarked about US$ 1 billion dollars, and next year we plan to set aside US$ 1.2 billion.

Of course, not all of the donors are governments and wealthy corporations. In many countries, children contributed their lunch allowance, and elderly people sent money out of their pensions. Girl scouts contributed money from selling cookies; school districts and other civic groups worked countless hours to collect donations to help us.

Every donation, whether it is one dollar or a million, counts ! And they helps to ensure that people who had lost their livelihoods were fed, housed, and cared for.

That is why we are absolutely determined that not a single cent is lost along the way. We have an obligation to use all funds that have been entrusted to us effectively, responsibly and transparently.

And I tell you, there is something very special going on in Aceh today. As I am sure all your correspondents know, a month ago we established the Agency for the Reconstruction of Aceh and Nias.

The Agency, led by Dr. Kuntoro, is comprised of a team of dedicated individuals that is so committed to what they are doing and to making sure they are doing it right.

We are determined that the reconstruction of Aceh and Nias will be clean, transparent, and will, above all, be in accordance with the real needs and the sensitivities of the people. The Acehnese are the ones who have suffered, and they are the ones who want so desperately to rebuild their lives and homes. Their wishes must be respected.

The people of Aceh and Nias are strong, resilient, and proud, and they will recover and become even stronger than before. My favorite story is about an Acehnese kid named Martunis, only 7 years old. Martunis survived the tsunami after being adrift for 21 days in the open sea. He taught himself to eat instant noodles, and survived on just a few bottles of mineral water that floated by him. He was found on January 15th. Because Martunis was wearing a replica of famous footballer Rui Costa, the Portuguese national players are looking after his rehabilitation.

There are countless Martunis-type stories in Aceh and Nias. They tell stories of courage, and of an incredible will to live and move on.

Ever since I stood with disbelief on the shores of Aceh the day after the tsunami, I have always known that the key challenge would be to keep international attention and commitment long after the dead were found and buried. I want to remind all the journalists that there are great stories to be told about how the tsunami victims rise up from despair, and rebuild their lives.

And nowadays, you do not have to look hard to see signs of that. Everywhere you look in the province, you can see people helping themselves and one another.

You would see, a group of artists, musicians and dancers who survived the tsunami, who are now teaching dance and music to children in the temporary camps for tsunami victims. They are thus helping ensure that invaluable Acehnese traditions are not lost. And many displaced persons, despite having lost their homes and most of their families, have started up their businesses – building boats to fish again, operating automobile repair shops, and opening market stalls to sell spices.

Indonesians from other islands have also come to Aceh and Nias to help. If you drive around Aceh, you will see banners identifying "support teams" from different regions in Indonesia. Many of them are volunteers, who have given up their jobs, to help in the relief and reconstruction efforts.

You will also see groups organizing games and useful activities for children in the centers for tsunami victims. And others are training women in how to make handicrafts.

As you can see, signs of life, of hope, of recovery are ALL around. Those who were affected by the tsunami don't want to live on charity forever. They want to work again. They also want to find emotional healing from this horrible crises.

As to the challenges still facing us in Aceh, I can only say that the need is immense. The Government has estimated that almost US$5 billion will be required to rebuild Aceh properly across a variety of sectors. This need will be met by funds from the Indonesia Government, Foreign Governments, international institutions, and private individuals.

While an enormous amount of money has been pledged, all of those pledges need to be realized soon for reconstruction and rehabilitation activities to move forward in an expedited manner.

In addition to funding, technical expertise is also needed, especially on the ground in the affected areas. We would appreciate your partnership and cooperation.

Before I conclude, I want to leave you with one thought. We have never seen a tsunami like this in our life time, but we also never seen the kind of intense global solidarity that came out of it, both on the part of Governments, international institutions and individuals. I'd like to think that this is a new phenomenon in international affairs. For the benefit of humanity, we should build on this tremendous reserve of global goodwill and compassion.

The world must become a solid community, even without a crisis, so that we can secure ourselves not only from the fury of natural disasters, but also from the folly of human conflicts.

Again, I thank you for this opportunity to address you all, and share with you our experiences. I am confident that next time we meet, with your good wishes and support, I will have more good news to share.

Have a good conference, and as we say in Indonesia, "terima kasih", or thank you, or in literal translation, "accept our love".

Thank you.

Tokyo, June 1, 2005

"*Now I think investments will take over from consumption...* *Indonesia is back on the map.*"—Manu Bhaskaran, Head of Economic Research, Centennial Group Holdings, Singapore.

(The New York Times, 17 February 2005)

"We envision a dynamic Indonesia dotted from east to west and north to south by numerous growth centers — each having dynamism of its own, each running on its own steam."

President Susilo Bambang Yudhoyono
Medan, March 10, 2005

"'Governance' is the ideology of the New Millennium."

President Susilo Bambang Yudhoyono
Medan, March 10, 2005

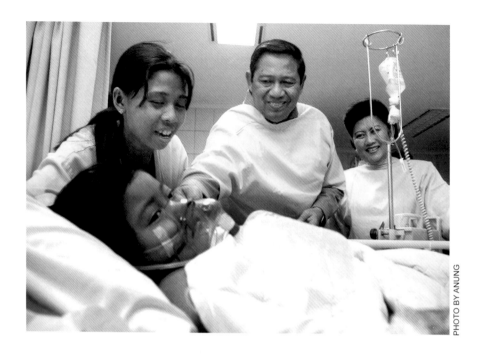

"I hope you see beyond such snapshots and see a nation that, given our seemingly endless natural disasters, has been down on luck lately, but remains high in spirit and strong in will."

President Susilo Bambang Yudhoyono
Canberra-Australia, April 4, 2005

32

"Reasons to Invest in Indonesia"

Keynote Speech at Nihon Keizai Shimbun, Inc
(Nikkei)

Okura Hotel-Tokyo, Japan
June 2, 2005

♦ ♦ ♦ ♦ ♦

Excellencies,
Ladies and gentlemen,
And my good friends from the Japanese business community,

Let me begin by saying something that I have been saying to everybody I meet in Japan in the past few days.

Thank you for the sympathy, solidarity and generosity you have shown us since the day of the tsunami. You might like to know that the first thing I did upon my arrival in Tokyo was to personally thank members of the Self-Defence Force, Japanese volunteers and medics who did humanitarian work in Aceh and Nias.

These people truly have big hearts, and it was a pleasure for me to meet and thank them.

Today, I wish to begin my remarks by referring to a subject that may sound a little unfamiliar to the ear: "national growth".

"National growth" is something that defines and summarizes Indonesia's key challenge, and encapsulates exactly what I intend to achieve with my Presidency.

We are used to hearing the term "economic growth". But "national growth", or growth of a nation is something else, something more, something fundamental.

National growth cannot be measured by statistics and numbers alone. In fact, economic growth does not automatically lead to growth of the nation.

Employment may rise, inflation may go down, the GDP may go up, and the stock market may hit a record high, but none of these things mean much if the nation as a whole becomes insecure, if conflicts persist, if the people loses faith in its values, if the country loses direction and confidence, if nation loses its sense of identity.

The real challenge is not just about ensuring the growth of the economy, but also the growth of the nation. Not just economic growth, but national growth.

My aim as President is to see to it that the Indonesian nation grows to be economically prosperous, but also resilient, cohesive, competitive, peaceful and confident about its identity, its values and its future.

That is what I call true "national growth". And this, ultimately, is what my Government is aiming for.

I believe that now is the best time for Indonesia to achieve its national growth.

Indonesia now has the historic chance to grow strongly, grow confidently, grow sustainably.

There are several reasons why I believe this.

First, for the first time in our history we have finally gotten democracy locked-in. Our elections last year in 2004 was the second free and fair elections since 1999. We have achieved a point of no return in our democratic development.

From now on, we will grow as a democracy, we will prosper as a democracy, and we will find peace as a democracy.

Second, I believe that we have found the key to unlock the enormous creative potentials of our nation. That key is called: governance. With good governance, we will fulfill the promise of reformasi. And with governance, we will transform Indonesia. And with governance we can capitalize on the massive new "energy" for change that was unleashed after our last elections of 2004.

Third, we will achieve national growth because we are harnessing the most important factor: the human capital. Which is why my Government attaches great importance to two key areas that will dramatically improve and enlarge our pool of human capital: investment and education. History teaches us that if you develop these two areas—investment and education-- everything will fall into place, everything will grow.

<u>Fourth</u>, we feel that there is solid international confidence and support towards Indonesia. This is the message that I have received from the many foreign leaders that I have met so far. And this is certainly the message that I have received from your government and your political parties. And we will do our best to live up to your high expectation.

Indonesia, thus, is on the verge of achieving its optimal national growth.

And herein lies Japan's opportunity.

I come here to reaffirm the long-standing partnership between Indonesia and Japan. But I also come here to raise the bar in our relationship. We in Indonesia want to see a greater engagement and a stronger partnership with Japan.

And the key part of that partnership have much to do with our common prosperity.

In my meetings with Japanese friends, I have been told that some Japanese companies are still considering whether or not to invest in Indonesia.

Well, let me offer you 6 (six) reasons why NOW—not later, now !-- is the right time to invest or to expand your investment in Indonesia.

Let me begin with reason number 1: We in Indonesia now have a political order which is guaranteed to last 5 years. The next elections is not until 2009, a long way from now. The President is directly elected by the people, not by political parties, which means he has a very strong mandate to govern.

There is also now a clearly defined relationship between the executive, the legislative and the judicial branches, which means political procedures are more certain. For you, this stable and predictable political order means that you can conveniently plan, invest and profit for the medium and long-term.

Reason number 2: We now have a government that is very pro-business.

You know, there is a very simple reason why I am pro-business. Pro-business means pro-job, it means pro-growth, and by extension it means pro-poor because of the jobs created by business. And precisely because I am pro-business, my Government is actively reviewing regulations and Laws which have created uncertainty and have not proven to be pro-market. Yes, this means reviewing our tax and customs laws. It also means reviewing our labor laws so as to achieve a more balanced terms where both business and labor can prosper together in partnership.

I also plan to establish, in the near future, a Task Force which would be solely dedicated to solving business disputes involving the private sector. This will ensure that problems and disputes involving the private sector will NOT be neglected; on the contrary, they will be tended to very seriously by the Government with a constructive attitude.

Reason number 3: Indonesia is very hospitable and accustomed to Japanese, and Japanese investments. Japanese companies have been in Indonesia for a very long time. They have been part of our economic success. There are around 900 Japanese companies operating in Indonesia, with equity investments of $11 billion and employing some 282,000 people.

Indonesians are very used to the Japanese way of life, and to their corporate culture. Many Indonesians speak Japanese. And Indonesian and Japanese workers have something in common: they both like to work hard to earn a good living. Moreover, Japanese products, especially automobiles and electronics, television personalities, play station, comic books, even Japanese hair style are very popular in Indonesia. And of course, Prime Minister Koizumi has many fans in Indonesia.

Reason number 4: Indonesia is now a place where you see a very strong anti- corruption drive, both on the part of Government and the people. I am very conscious of the fact that I was elected, among others, on an anti-corruption platform. Open up the internet, read our daily papers, or turn on the tv, and you will see endless news about government officials being investigated for corruption, about illegal loggers getting caught and thrown in jail, about bankers in trouble for doing shady dealings, or about the Electoral Commission mismanaging their funds.

Nobody is above the law in today's Indonesia, and I want to see an Indonesia where integrity is the rule, not the exception. And it will continue like this for the rest of my term.

Reason number 5: Indonesia now has good macro-economic conditions, which we were fortunate to inherit from the previous Government. We grew by 6,4 % last quarter, despite the tsunami, and I expect growth this year to be 5,5 %, and we are aiming at average of 6,6 % for the next 5 years, which in my view is totally achievable and realistic. You will also be interested to know that my Government is committed to fiscal prudence. Our budget deficit this year is aimed at 0,8 % and we are targeting a balanced budget by 2009. The Rupiah is stable and inflation is around 7.5 %.

And if you still want more reasons, let me throw in another one. Reason number 6: Indonesia has great weather, you can be out in open air 24 hours a day, we have gentle people who love to smile, to learn and to work hard, and we have great food. And if you are really homesick, you can find Japanese food at every street.

So there you have it. 6 great reasons to take advantage of Indonesia's business opportunities. If you want more reasons, you can ask my two Ministers in their presentations later.

The bottom line is that Indonesians are keen to see a stronger entrepreneurial presence of Japan in a wider range of businesses.

We hope to see your existing subsidiaries expand and new ones to come.

There is still wide opportunities for Japanese companies to expand in the traditional areas of Japanese investment such as electronics,

If we in Indonesia continue to do the right thing to promote our national growth, we will carve our own geopolitical space which will take the form of a vast oasis of democracy, peace, and prosperity.

That oasis of democracy, peace and prosperity is good for Indonesia, good for the region, and is good for Japan.
I thank you.

Tokyo, June 2, 2005

"The good news is that Indonesia has jumped onto the foreign investment radar screen. Yudhoyono has met with investors to promote the country and has pressed the bureaucracy to speed up license approvals. That has paid off in deals. Malaysia's Maxis Communications ponied up $100 million for Lippo Telecom in February, while Hong Kong's Hutchison Telecom (HUWHT) spent $120 million for mobile carrier Cyber Access Communications in March. That same month, Philip Morris International Inc. agreed to a $5.2 billion takeover of Indonesia's No. 3 cigarette maker, Hanjaya Mandala Sampoerna"—Brian Bremner and Assif Shameen.

(BusinessWeek, 4 July 2005)

"Prime Minister Lee and I have agreed to develop a new framework for bilateral cooperation. While continuing to actively deal with pending issues, we will move ahead to find new opportunities of cooperation in various areas of common interest."

President Susilo Bambang Yudhoyono
Singapore, February 16, 2005

"I know, it is the natural instinct of Americans to want to change the world. What I would like to tell you is that the best way for America to change the world is to share your knowledge with the world."

President Susilo Bambang Yudhoyono
Washington DC, USA , May 25, 2005

Memorable Speeches
by
Susilo Bambang Yudhoyono
before
His Presidency

Editor's note

Susilo Bambang Yudhoyono, then Coordinating Minister for Political and Security Affairs, delivered this speech on the occasion of the one-year remembrance of the Bali Bombing. The event, hosted by Prime Minister John Howard, was attended by families of the victims from Australia. In a 6-minute speech described by Greg Sheridan as 'eloquent, personal, and powerful', Susilo Bambang Yudhoyono moved many in the audience to tears, and left a deep impression on million others who watched him on TV. The speech gave mainstream Australians their first introduction to Susilo Bambang Yudhoyono. When Susilo Bambang Yudhoyono ran for President in 2004, the Australian media referred to him as 'the man delivered that Bali speech'.

REMARKS BY
H.E. SUSILO BAMBANG YUDHOYONO
COORDINATING MINISTER FOR POLITICS AND SECURITY
REPUBLIC OF INDONESIA

ON THE OCCASION OF
THE REMEMBRANCE FOR
THE VICTIMS OF THE BALI BOMBING

BALI
OCTOBER 12, 2003

Bismillah Hirrahmanirrahim
Assalamu'alaikum Warrahmatullahi Wabarakatuh
Oom Swasti Astu

His Excellency Prime Minister John Howard and Mrs. Howard
The leader of the opposition the Honorable Simon Crean and Mrs. Crean,
Distinguished Ambassadors,
Families and friends of victims,
Distinguished guests,

On behalf of the President Megawati Soekarnoputri, and on behalf of the Government and people of Indonesia, I take great pleasure in welcoming you to Indonesia, and especially to this solemn day of remembrance of the victims of the Bali bombings.

Exactly a year ago this day, three bombs exploded on this beautiful peaceful island of God. Two-hundred-and-two-men and women perished that evening.

Never mind their nationalities. Never mind their race, religions or ethnicity or profession.

They were our sons, our daughters, our fathers and mothers, brothers and sisters, our cousins, our best friends, our soul mates. And they were all innocents. They all had happy plans to spend "tomorrow" under the sun. They all had families to write and come home to.

But they were all rudely taken away from our midst by terrorists who wanted to make a senseless point of their hatred for others.

To this day, we still do not understand why these loved ones had to meet such tragic, undeserved fate. Many of us had been lost trying to search for answers and meaning out this nightmare.

But there is a time for shock and disbelief. There is a time to grieve. There is a time to fight. There is a time for justice. There is a time for reflection. There is a time for remembrance. And there is a time to let go and move on.

We let go knowing that our loved ones are in a better place, by God's side, the most precious place of all.

We let go knowing that we will miss them forever, and knowing that our lives will never be the same without the realness and sweetness of their physical presence in our daily lives.

We let go knowing that we will honor their memory by becoming a better person, by cherishing life even more, by striving to be happy, and by always promoting goodness over evil.

And we let go by promising them the best kind of justice of all: we shall ensure that the noble values which the terrorists aim to destroy will always remain dear to our hearts, and will bound all of us here ever closer as a grand family of nations and peoples.

What are these values? Freedom. Religiosity. Tolerance. Diversity. Unity. Democracy. Compassion. Fraternity. And Humanity. These are the core values that define our civilized ways of life. These are the values that no terrorist bombs can ever take away from us.

We gather here today with some measure of relief that justice is being delivered. Many of the terrorists had been caught, put behind bars, put on trial and sentenced by our courts. Some are still on the run but make no mistake: we will hunt them, we will find them, we will bring them to justice. These diabolical men and their brand of evil simply have no place in our society. They belong to our darkest dungeons, locked away deep beneath our children's playgrounds. History will condemn them forever.

The government and people of Indonesia are resolute in condemning the terrorist attacks as a travesty to the true teaching of all religions, which promotes peace, tolerance and brotherhood.

As a frontline state in the global coalition against terrorism, the Indonesian government and people will maximize our efforts to eradicate terrorism within Indonesia and around the world.

We will continue to wage a comprehensive strategy to combat terrorism for the short, medium and long-terms, which includes international cooperation and addressing the root causes of terrorism.

It is only fitting, therefore, that, as a Muslim myself, I should end my remarks with a verse from the Qur'an:

"Wa laa taqtulun latii harramallaahu illaa bil haqqi dzaalikum wash-shaakum bihii la'allakum ta'qiluun

...dan janganlah kamu membunuh jiwa yang diharamkan Allah (membunuhnya) melainkan dengan sesuatu (sebab) yang benar". Demikian itu yang diperintahkan oleh Tuhanmu kepadamu supaya kamu memahami (nya). (Q.S. al-An'am/6:151).

...take not life, which Allah hath made sacred, except by way of justice and law: thus doth He command you, that ye may learn wisdom. (Q.S. al-An'am/6:151)

Amin.

Wassalamualaikum Warrahmatullahi Wabarrakatuh
Oom Shanti Shanti Shanti oom

"I would venture to say that in some cases, tolerance is more important than freedom. It is tolerance that sets us free. It is through tolerance that we can attain genuine peace. It is tolerance that protects freedom, harness diversity and delivers progress. It is tolerance that makes openness manageable."

President Susilo Bambang Yudhoyono
Washington DC, USA , May 25, 2005

REMARKS BY
H.E. SUSILO BAMBANG YUDHOYONO

AT THE OPENING OF
THE WAHID INSTITUTE

JAKARTA
SEPTEMBER 7, 2004

Ass Wr Wb
Bismillah Hirrahmanirrahim,
Ladies and gentlemen,
Brothers and sisters,

Let me begin by saying how delightful I am to see the establishment of the Wahid Institute. I am given to understand that the Wahid Institute aims to promote greater understanding of Islam and to project Islam's true face : peaceful, tolerant and moderate.

Our theme tonight is: "Seeding Plural and Peaceful Islam". It is a very appropriate theme, particularly if we consider the world of challenges faced by the Ummah today.

Let me outline at least 3 particular challenges which I think the Ummah should have answers to.

First, is how we address the growing restlessness both within many Islamic countries and between Islamic communities. King

Abdullah of Jordan once called this "the battle for the soul of Islam". We see this "battle for the soul" of Islam in many places, in Afghanistan, in Pakistan, in Saudi Arabia, in Algiers, in Jordan, in Egypt, in Iraq, in Iran, and we have also seen it in our corner of the world : in Malaysia and Indonesia. Each of them has its own unique circumstances. But in general, you can draw that the battle for the soul of Islam involves two competing forces : those who are rather intolerant, exclusive and seek to impose their views on others, and those embrace tolerant and pluralistic Islam. They are both fundamentalists, and but they are driven by different visions, different self-conceptions and different worldviews.

As this struggle is something that has gone on for centuries, I do not see it being resolved in the short-term. What this means is that we will have to live with its consequences for some time.

Secondly, is how to address the see rising tension between the western world and the Islamic world. These days, it is fashionable to talk about "Islam versus the west", or even "Islam versus the rest". About a decade or so ago, Samuel Huntington warned about the spectre of a "clash of civilizations". But I do not believe that the western world and the Islamic world are necessarily poised for conflict and collision. I note, for example, that many Islamic communities have embraced some forms of the "western" way of life, and, on the other spectrum, Islam itself has become the fastest growing religion in the United States. The western and the Islamic worlds certainly can live, work and prosper together.

But certainly the western world needs to address the plight, grievances and anger felt by many muslims throughout the world, many of whom are suffering from injustice, abject poverty and violence. The western world need to recognize that many muslims feel marginalized in their own countries and in world affairs. Among the most important of these "hot issues" is the need to ensure the speedy resolution of the long-standing Arab-Israeli conflict, and the creation of an independent, viable and sovereign Palestinian state in the near future, hopefully by 2005.

The third challenge, is how do we improve living conditions in muslim societies.

Take a good look at the world's 20 biggest economies : rank number 1 is the US with a GDP over USD$ 10 trillion, and rank 20 is Belgium with a GDP of 229. In between them, there is not a single muslim country. If you expand it to the world's biggest 50 economies, then you have only 9 (nine) muslim populated countries among them: Saudi Arabia, Turkey, Indonesia, Iran, Egypt, Malaysia, UAE, Pakistan, Algeria.

Of the world's 20 biggest trading nations, none are muslim societies. Only if you expand to top 50 trading nations, only 5 muslim countries are on that list : Malaysia, Saudi Arabia, Indonesia, Turkey, and United Arab Emirates.

Of the world's top 20 countries in terms of human development index, none are muslim societies. And of the top 50, there are only 5 muslim societies : Brunei, Bahrain, Kuwait, United Arab Emirates, Qatar.

Of the world's top 20 in terms of overall global competitiveness, you have only 1 muslim country—Malaysia—ranked number 17, and there isn't another muslim society in the top 40 of that category.

Do you get the picture ? Islamic societies are lagging behind in terms of worldwide socio-economic progress. This is in stark contrast to the heritage of Islam as a religion of progress and the most advanced civilization in the world for centuries, where Islamic cities became the centers of learning for philosophy, literature, astronomy, mathematics, medicine, optics, architecture.

All these challenges require answers from the Ummah, and especially from the Islamic intellectuals worldwide. It requires the Ummah to think hard about where we have been and where we intend to be in the future, and how we go about achieving it.

With regard to the "battle for the soul of Islam", we have to remember that we do have a say in this debate, we have an important voice, and we cannot be relegated to the sidelines as silent observers. Indonesians have much to say about the kind of Islam that lives in our soul—a moderate, peace-loving, tolerant and pluralistic Islam. We can lead by example : by proving that Indonesian muslims can live in peace and harmony with non-muslims, as our forefathers have done for centuries.

With regard to "Islam and the west", we need to make the West understand Islam, and muslims, better. They need to know the issues that concern us, and how strongly we feel about them. But we also need to reach out to the West, we need to build bridges and promote a two-way dialogue. We have to speak up against injustices faced by muslims, but we must equally be resolute in stressing that Islam rejects terrorism and would protest anyone who suggests otherwise.

On the issues of "modernity", we need to define ways by which the Ummah can deal with globalization and progress. The Ummah already missed out the industrial revolution which was dominated by Europe in the 18th century. The Ummah did not start the present information revolution, and it remains to be seen if the Ummah can master the information technology to our own betterment. But I strongly believe that the Ummah can take a front seat in the global marketplace of ideas, in global innovations, in global progress. They just need to be enlightened and organized in the right way.

We in Indonesia also can also show that Islam and democracy do go hand-in-hand. I truly believe that the two are perfectly compatible. Why ? Look at the first muslims who spread the religion of Islam under the leadership of our Great Prophet Muhammad. These first muslims transformed their society from a condition of Jahilliyah to a civilized society driven by compassion, equality, brotherhood, justice tolerance, and respect for human dignity. These were the hallmarks of the society built by the first muslims, which revolutionized society in ways which were very democratic. The Ummah of today must strive to strengthen our faith and to practice Islamic teachings in our daily lives, but we must also do all we can to seek ways to embrace democracy, modernity, technology and progress.

So, these, Yenny, in a nutshell, are your homeworks as you and your colleagues begin the noble work of The Wahid Institute. Of course,

I expect a full report from you on these hard issues in the next few months.

I wish all the best for the Wahid Institute. Yenny is young, resourceful, bright, idealistic, and comes from a distinguished family of prominent Islamic thinkers. I understand that the establishment of the Wahid Institute was inspired by Kiai Haji Abdurrahman Wahid, Gus Dur, whom I respect, and who is known in our country and the world over as a leader and an Islamic intellectual who tirelessly promotes the moderate, tolerant and pluralistic Islam.

I have therefore every confidence that the Wahid Institute will play its rightful role to "seed a plural and peaceful Islam", to give light to the Ummah in Indonesia and abroad, to become a voice of reason, and to be a proponent for justice and progress, in the footsteps of our Great Prophet Muhammad SAW.

Thank you, and enjoy the evening.

Wass Wr Wb

"I strongly believe that the Ummah can take a front seat in the global marketplace of ideas, in global innovations, in global progress."

Susilo Bambang Yudhoyono
Jakarta, September 7, 2004

Dr. H. SUSILO BAMBANG YUDHOYONO
President of the Republic of Indonesia

General TNI (Ret) Susilo Bambang Yudhoyono, popularly known as SBY, was born in Pacitan, East Java, on 9 September 1949. He graduated from the Military Academy in 1973—top in his class. He received his fourth star in 2000. In the first-ever direct presidential election in Indonesia in 2004, Susilo Bambang Yudhoyono, running on a platform for "more just, more peaceful, more prosperous, and more democratic Indonesia", was elected as the 6th President of the Republic of Indonesia, gaining a landslide 60% of the popular vote over the incumbent President Megawati Soekarnoputri.

President Yudhoyono is also an accomplished scholar. He was educated in the United States, where he received his Masters degree in Management from Webster University in 1991. He continued his study and earned a Doctorate Degree in Agricultural Economics from Bogor Institute of Agriculture, West Java, Indonesia, in 2004.

During his 27-year distinguished military service, President Yudhoyono took an extensive range of training, education and courses, both in Indonesia and overseas. President Yudhoyono also held numerous important posts and positions as troop and territorial commander, staff officer, trainer and lecturer. He served both in the field and at headquarters, as well as missions overseas. He was the Commander of the United Nations Military Observers and Commander of the Indonesian Military Contingent in Bosnia-Herzegovina from 1995-1996.

For his outstanding service, President Yudhoyono was decorated with 24 medals and awards, including the UNPKF Medal, the *Bintang Dharma*, the *Bintang Mahaputera Adipurna* and the *Bintang Republik Indonesia Adipurna*, the highest national medal for excellent service beyond the calls of duty.

Prior to being elected, President Yudhoyono held various important government positions, including Minister of Mining and Energy and Co-ordinating Minister for Political, Social, and Security Affairs in the National Unity Cabinet under President Abdurrahman Wahid. He again served the in latter post in the *Gotong Royong* Cabinet under President Megawati Soekarnoputri. It was in his capacity as Coordinating Minister for Political, Social, and Security Affairs that he became internationally recognized for leading Indonesia's counter-terrorism efforts.

President Yudhoyono is also known for his activities in various civil society organizations. He served as Co-Chairman of the Governing Board of the Partnership for the Governance Reform, a joint Indonesian-international organization focused on the improvement of governance in Indonesia. He also served as Chairman of the Advisory Board of the Brighten Institute, an institution devoted to studying the theory and practice of national development policy.

President Yudhoyono is a keen reader and has authored a number of books and articles including: *Revitalization of the Indonesian Economy: Business, Politics and Good Governance* (2002), and *Coping with the Crisis - Securing the Reform* (1999). *Taman Kehidupan* (Garden of Life) is his anthology published in 2004. President Yudhoyono speaks English fluently.

President Yudhoyono is a devoted Moslem. He is married to Madam Ani Herawati. The first couple is blessed with two sons. The oldest is First Lieutenant Agus Harimurti Yudhoyono, who graduated top in his class from the Military Academy in 2000 and is now serving at the elite 305th Airborne Battalion of the Army Strategic Reserves Command (KOSTRAD). The youngest, Edhie Baskoro Yudhoyono, earned his degree in Economics from Curtin University, Australia.